NON SANZ DROICT.

William Shakespeare

The Tragedy of
MACBETH

**With New Dramatic
Criticism and an
Updated Bibliography**

Edited by Sylvan Barnet

The Signet Classic Shakespeare
GENERAL EDITOR: SYLVAN BARNET

A SIGNET CLASSIC

SIGNET CLASSIC
Published by the Penguin Group
Penguin Books USA Inc., 375 Hudson Street,
New York, New York 10014, U.S.A.
Penguin Books Ltd, 27 Wrights Lane,
London W8 5TZ, England
Penguin Books Australia Ltd, Ringwood,
Victoria, Australia
Penguin Books Canada Ltd, 10 Alcorn Avenue,
Toronto, Ontario, Canada M4V 3B2
Penguin Books (N.Z.) Ltd, 182–190 Wairau Road,
Auckland 10, New Zealand

Penguin Books Ltd, Registered Offices:
Harmondsworth, Middlesex, England

Published by Signet Classic, an imprint of Dutton Signet,
a division of Penguin Books USA Inc.

39 38 37

REGISTERED TRADEMARK—MARCA REGISTRADA

Library of Congress Catalog Card Number: 86-60161

Printed in the United States of America

Contents

Shakespeare: Prefatory Remarks   *vii*

Introduction   *xxii*

The Tragedy of Macbeth   37

Textual Note   132

The Source of *Macbeth*   136

    Selections from Raphael Holinshed:
    *Chronicles of England, Scotland and
    Ireland*   137

Commentaries:

    Samuel Johnson: *Macbeth*   156

    A. C. Bradley: from *Shakespearean
    Tragedy*   166

    Elmer Edgar Stoll: Source and Motive in
    Macbeth and *Othello*   183

    Cleanth Brooks: The Naked Babe and the
    Cloak of Manliness   196

    Oscar James Campbell: From
    "Shakespeare and the 'New' Critics"   222

    Mary McCarthy: General Macbeth   229

    Joan Larsen Klein: Lady Macbeth:
    "Infirm of Purpose"   241

    Sylvan Barnet: *Macbeth* on Stage
    and Screen   254

Suggested References   268

Shakespeare: Prefatory Remarks

Between the record of his baptism in Stratford on 26 April 1564 and the record of his burial in Stratford on 25 April 1616, some forty documents name Shakespeare, and many others name his parents, his children, and his grandchildren. More facts are known about William Shakespeare than about any other playwright of the period except Ben Jonson. The facts should, however, be distinguished from the legends. The latter, inevitably more engaging and better known, tell us that the Stratford boy killed a calf in high style, poached deer and rabbits, and was forced to flee to London, where he held horses outside a playhouse. These traditions are only traditions; they may be true, but no evidence supports them, and it is well to stick to the facts.

Mary Arden, the dramatist's mother, was the daughter of a substantial landowner; about 1557 she married John Shakespeare, who was a glove-maker and trader in various farm commodities. In 1557 John Shakespeare was a member of the Council (the governing body of Stratford), in 1558 a constable of the borough, in 1561 one of the two town chamberlains, in 1565 an alderman (entitling him to the appellation "Mr."), in 1568 high bailiff—the town's highest political office, equivalent to mayor. After 1577, for an unknown reason he drops out of local politics. The birthday of William Shakespeare, the eldest son of this locally prominent man, is unrecorded; but the Stratford parish register records that the infant was baptized on 26 April 1564. (It is quite possible that he was born on 23 April, but this date has probably been assigned by tradition because it is the date on which, fifty-two years later, he died.) The attendance records of the Stratford grammar school of the period are not extant, but it is reasonable to assume that the son of a local official attended the school and received substantial training in Latin. The masters of the school from Shakespeare's seventh to fifteenth years held Oxford degrees; the Elizabethan curriculum excluded mathematics and the natural sciences but taught a good deal of Latin rhetoric, logic, and literature. On 27 November 1582 a marriage license was issued to Shakespeare and Anne Hathaway, eight years his senior. The couple had a child in May, 1583. Perhaps the marriage was necessary, but perhaps the couple had earlier engaged in a formal "troth plight" which would render their children legitimate even if no further ceremony were performed. In 1585 Anne Hathaway bore Shakespeare twins.

That Shakespeare was born is excellent; that he married and had children is pleasant; but that we know nothing about his departure from Stratford to London, or about the beginning of his theatrical career, is lamentable and must be admitted. We would gladly sacrifice details about his children's baptism for details about his earliest days on the stage. Perhaps the poaching episode is true (but it is first reported almost a century after Shakespeare's death), or perhaps he first left Stratford to be a schoolteacher, as another tradition holds; perhaps he was moved by

Such wind as scatters young men through the world,
To seek their fortunes further than at home
Where small experience grows.

In 1592, thanks to the cantankerousness of Robert Greene, a rival playwright and a pamphleteer, we have our first reference, a snarling one, to Shakespeare as an actor and playwright. Greene warns those of his own educated friends who wrote for the theater against an actor who has presumed to turn playwright:

There is an upstart crow, beautified with our feathers, that with his *tiger's heart wrapped in a player's hide* supposes he is as well able to bombast out a blank verse as the best of you, and being an absolute Johannes-factotum is in his own conceit the only Shake-scene in a country.

The reference to the player, as well as the allusion to Aesop's crow (who strutted in borrowed plumage, as an actor struts in fine words not his own), makes it clear that by this date Shakespeare had both acted and written. That Shakespeare is meant is indicated not only by "Shake-scene" but by the parody of a line from one of Shakespeare's plays, *3 Henry VI*: "O, tiger's heart wrapped in a woman's hide." If Shakespeare in 1592 was prominent enough to be attacked by an envious dramatist, he probably had served an apprenticeship in the theater for at least a few years.

In any case, by 1592 Shakespeare had acted and written, and there are a number of subsequent references to him as an actor: documents indicate that in 1598 he is a "principal comedian," in 1603 a "principal tragedian," in 1608 he is one of the "men players." The profession of actor was not for a gentleman, and it occasionally drew the scorn of university men who resented writing speeches for persons less educated than themselves, but it was respectable enough: players, if prosperous, were in effect members of the bourgeoisie, and there is nothing to suggest that Stratford considered William Shakespeare less than a solid citizen. When, in 1596, the Shakespeares were granted a coat of arms, the grant was made to Shakespeare's father, but probably William Shakespeare (who the next year bought the second-largest house in town) had arranged the matter on his own behalf. In subsequent transactions he is occasionally styled a gentleman.

Although in 1593 and 1594 Shakespeare published two narrative poems dedicated to the Earl of Southampton, *Venus and Adonis* and *The Rape of Lucrece*, and may well have written most or all of his sonnets in the middle nineties, Shakespeare's literary activity seems to have been almost entirely devoted to the theater. (It may be significant that the two narrative poems were written in years when the plague closed the theaters for several months.) In 1594 he was a charter member of a theatrical company called the Chamberlain's Men (which in 1603 changed its name to the King's Men); until he retired to Stratford (about 1611, apparently), he was with this remarkably stable company. From 1599 the company acted primarily at the Globe Theatre, in which Shakespeare held a one-tenth interest. Other Elizabethan dramatists are known to have acted, but no other is known also to have been entitled to a share in the profits of the playhouse.

Shakespeare's first eight published plays did not have his name on them, but this is not remarkable; the most popular play of the sixteenth century, Thomas Kyd's *The Spanish Tragedy,* went through many editions without naming Kyd, and Kyd's authorship is known only because a book on the profession of acting happens to quote (and attribute to Kyd) some lines on the interest of Roman emperors in the drama. What is remarkable is that after 1598 Shakespeare's name commonly appears on printed plays—some of which are not his. Another indication of his popularity comes from Francis Meres, author of *Palladis Tamia: Wit's Treasury* (1598): in this anthology of snippets accompanied by an essay on literature, many playwrights are mentioned, but Shakespeare's name occurs more often than any other, and Shakespeare is the only playwright whose plays are listed.

From his acting, playwriting, and share in a theater, Shakespeare seems to have made considerable money. He put it to work, making substantial investments in Stratford real estate. When he made his will (less than a month before he died), he sought to leave his property intact to his descendants. Of small bequests to relatives and to friends (including three actors, Richard Burbage, John Heminges, and Henry Condell), that to his wife of the second-best bed has provoked the most comment; perhaps it was the bed the couple had slept in, the best being reserved for visitors. In any case, had Shakespeare not excepted it, the bed would have gone (with the rest of his household possessions) to his daughter and her husband. On 25 April 1616 he was buried within the chancel of the church at Stratford. An unattractive monument to his memory, placed on a wall near the grave, says he died on 23 April. Over the grave itself are the lines, perhaps by Shakespeare, that (more than his literary fame) have kept his bones undisturbed in the crowded burial ground where old bones were often dislodged to make way for new:

> Good friend, for Jesus' sake forbear
> To dig the dust enclosèd here.
> Blessed be the man that spares these stones
> And cursed be he that moves my bones.

Thirty-seven plays, as well as some nondramatic poems, are held to constitute the Shakespeare canon. The dates of composition of most of the works are highly uncertain, but there is often evidence of a *terminus a quo* (starting point) and/or a *terminus ad quem* (terminal point) that provides a framework for intelligent guessing. For example, *Richard II* cannot be earlier than 1595, the publication date of some material to which it is indebted; *The Merchant of Venice* cannot be later than 1598, the year Francis Meres mentioned it. Sometimes arguments for a date hang on an alleged topical allusion, such as the lines about the unseasonable weather in *A Midsummer Night's Dream,* II.i.81-117, but such an allusion (if indeed it is an illusion) can be variously interpreted, and in any case there is always the possibility that a topical allusion was inserted during a revision, years after the composition of a play. Dates are often attributed on the basis of style, and although conjectures about style usually rest on other conjectures, sooner or later one must rely on one's literary sense. There is no real proof, for example, that *Othello* is not as early as *Romeo and Juliet,* but one feels *Othello* is later, and because the first record of its performance is 1604, one is glad enough to set its composition at that date and not push it back into Shakespeare's early years. The following chronology, then, is as much indebted to informed guesswork and sensitivity as it is to fact. The dates, necessarily imprecise, indicate something like a scholarly consensus.

PLAYS

1588–93	*The Comedy of Errors*
1588–94	*Love's Labor's Lost*
1590–91	*2 Henry VI*
1590–91	*3 Henry VI*
1591–92	*1 Henry VI*
1592–93	*Richard III*
1592–94	*Titus Andronicus*
1593–94	*The Taming of the Shrew*
1593–95	*The Two Gentlemen of Verona*
1594–96	*Romeo and Juliet*
1595	*Richard II*
1594–96	*A Midsummer Night's Dream*
1596–97	*King John*
1596–97	*The Merchant of Venice*
1597	*1 Henry IV*
1597–98	*2 Henry IV*
1598–1600	*Much Ado About Nothing*
1598–99	*Henry V*
1599	*Julius Caesar*
1599–1600	*As You Like It*
1599–1600	*Twelfth Night*
1600–01	*Hamlet*
1597–1601	*The Merry Wives of Windsor*
1601–02	*Troilus and Cressida*
1602–04	*All's Well That Ends Well*
1603–04	*Othello*
1604	*Measure for Measure*
1605–06	*King Lear*
1605–06	*Macbeth*
1606–07	*Antony and Cleopatra*
1605–08	*Timon of Athens*
1607–09	*Coriolanus*

1608-09	*Pericles*
1609-10	*Cymbeline*
1610-11	*The Winter's Tale*
1611	*The Tempest*
1612-13	*Henry VIII*

POEMS

1592	*Venus and Adonis*
1593-94	*The Rape of Lucrece*
1593-1600	*Sonnets*
1600-01	*The Phoenix and the Turtle*

Shakespeare's Theater

In Shakespeare's infancy, Elizabethan actors performed wherever they could—in great halls, at court, in the courtyards of inns. The innyards must have made rather unsatisfactory theaters: on some days they were unavailable because carters bringing goods to London used them as depots; when available, they had to be rented from the innkeeper; perhaps most important, London inns were subject to the Common Council of London, which was not well disposed toward theatricals. In 1574 the Common Council required that plays and playing places in London be licensed. It asserted that

> sundry great disorders and inconveniences have been found to ensue to this city by the inordinate haunting of great multitudes of people, specially youth, to plays, interludes, and shows, namely occasion of frays and quarrels, evil practices of incontinency in great inns having chambers and secret places adjoining to their open stages and galleries,

and ordered that innkeepers who wished licenses to hold performances put up a bond and make contributions to the poor.

The requirement that plays and innyard theaters be licensed, along with the other drawbacks of playing at inns, probably drove James Burbage (a carpenter-turned-actor) to rent in 1576 a plot of land northeast of the city walls and to build here—on property outside the jurisdiction of the city—England's first permanent construction designed for plays. He called it simply the Theatre. About all that is known of its construction is that it was wood. It soon had imitators, the most famous being the Globe (1599), built across the Thames (again outside the city's jurisdiction), out of timbers of the Theatre, which had been dismantled when Burbage's lease ran out.

There are three important sources of information about the structure of Elizabethan playhouses—drawings, a contract, and stage directions in plays. Of drawings, only the so-called De Witt drawing (c. 1596) of the Swan—really a friend's copy of De Witt's drawing—is of much significance. It shows a building of three tiers, with a stage jutting from a wall into the yard or center of the building. The tiers are roofed, and part of the stage is covered by a roof that projects from the rear and is supported at its front on two posts, but the groundlings, who paid a penny to stand in front of the stage, were exposed to the sky. (Performances in such a playhouse were held only in the daytime; artificial illumination was not used.) At the rear of the stage are two doors; above the stage is a gallery. The second major source of information, the contract for the Fortune, specifies that although the Globe is to be the model, the Fortune is to be square, eighty feet outside and fifty-five inside. The stage is to be forty-three feet broad, and is to extend into the middle of the yard (i.e., it is twenty-seven and a half feet deep). For patrons willing to pay more than the general admission charged of the groundlings, there were to be three galleries provided with seats. From the third chief source, stage directions, one learns that entrance to the stage was by doors, presumably spaced widely apart at the rear ("Enter one citizen at one door, and another at the other"), and that in addition to the platform stage there was occasionally some sort of curtained booth or alcove allowing for "discovery" scenes, and some sort of playing space "aloft" or "above" to represent (for example) the top of a city's walls or a room above the street. Doubtless each theater had its own peculiarities, but perhaps we can talk about a "typical" Elizabethan theater if we realize that no theater need exactly have fit the description, just as no father is the typical father with 3.7 children. This hypothetical theater is wooden, round or polygonal (in *Henry V* Shakespeare calls it a "wooden *O*"), capable of holding some eight hundred spectators standing in the yard around the projecting elevated stage and some fifteen hundred additional spectators seated in the three roofed galleries. The stage, protected by a "shadow" or "heavens" or roof, is entered by two doors; behind the doors is the "tiring house" (attiring house, i.e., dressing room), and above the doors is some sort of gallery that may sometimes hold spectators but that can be used (for example) as the bedroom from which Romeo—according to a stage direction in one text—"goeth down." Some evidence suggests that a throne can be lowered onto the platform stage, perhaps from the "shadow"; certainly characters can descend from the stage through a trap or traps into the cellar or "hell." Sometimes this space beneath the platform accommodates a sound-effects man or musician (in *Antony and Cleopatra* "music of the hautboys is under the stage") or an actor (in *Hamlet* the "Ghost cries under the stage"). Most characters simply walk on and off, but because there is no curtain in front of the platform, corpses will have to be carried off (Hamlet must lug Polonius' guts into the neighbor room), or will have to fall at the rear, where the curtain on the alcove or booth can be drawn to conceal them.

Such may have been the so-called "public theater." Another kind of theater, called the "private theater" because its much greater admission charge limited its audience to the wealthy or the prodigal, must be briefly mentioned. The private theater was basically a large

room, entirely roofed and therefore artificially illuminated, with a stage at one end. In 1576 one such theater
was established in Blackfriars, a Dominican priory in
London that had been suppressed in 1538 and confiscated
by the Crown and thus was not under the city's jurisdiction. All the actors in the Blackfriars theater were boys
about eight to thirteen years old (in the public theaters
similar boys played female parts; a boy Lady Macbeth
played to a man Macbeth). This private theater had a
precarious existence, and ceased operations in 1584. In
1596 James Burbage, who had already made theatrical
history by building the Theater, began to construct a second Blackfriars theater. He died in 1597, and for several
years this second Blackfriars theater was used by a
troupe of boys, but in 1608 two of Burbage's sons and
five other actors (including Shakespeare) became joint
operators of the theater, using it in the winter when the
open-air Globe was unsuitable. Perhaps such a smaller
theater, roofed, artificially illuminated, and with a tradition of a courtly audience, exerted an influence on
Shakespeare's late plays.

·Performances in the private theaters may well have
had intermissions during which music was played, but
in the public theaters the action was probably uninter-
rupted, flowing from scene to scene almost without a
break. Actors would enter, speak, exit, and others would
immediately enter and establish (if necessary) the new
locale by a few properties and by words and gestures.
Here are some samples of Shakespeare's scene painting:

> This is Illyria, lady.

> Well, this is the Forest of Arden.

> This castle hath a pleasant seat; the air
> Nimbly and sweetly recommends itself
> Unto our gentle senses.

On the other hand, it is a mistake to conceive of the
Elizabethan stage as bare. Although Shakespeare's

Chorus in *Henry V* calls the stage an "unworthy scaffold" and urges the spectators to "eke out our performance with your mind," there was considerable spectacle. The last act of *Macbeth,* for example, has five stage directions calling for "drum and colors," and another sort of appeal to the eye is indicated by the stage direction "Enter Macduff, with Macbeth's head." Some scenery and properties may have been substantial; doubtless a throne was used, and in one play of the period we encounter this direction: "Hector takes up a great piece of rock and casts at Ajax, who tears up a young tree by the roots and assails Hector." The matter is of some importance, and will be glanced at again in the next section.

The Texts of Shakespeare

Though eighteen of his plays were published during his lifetime, Shakespeare seems never to have supervised their publication. There is nothing unusual here, when a playwright sold a play to a theatrical company he surrendered his ownership of it. Normally a company would not publish the play, because to publish it meant to allow competitors to acquire the piece. Some plays, however, did get published: apparently treacherous actors sometimes pieced together a play for a publisher, sometimes a company in need of money sold a play, and sometimes a company allowed a play to be published that no longer drew audiences. That Shakespeare did not concern himself with publication, then, is scarcely remarkable; of his contemporaries only Ben Jonson carefully supervised the publication of his own plays. In 1623, seven years after Shakespeare's death, John Heminges and Henry Condell (two senior members of Shakespeare's company, who had performed with him for about twenty years) collected his plays—published and unpublished —into a large volume, commonly called the First Folio. (A folio is a volume consisting of sheets that have been folded once, each sheet thus making two leaves, or four pages. The eighteen plays published during Shakespeare's lifetime had been issued one play per volume in small books called quartos. Each sheet in a quarto has been folded twice, making four leaves, or eight pages.) The First Folio contains thirty-six plays; a thirty-seventh, *Pericles*, though not in the Folio is regarded as canonical. Heminges and Condell suggest in an address "To the great variety of readers" that the republished plays are presented in better form than in the quartos: "Before you were abused with diverse stolen and surreptitious copies, maimed and deformed by the frauds and stealths of injurious impostors that exposed them; even those, are now offered to your view cured and perfect of their limbs, and all the rest absolute in their numbers, as he [i.e., Shakespeare] conceived them."

Whoever was assigned to prepare the texts for publication in the First Folio seems to have taken his job seriously and yet not to have performed it with uniform care. The sources of the texts seem to have been, in general, good unpublished copies or the best published copies. The first play in the collection, *The Tempest*, is divided into acts and scenes, has unusually full stage directions and descriptions of spectacle, and concludes with a list of the characters, but the editor was not able (or willing) to present all of the succeeding texts so fully dressed. Later texts occasionally show signs of carelessness: in one scene of *Much Ado About Nothing* the names of actors, instead of characters, appear as speech prefixes (presumably evidence that the printer's copy for this play was a prompt copy); proofreading throughout the Folio is spotty and apparently was done without reference to the printer's copy; the pagination of *Hamlet* jumps from 156 to 257.

A modern editor of Shakespeare must first select his copy; no problem if the play exists only in the Folio, but a considerable problem if the relationship between a quarto and the Folio—or an early quarto and a later one—is unclear. When an editor has chosen what seems to him to be the most authoritative text or texts for his copy, he has not done with making decisions. First of all, he must reckon with Elizabethan spelling. If he is not producing a facsimile, he probably modernizes it, but ought he to preserve the old form of words that apparently were pronounced quite unlike their modern forms—"lanthorn," "alablaster"? If he preserves these forms, is he really preserving Shakespeare's forms or perhaps those of a compositor in the printing house? What is one to do when one finds "lanthorn" and "lantern" in adjacent lines? (The editors of this series in general, but not invariably, assume that words should be spelled in their modern form.) Elizabethan punctuation, too, presents problems. For example in the First Folio, the only text for the play, Macbeth rejects his wife's idea that he can wash the blood from his hand:

> no: this my Hand will rather
> The multitudinous Seas incarnardine,
> Making the Greene one, Red.

Obviously an editor will remove the superfluous capitals, and he will probably alter the spelling to "incarnadine," but will he leave the comma before "red," letting Macbeth speak of the sea as "the green one," or will he (like most modern editors) remove the comma and thus have Macbeth say that his hand will make the ocean *uniformly* red?

An editor will sometimes have to change more than spelling or punctuation. Macbeth says to his wife:

> I dare do all that may become a man,
> Who dares no more, is none.

For two centuries editors have agreed that the second line is unsatisfactory, and have emended "no" to "do": "Who dares do more is none." But when in the same play Ross says that fearful persons

> floate vpon a wilde and violent Sea
> Each way, and moue,

need "move" be emended to "none," as it often is, on the hunch that the compositor misread the manuscript? The editors of the Signet Classic Shakespeare have restrained themselves from making abundant emendations. In their minds they hear Dr. Johnson on the dangers of emending: "I have adopted the Roman sentiment, that it is more honorable to save a citizen than to kill an enemy." Some departures (in addition to spelling, punctuation, and lineation) from the copy text have of course been made, but the original readings are listed in a note following the play, so that the reader can evaluate them for himself.

The editors of the Signet Classic Shakespeare, following tradition, have added line numbers and in many cases act and scene divisions as well as indications of locale at the beginning of scenes. The Folio divided most of the plays into acts and some into scenes. Early eighteenth-century editors increased the divisions. These divisions, which provide a convenient way of referring to passages in the plays, have been retained, but when not in the text chosen as the basis for the Signet Classic text they are enclosed in square brackets [ ] to indicate that they are editorial additions. Similarly, although no play of Shakespeare's published during his lifetime was equipped with indications of locale at the heads of scene divisions, locales have here been added in square brackets for the convenience of the reader, who lacks the information afforded to spectators by costumes, properties, and gestures. The spectator can tell at a glance he is in the throne room, but without an editorial indication the reader may be puzzled for a while. It should be mentioned, incidentally, that there are a few authentic stage directions—perhaps Shakespeare's, perhaps a prompter's—that suggest locales: for example, "Enter Brutus in his orchard," and "They go up into the Senate house." It is hoped that the bracketed additions provide the reader with the sort of help provided in these two authentic directions, but it is equally hoped that the reader will remember that the stage was not loaded with scenery.

No editor during the course of his work can fail to recollect some words Heminges and Condell prefixed to the Folio:

It had been a thing, we confess, worthy to have been wished, that the author himself had lived to have set forth and overseen his own writings. But since it hath been ordained otherwise, and he by death departed from that right, we pray you do not envy his friends the office of their care and pain to have collected and published them.

Nor can an editor, after he has done his best, forget Heminges and Condell's final words: "And so we leave you to other of his friends, whom if you need can be your guides. If you need them not, you can lead yourselves, and others. And such readers we wish him."

SYLVAN BARNET
Tufts University

Introduction

The date of *Macbeth*, like that of many of Shakespeare's plays, is not beyond all dispute, but there are good reasons for believing it was written in 1605–06 and was performed at Hampton Court in 1606 before James I of England and his brother-in-law, Christian of Denmark. The play, indeed, seems to have been written to please James (and perhaps thus to further the fortunes of Shakespeare's theatrical company, which in 1603 had been named the King's Men). The evidence that Shakespeare sought to please James ranges from the highly favorable portrait of Banquo, from whom the Stuarts claimed descent (the pageant in IV.i of Banquo and the eight kings seems to be a polite tribute to James, who was the ninth Stuart monarch), to such a small detail as the omission of a defeat of the Danes—this to avoid embarrassing the visiting Danish king. But for a discussion of all such evidence, the reader must consult Henry N. Paul's *The Royal Play of Macbeth*. Our concern here will not be with the play Shakespeare wrote for the two kings, but with the play he wrote for us.

Although *Macbeth* draws its material from Holinshed's *Chronicles*, a historical compilation that provided Shakespeare with much of the material for the ten plays that in the Folio of 1623 comprise the section labeled "Histories," *Macbeth* was entitled a tragedy and was printed among the tragedies in the Folio. James may have looked on the play as history, but it is not history. (Banquo, for example, was a convenient invention of a Scottish historian who in the early sixteenth century needed to give the Stuart line a proper beginning.) It is something that poets and literary critics customarily consider superior to history: a vision of life that has the concreteness of history and yet the wisdom of philosophy. Of course none of Shakespeare's history plays is satisfactory history; the exclusion of *Macbeth* from the "Histories" does not mean that the editors of the Folio recognized in it any unusual departure from fact. Perhaps *Macbeth* was excluded simply because its dramatis personae are Scottish, not English. But its presence among the "Tragedies" may mean that the editors saw a fundamental difference between *Macbeth* and, say, *Richard III*, which had earlier been published as a tragedy and which is called a tragedy even while it is placed among the "Histories." When one reads or sees *Richard III*, one cannot help feeling—even despite some familiarity with modern historical accounts that have demonstrated Shakespeare's distortions of fact—that one is experiencing a re-creation or re-presentation of what men did to other men during a segment of English history. When one reads or sees *Macbeth*, one cannot help feeling that one is experiencing a re-creation or re-presentation of what a man is, in the present, even in the timeless.

Suppose we take a definition of tragedy and apply it to *Macbeth*. We may find that the play helps to support the definition, and that when we apply this touchstone we see things in the play that we might otherwise have missed. (But we will also see that the definition shrinks the play, and that after it has served its purpose it must be discarded for another that may further illuminate the play.) Let us take as our first touchstone a line uttered in Cyril Tourneur's *The Revenger's Tragedy,* a play apparently written about the same time as *Macbeth*:

When the bad bleed, then is the tragedy good.

In this view, tragedy shows the punishment of evildoers;

at its conclusion (to quote the Duke of Albany, in *King Lear*)

> All friends shall taste
> The wages of their virtue, and all foes
> The cup of their deservings.

What is there of this in *Macbeth*? If Tourneur's "bad" includes, as it must, a man who knowingly kills his benefactor, and who follows this murder with tyrannical assaults upon the lives of his countrymen (including women and children), then the formula has some relevance to *Macbeth*. For although most discussions of tragedy start from Aristotle's assumption that the best tragedy concerns a man who does a deed of horror in ignorance (Oedipus kills an old man who unknown to him is his father, Othello kills Desdemona in the mistaken belief that she is unchaste, Brutus makes errors of judgment that undercut his high-minded aspirations), Macbeth is not confused about the criminal nature of his deed. When he kills the king who is his guest and generous lord, he knows, as Oedipus, Othello, and Brutus do not, that he does a "horrid deed." Even before he does the deed he foresees the outcome, apparently sensing that in the nature of things something rather like Albany's view will come about through the workings of even-handed justice. In his first soliloquy he says:

> . . . we but teach
> Bloody instructions, which, being taught, return
> To plague th' inventor: this even-handed justice
> Commends th' ingredients of our poisoned chalice
> To our own lips.[1]

> (I.vii.8-12)

---

[1] By the way, although the idea that an evil act engenders its own punishment is scarcely novel, Shakespeare's use of it here is probably indebted to a passage in Holinshed's *Chronicles*: "For the prick of conscience, as it chanceth ever in tyrants and such as attain to any estate by unrighteous means, caused him ever to fear, lest he should be served of the same cup as he had ministered to his predecessors."

Nor does Macbeth lose his moral sense after his first crime. Midway in the play, when he has already suffered violent feelings of guilt, he determines to toughen himself in villainous practice; he has seen the ghost of one of his victims because (he thinks) he is still a fearful novice in crime and he has not yet inured himself by "hard use." A little later, when he fears he is losing his control, he determines that his course must be bloodier:

> From this moment
> The very firstlings of my heart shall be
> The firstlings of my hand. And even now,
> To crown my thoughts with acts, be it thought and
>   done:
> The castle of Macduff I will surprise;
> Seize upon Fife; give to th' edge o' th' sword
> His wife, his babes, and all unfortunate souls
> That trace him in his line. No boasting like a fool;
> This deed I'll do before this purpose cool.
>   (IV.i.146-54)

Another way of seeing something of Macbeth's calculated villainy—something of the quality that puts him in Tourneur's classification of "the bad"—is to see what his opponents are like. Who are they? Chief of them is Malcolm, the heir to the throne—a man chaste, trustworthy, and patriotic—and they include men who are distressed to hear that Macbeth has made "each new morn/ New widows howl, new orphans cry." To these enemies of Macbeth, he is a butcher, a tyrant, a hell-kite, a hellhound. Malcolm and his allies, on the other hand, are the instruments of the powers above, and are God's soldiers. The concluding speech sharply contrasts the defeated tyrant (at whose fall, Dr. Johnson says, "every reader rejoices") and the rightful king:

> What's more to do,
> Which would be planted newly with the time—
> As calling home our exiled friends abroad
> That fled the snares of watchful tyranny,

> Producing forth the cruel ministers
> Of this dead butcher and his fiendlike queen,
> Who, as 'tis thought, by self and violent hands
> Took off her life—this, and what needful else
> That calls upon us, by the grace of Grace
> We will perform in measure, time, and place:
> So thanks to all at once and to each one,
> Whom we invite to see us crowned at Scone.
>
> (V.viii.64-75)

Macbeth has been allied with witches or fiends, but the rightful ruler will work "by the grace of Grace." Macbeth has been unable to "buckle his distempered cause/Within the belt of rule," but the rightful ruler will perform his actions "in measure, time, and place." Macbeth had heard Duncan say to him "I have begun to plant thee, and will labor/To make thee full of growing," yet he had turned against the source of his growth, killed Duncan (and so made of himself a rootless branch that must become desiccated); the rightful ruler's mind turns to planting newly with the time.

It can be put this way: Macbeth's action is contrary to nature, and he knows it. The mere thought of his deed makes his body function unnaturally. The witches' solicitation, he says,

> doth unfix my hair
> And make my seated heart knock at my ribs,
> Against the use of nature.
>
> (I.iii.135-37)

The wounds inflicted on Duncan look like "a breach in nature," and the sun feels the effect of the murder:

> By the clock 'tis day,
> And yet dark night strangles the traveling lamp:
> Is't night's predominance, or the day's shame,
> That darkness does the face of earth entomb,
> When living light should kiss it?
>
> (II.iv.6-10)

To which the Old Man replies: " 'Tis unnatural,/ Even like the deed that's done."

By turning against the source of his growth, then, Macbeth becomes infected:

> Who then shall blame
> His pestered senses to recoil and start,
> When all that is within him does condemn
> Itself for being there?
>   (V.ii.22-25)

But of course this is not the whole story, and the Macbeth that has been thus far discussed is only a part of Shakespeare's Macbeth. At the outset of the play we meet not Macbeth but the Weird Sisters. The next time they assemble, the third one says, it will be to meet with Macbeth. The incantatory quality of their verse—the power of the rhyme, the alliteration, and the mysterious paradoxes —can be felt even in a single couplet:

> Fair is foul, and foul is fair.
> Hover through the fog and filthy air.
>   (I.i.10-11)

We may insist, on reflection, that Macbeth is a free agent who need not have yielded to the witches' hints; certainly he harbors within him what they present to our eye. Yet can we feel sure that he has not been ensnared: the charm has been wound up, and if he is the tyrant, viewed another way he is the victim of infernal tyranny. "The instruments of darkness tell us truths,/Win us with honest trifles, to betray 's/In deepest consequence." The witches can control the winds, and we first see Macbeth on a "blasted heath." The very air he breathes, as it is in part made up of the witches who "melted as breath into the wind," is infected. This second view, of Macbeth as victim, though it must not be pressed (the noble Duncan finds the air sweet—but, in another way, he too is a victim), finds support in Shakespeare's other tragedies and even in his use of the word "tragedy" and its derivatives. He seems never to use it in a context that bears much resemblance to Tourneur's line, "When the bad bleed, then is the tragedy good." Always, or almost always, the word is linked with a violent death that evokes woe or is said to be woeful. Because he does not mention "tragedy" in *Macbeth,* an example must be drawn from another play. One of his earliest uses of the word will suffice. In *1 Henry VI,* Salisbury, an English Commander, has been killed by a hidden French gunner. Talbot, Salisbury's cohort, laments the sudden fall:

> Accursed tower! Accursed fatal hand
> That hath contrived this woeful tragedy.
> (I.iv)

The reference to the tower, and the word "fatal" ("destined," "fated") are important, for they suggest that tragedy sets its woeful happenings against a mysterious backdrop of inhuman and inscrutable forces.

The Weird Sisters in *Macbeth* are of course part of this inscrutable surrounding. In the Folio their name is spelled "weyard" or "weyward" (perhaps with a glance at "wayward"?) but the stage directions and speech prefixes call them witches. They have the traditional petty malice (and beards) of witches, and they acknowledge "masters," but they also have properties not associated with witches: they vanish like bubbles, and they speak authoritatively. In the fourth act they are closer to the Furies than to mischievous hags. No English play before *Macbeth* has such imposing witches, and if the Weird Sisters resemble witches in their ability to sail in a sieve and in their animal-killing and in their cookery and in their revenge on the sailor's wife, they nevertheless seem also to merit the title Macbeth gives them—"juggling fiends." Their name suggests the Fates (Old English *wyrd,* fate), and Holinshed conjectures that they may be "The goddesses of destiny," though of course Holinshed's view need not be Shakespeare's.

Is it, then, Macbeth's bad luck that the witches wait for him? Or is there something within himself that has at-

tracted them, and that makes him recognize his kinship
with them? Are they the dramatist's concrete embodi-
ments of a part of Macbeth? As soon as we ask these
questions we realize that debate is futile; we cannot reply
by pointing to Elizabethan treatises on demonology; we can
only repeat portions of the play; and the play does
not provide unequivocal answers.

Equivocation, in fact, is in part what the play is about.
The Porter (II.iii) soliloquizes about an equivocator,
but we do not have to wait for him to introduce the
theme of doubleness or ambiguity. The Weird Sisters,
in the first scene, will meet "when the battle's lost and
won," and for them "fair is foul, and foul is fair." A few
moments later Macbeth will enter, and his first line will
be

So foul and fair a day I have not seen.

One aspect of this pervasive doubleness is in the wordplay. The Porter has his quibbles, of course, but so do
Macbeth and Lady Macbeth. Second meanings, however,
lurk not only under words (e.g., *gild-guilt*); there are
second meanings under whole speeches and actions. This
is not surprising in a play in which the protagonist is advised to "look like th' innocent flower,/But be the
serpent under 't," and in which we hear "Away, and mock
the time with fairest show:/False face must hide what
the false heart doth know." Still, it was not inevitable that
Shakespeare should so brilliantly follow the innocent Duncan's observation that "There's no art/To find the
mind's construction in the face:/He was a gentleman
on whom I built/An absolute trust" with a stage direction, *"Enter Macbeth,"* i.e., enter another whose appearance will deceive Duncan.

It is time that we look more closely at Macbeth's double
nature, for if he is the "devilish Macbeth" that Malcolm
says he is, he is also something else.

Very early in the play—immediately after the odd
ritual of a dozen lines in which the Weird Sisters inform
us that they will meet with Macbeth, we get a report of

Macbeth's loyalty and courage. He is "brave Macbeth," "valiant cousin! Worthy gentleman," and "noble Macbeth," and by his deeds against rebels and foreign invaders he has earned these words. His first appearance on the stage does not quite confirm this report, but if anything it even more potently engages our sympathetic interest; he starts and seems "to fear/Things that do sound so fair." With hindsight we can say that he starts because he has already harbored criminal impulses that respond to the witches' words, but what is more important is that his apprehensiveness suggests both an apartness from others and a self-division that will make us see in him a good deal more than the blackguard. Twice in this first view of Macbeth we hear him described as "rapt," and his asides—confessing his uncertainties—complicate him and make him more than the hero described in the previous scene. There he had unseamed a rebel from the nave to the chops, had been an eagle, a cannon, and valor's minion. That is, when we first hear of Macbeth we hear of a man of noble and unambiguous action; when we first see Macbeth, we see a man of uncertainty. His first appearance puts him in the company of sympathetic tragic heroes such as Hamlet and Romeo. (Hamlet's first remark is an aside, and his next few speeches reveal he is not at one with his surroundings or himself. When we first see Romeo he is so abstracted that he is unaware of the time of day, and he endures "sad hours.") Conversely, Macbeth is far from the evil Richard III, whose history Shakespeare presented in the tragic shape of a rise and fall. Richard is unambiguously a villain. As early as the thirtieth line of the play he begins

> I am determined to prove a villain,
> And hate the idle pleasures of these days.
> Plots have I laid, inductions dangerous,
> By drunken prophecies, libels, and dreams,
> To set my brother Clarence and the King
> In deadly hate, the one against the other.
> And if King Edward be as true and just

As I am subtle, false, and treacherous . . .

This unmitigated villainy is not without its attractions,
but contrast it with Macbeth's recoil at his own murderous thoughts:

> My thought, whose murder yet is but fantastical,
> Shakes so my single state of man that function
> Is smothered in surmise, and nothing is
> But what is not.
>
> (I.iii. 139-42)

It is not, then, that he commits crimes and at the end
suffers; he suffers even before he commits his first criminal action, and because he is his own tormentor he
scarcely needs the spectator's punishing eyes. Immediately after killing Duncan he is afflicted with doubts and
has a premonition of the sleeplessness that will ensue.
Lady Macbeth takes a simpler view: "Consider it not so
deeply," "These deeds must not be thought/After these
ways; so, it will make us mad," "A little water clears
us of this deed:/How easy is it then!" (But if she here
seems as black as the evil angel that prompts Mankind
to illicit deeds in the old morality plays, she too reveals
inner depths in the sleepwalking scene, when we see that
like her husband she is troubled with thick-coming fancies
that keep her from her rest.)

Macbeth early recognizes the unnaturalness of his
thoughts, and, as the asides in the first act make clear,
they estrange him from his fellows and even almost from
himself. They

> make my seated heart knock at my ribs,
> Against the use of nature.
>
> (I.iii.136-37)

The soldier who fought along with his countrymen—who
is described as a savior—becomes, by the last act, a
man who knows that he has no friends (enemy troops,
rather than troops of friends, surround him); his sol-

diers at the end—those who do not desert him—are mere "constrainèd things/Whose hearts are absent too." His course in blood has separated him not only from God ("wherefore could I not pronounce 'Amen'?"), and from his subjects (he cannot banquet at ease with them), but even from his wife. At the start of the play she is his "dearest partner of greatness," and his "dearest love." But midway in the play (though she is "dearest chuck") he keeps from her the plot against Banquo, and at the end he seems almost insensible to her death: "She should have died hereafter." There are many ways of responding to the news of the death of a beloved one, and in this play Shakespeare gives us three. It is instructive to compare Macduff's response (IV.iii) and Old Siward's (V.viii), very different yet not totally so, and to contrast them to Macbeth's utterly dissimilar response.

What of Macbeth's own death? Its effect on us is complex. When his severed head is brought in, perhaps we sense a parallel between Macbeth's career and that of the treacherous Macdonwald, whose head Macbeth had justly fixed upon the battlements, and a contrast between, first, Macbeth and the Thane of Cawdor, who confessed his treasons and yielded up his life "as 'twere a trifle," and, second, between Macbeth and Young Siward, who died as "God's soldier"; but perhaps too we feel that there is something of the soldierly Macbeth in his final contest, and, equally important, that his death is the release (hence it is not wholly painful to him) of one who knows he harvested what he sowed, and who is aweary of the sun.

The speech Macbeth makes before he dies can here be used to remind us that he holds our interest partly by his language. It is not a matter of confusing the character with the author, but simply a matter of recognizing that one of the things that makes us interested in Macbeth (and in all of the people embodied in the play, or, rather, the people who embody the play) is memorable speech. The point might be made by printing the lines he utters on the nothingness of life just after he learns of Lady Macbeth's death—lines so potent that although they fit exactly into their place in the drama they have often been taken out and held to represent Shakespeare's own view—yet the role that Macbeth's language plays can be still better seen by quoting a dying speech that David Garrick composed for Macbeth in the eighteenth century. Even the reader who has read only as much of the play as has been quoted in this introduction must recognize that every word of Shakespeare's Macbeth will engage him as Garrick's does not. Garrick's Macbeth says:

> Hell drags me down. I sink,
> I sink. Oh! my soul is lost forever.
> Oh!   *Dies.*

The final speech of Shakespeare's Macbeth is an almost indescribable blend of corrupted pride, desperation, animal fury, and courage; it is not one of the meditative or descriptive passages that even out of context has a life of its own, but like all the other lines in the play it holds us rapt.

SYLVAN BARNET

The Tragedy of
MACBETH

Duncan, King of Scotland
Malcolm ⎫
Donalbain ⎭ his sons
Macbeth ⎫
Banquo ⎪
Macduff ⎪
Lennox ⎪
Ross ⎬ noblemen of Scotland
Menteith ⎪
Angus ⎪
Caithness ⎭
Fleance, son to Banquo
Siward, Earl of Northumberland, general of the
    English forces
Young Siward, his son
Seyton, an officer attending on Macbeth
Son to Macduff
An English Doctor
A Scottish Doctor
A Porter
An Old Man
Three Murderers
Lady Macbeth
Lady Macduff
A Gentlewoman attending on Lady Macbeth
Hecate
Witches
Apparitions
Lords, Officers, Soldiers, Attendants, and Mes-
    sengers

Scene: Scotland; England]

The Tragedy of Macbeth

ACT I

Scene I. [*An open place.*]

Thunder and lightning. Enter Three Witches.

First Witch. When shall we three meet again?
  In thunder, lightning, or in rain?

Second Witch. When the hurlyburly's done,
  When the battle's lost and won.

Third Witch. That will be ere the set of sun.   5

First Witch. Where the place?

Second Witch.   Upon the heath.

Third Witch. There to meet with Macbeth.

First Witch. I come, Graymalkin.° ¹

Second Witch. Paddock° calls.

Third Witch.   Anon!°

All. Fair is foul, and foul is fair.   10

  Hover through the fog and filthy air.

                                        Exeunt.

¹ The degree sign (°) indicates a footnote, which is keyed to the text by line number. Text references are printed in *italic* type; the annotation follows in roman type.
I.i. 8 *Graymalkin* (the witch's attendant spirit, a gray cat) 9 *Paddock* toad 9 *Anon* at once

37

Scene II. [*A camp.*]

Alarum within.°   Enter King [Duncan], Mal-
colm, Donalbain, Lennox, with Attendants, meet-
ing a bleeding Captain.

King. What bloody man is that? He can report,
As seemeth by his plight, of the revolt
The newest state.

Malcolm.   This is the sergeant°
Who like a good and hardy soldier fought
5 'Gainst my captivity. Hail, brave friend!
Say to the king the knowledge of the broil°
As thou didst leave it.

Captain.   Doubtful it stood,
As two spent swimmers, that do cling together
And choke their art.° The merciless Macdonwald—
10 Worthy to be a rebel for to that
The multiplying villainies of nature
Do swarm upon him—from the Western Isles°
Of kerns and gallowglasses° is supplied;
And Fortune, on his damnèd quarrel° smiling,
15 Showed like a rebel's whore:° but all's too weak:
For brave Macbeth—well he deserves that name—
Disdaining Fortune, with his brandished steel,
Which smoked with bloody execution,
Like valor's minion° carved out his passage

I.ii.s.d. *Alarum within* trumpet call offstage   3 *sergeant* i.e., officer
(he is called, perhaps with no inconsistency in Shakespeare's day,
a captain in the s.d. and speech prefixes. *Sergeant* is trisyllabic)
6 *broil* quarrel   9 *choke their art* hamper each other's doings   12 *West-*
ern Isles Hebrides   13 *Of kerns and gallowglasses* with lightly armed
Irish foot soldiers and heavily armed ones   14 *damnèd quarrel* accursed
cause   15 *Showed like a rebel's whore* i.e., falsely appeared to favor
Macdonwald   19 *minion* (trisyllabic) favorite

Till he faced the slave;   20
Which nev'r shook hands, nor bade farewell to him,
Till he unseamed him from the nave to th' chops,°
And fixed his head upon our battlements.

King. O valiant cousin! Worthy gentleman!

Captain. As whence the sun 'gins his reflection°   25
Shipwracking storms and direful thunders break,
So from that spring whence comfort seemed to come
Discomfort swells. Mark, King of Scotland, mark:
No sooner justice had, with valor armed,
Compelled these skipping kerns to trust their heels   30
But the Norweyan lord, surveying vantage,°
With furbished arms and new supplies of men,
Began a fresh assault.

King.   Dismayed not this
Our captains, Macbeth and Banquo?

Captain.   Yes;
As sparrows eagles, or the hare the lion.   35
If I say sooth,° I must report they were
As cannons overcharged with double cracks;°
So they doubly redoubled strokes upon the foe.
Except° they meant to bathe in reeking wounds,
Or memorize another Golgotha,°   40
I cannot tell—
But I am faint; my gashes cry for help.

King. So well thy words become thee as thy wounds;
They smack of honor both. Go get him surgeons.

                        [*Exit Captain, attended.*]

                Enter Ross and Angus.
Who comes here?

---

22 *nave to th' chops* navel to the jaws   25 *reflection* (four syllables;
the ending—*ion* here and often elsewhere in the play— is disyllabic)
31 *surveying vantage* seeing an opportunity   36 *sooth* truth   37 *cracks*
explosives   39 *Except* unless   40 *memorize another Golgotha* make
the place as memorable as Golgotha, "the place of the skull"

45 *Malcolm.*   The worthy Thane° of Ross.

Lennox. What a haste looks through his eyes! So
        should he look
   That seems to° speak things strange.

Ross.   God save the king!

King. Whence cam'st thou, worthy Thane?

Ross.   From Fife, great King;
   Where the Norweyan banners flout the sky
50 And fan our people cold.
   Norway° himself, with terrible numbers,
   Assisted by that most disloyal traitor
   The Thane of Cawdor, began a dismal° conflict;
   Till that Bellona's bridegroom, lapped in proof,°
55 Confronted him with self-comparisons,°
   Point against point, rebellious arm 'gainst arm,
   Curbing his lavish° spirit: and, to conclude,
   The victory fell on us.

King.   Great happiness!

Ross.   That now
   Sweno, the Norways' king, craves composition;°
60 Nor would we deign him burial of his men
   Till he disbursèd, at Saint Colme's Inch,°
   Ten thousand dollars° to our general use.

King. No more that Thane of Cawdor shall deceive
   Our bosom interest:° go pronounce his present°
        death,
65 And with his former title greet Macbeth.

Ross. I'll see it done.

King. What he hath lost, noble Macbeth hath won.
                                        Exeunt.

---

⁴⁵ *Thane* (a Scottish title of nobility)   ⁴⁷ *seems to* seems about to
⁵¹ *Norway* the King of Norway   ⁵³ *dismal* threatening   ⁵⁴ *Bellona's
. . . proof* the mate of the goddess of war, clad in tested (proved)
armor   ⁵⁵ *self-comparisons* counter-movements   ⁵⁷ *lavish* insolent
⁵⁹ *composition* terms of peace   ⁶¹ *Inch* island   ⁶² *dollars* (Spanish and
Dutch currency)   ⁶⁴ *Our bosom interest* my (plural of royalty)
heart's trust   ⁶⁴ *present* immediate

Scene III. [*A heath.*]

Thunder. Enter the Three Witches.

First Witch. Where hast thou been, sister?

Second Witch. Killing swine.

Third Witch. Sister, where thou?

First Witch. A sailor's wife had chestnuts in her lap,
And mounched, and mounched, and mounched.
   "Give me," quoth I.   5
"Aroint thee,° witch!" the rump-fed ronyon° cries.
Her husband's to Aleppo gone, master o' th' Tiger:
But in a sieve I'll thither sail,
And, like a rat without a tail,
I'll do, I'll do, and I'll do.   10

Second Witch. I'll give thee a wind.

First Witch. Th' art kind.

Third Witch. And I another.

First Witch. I myself have all the other;
And the very ports they blow,°   15
All the quarters that they know
I' th' shipman's card.°
I'll drain him dry as hay:
Sleep shall neither night nor day
Hang upon his penthouse lid;°   20
He shall live a man forbid:°
Weary sev'nights nine times nine
Shall he dwindle, peak,° and pine:

I.iii. 6 *Aroint thee* begone   6 *rump-fed ronyon* fat-rumped scabby creature   15 *ports they blow* harbors to which the winds blow (?)
17 *card* compass card   20 *penthouse lid* eyelid (the figure is of a lean-to)
21 *forbid* cursed   23 *peak* waste away

Though his bark cannot be lost,
25   Yet it shall be tempest-tossed.
Look what I have.

Second Witch. Show me, show me.

First Witch. Here I have a pilot's thumb,
Wracked as homeward he did come.

                    Drum within.

30   *Third Witch.* A drum, a drum!
Macbeth doth come.

All. The weïrd° sisters, hand in hand,
Posters° of the sea and land,
Thus do go about, about:
35   Thrice to thine, and thrice to mine,
And thrice again, to make up nine.
Peace! The charm's wound up.

                Enter Macbeth and Banquo.

Macbeth. So foul and fair a day I have not seen.

Banquo. How far is 't called to Forres? What are these
40   So withered, and so wild in their attire,
That look not like th' inhabitants o' th' earth,
And yet are on 't? Live you, or are you aught
That man may question?° You seem to understand
          me,
By each at once her choppy° finger laying
45   Upon her skinny lips. You should be women,
And yet your beards forbid me to interpret
That you are so.

Macbeth.   Speak, if you can: what are you?

First Witch. All hail, Macbeth! Hail to thee, Thane of
Glamis!

Second Witch. All hail, Macbeth! Hail to thee, Thane of
Cawdor!

32 *weïrd* destiny-serving (?)   38 *Posters* swift travelers   43 *question* talk
to   44 *choppy* chapped

Third Witch. All hail, Macbeth, that shalt be King
   hereafter!   50

Banquo. Good sir, why do you start, and seem to fear
   Things that do sound so fair? I' th' name of truth,
   Are ye fantastical,° or that indeed
   Which outwardly ye show? My noble partner
   You greet with present grace° and great prediction   55
   Of noble having° and of royal hope,
   That he seems rapt withal:° to me you speak not.
   If you can look into the seeds of time,
   And say which grain will grow and which will not,
   Speak then to me, who neither beg nor fear   60
   Your favors nor your hate.

First Witch. Hail!

Second Witch. Hail!

Third Witch. Hail!

First Witch. Lesser than Macbeth, and greater.   65

Second Witch. Not so happy,° yet much happier.

Third Witch. Thou shalt get° kings, though thou be
   none.
   So all hail, Macbeth and Banquo!

First Witch. Banquo and Macbeth, all hail!

Macbeth. Stay, you imperfect° speakers, tell me more: 70
   By Sinel's° death I know I am Thane of Glamis;
   But how of Cawdor? The Thane of Cawdor lives,
   A prosperous gentleman; and to be King
   Stands not within the prospect of belief,
   No more than to be Cawdor. Say from whence   75
   You owe° this strange intelligence?° Or why
   Upon this blasted heath you stop our way

---

⁵³ *fantastical* imaginary ⁵⁵ *grace* honor ⁵⁶ *having* possession ⁵⁷ *rapt
withal* entranced by it ⁶⁶ *happy* fortunate ⁶⁷ *get* beget ⁷⁰ *imperfect*
incomplete ⁷¹ *Sinel* (Macbeth's father) ⁷⁶ *owe* own, have ⁷⁶ *intelligence* information

With such prophetic greeting? Speak, I charge
    you.

> *Witches vanish.*

Banquo. The earth hath bubbles as the water has,
80   And these are of them. Whither are they vanished?

Macbeth. Into the air, and what seemed corporal°
    melted
      As breath into the wind. Would they had stayed!

Banquo. Were such things here as we do speak about?
      Or have we eaten on the insane° root
85   That takes the reason prisoner?

Macbeth. Your children shall be kings.

Banquo.   You shall be King.

Macbeth. And Thane of Cawdor too. Went it not so?
Banquo. To th' selfsame tune and words. Who's here?

> *Enter Ross and Angus.*

Ross. The King hath happily received, Macbeth,
90   The news of thy success; and when he reads°
      Thy personal venture in the rebels' fight,
      His wonders and his praises do contend
      Which should be thine or his.° Silenced with that,
      In viewing o'er the rest o' th' selfsame day,
95   He finds thee in the stout Norweyan ranks,
      Nothing afeard of what thyself didst make,
      Strange images of death. As thick as tale
      Came post with post,° and every one did bear
      Thy praises in his kingdom's great defense,
      And poured them down before him.

100 *Angus.*   We are sent
      To give thee, from our royal master, thanks;

---

81 *corporal* corporeal   84 *insane* insanity-producing   90 *reads* considers
92–93 *His* wonders . . . *his* i.e., Duncan's speechless admiration, appropriate to him, contends with his desire to praise you (?)   97–98 *As
thick . . . post* as fast as could be counted came messenger after messenger

    Only to herald thee into his sight,
    Not pay thee.

Ross. And for an earnest° of a greater honor,
    He bade me, from him, call thee Thane of Cawdor;   *105*
    In which addition,° hail, most worthy Thane!
    For it is thine.

Banquo.   What, can the devil speak true?

Macbeth. The Thane of Cawdor lives: why do you dress
    me
    In borrowed robes?

Angus.   Who was the thane lives yet,
    But under heavy judgment bears that life   *110*
    Which he deserves to lose. Whether he was com-
        bined°
    With those of Norway, or did line° the rebel
    With hidden help and vantage,° or that with both
    He labored in his country's wrack,° I know not;
    But treasons capital, confessed and proved,   *115*
    Have overthrown him.

Macbeth.   [*Aside*] Glamis, and Thane of Cawdor:
    The greatest is behind.° [*To Ross and Angus*] Thanks
        for your pains.
    [*Aside to Banquo*] Do you not hope your children
        shall be kings,
    When those that gave the Thane of Cawdor to me
    Promised no less to them?

Banquo. [*Aside to Macbeth*] That, trusted home,° *120*
    Might yet enkindle you unto the crown,
    Besides the Thane of Cawdor. But 'tis strange:
    And oftentimes, to win us to our harm,
    The instruments of darkness tell us truths,
    Win us with honest trifles, to betray 's   *125*

---

104 *earnest* pledge   106 *addition* title   111 *combined* allied   112 *line* support   113 *vantage* opportunity   114 *wrack* ruin   117 *behind* i.e., to follow   120 *home* all the way

In deepest consequence.° \
Cousins,° a word, I pray you.

Macbeth. [*Aside*] Two truths are to \
As happy prologues to the swelling° act \
Of the imperial theme.—I thank you, gentlemen.—
130   [*Aside*] This supernatural soliciting° \
Cannot be ill, cannot be good. If ill, \
Why hath it given me earnest of success, \
Commencing in a truth? I am Thane of Cawdor: \
If good, why do I yield to that suggestion
135   Whose horrid image doth unfix my hair \
And make my seated° heart knock at my ribs, \
Against the use of nature?° Present fears \
Are less than horrible imaginings. \
My thought, whose murder yet is but fantastical,°
140   Shakes so my single° state of man that function \
Is smothered in surmise, and nothing is \
But what is not.

Banquo.   Look, how our partner's rapt.

Macbeth. [*Aside*] If chance will have me King, why, \
    chance may crown me, \
Without my stir.

Banquo.   New honors come upon him, \
Like our strange° garments, cleave not to their
145   mold \
But with the aid of use.

Macbeth.   [*Aside*] Come what come may \
Time and the hour runs through the roughest day.

Banquo. Worthy Macbeth, we stay upon your leisure.°

Macbeth. Give me your favor.° My dull brain was \
    wrought

---

126 *In deepest consequence* in the most significant sequel   127 *Cousins* i.e., fellow noblemen   128 *swelling* stately   130 *soliciting* inviting 136 *seated* fixed   137 *Against the use of nature* contrary to my natural way   139 *fantastical* imaginary   140 *single* unaided, weak (or "entire"?) 145 *strange* new   148 *stay upon your leisure* await your convenience 149 *favor* pardon

With things forgotten. Kind gentlemen, your pains   150
Are registered where every day I turn
The leaf to read them. Let us toward the King.
[*Aside to Banquo*] Think upon what hath
    chanced, and at more time,
The interim having weighed it,° let us speak
Our free hearts° each to other.

Banquo.   Very gladly.   155

Macbeth. Till then, enough. Come, friends.

                                        Exeunt.

Scene IV.   [*Forres. The palace.*]

Flourish.° Enter King [*Duncan*], *Lennox,
    Malcolm, Donalbain, and Attendants.*

King. Is execution done on Cawdor? Are not
    Those in commission° yet returned?

Malcolm.   My liege,
    They are not yet come back. But I have spoke
    With one that saw him die, who did report
    That very frankly he confessed his treasons,   5
    Implored your Highness' pardon and set forth
    A deep repentance: nothing in his life
    Became him like the leaving it. He died
    As one that had been studied° in his death,
    To throw away the dearest thing he owed°   10
    As 'twere a careless° trifle.

154 *The interim having weighed it* i.e., when we have had time to
think   155 *Our free hearts* our minds freely   I.iv.s.d. *Flourish* fanfare
2 *in commission* i.e., commissioned to oversee the execution   9 *studied.*
rehearsed   10 *owed* owned   11 *careless* uncared-for

King.   There's no art
To find the mind's construction in the face:
He was a gentleman on whom I built
An absolute trust.

    Enter Macbeth, Banquo, Ross, and Angus.

               O worthiest cousin!
15 The sin of my ingratitude even now
Was heavy on me: thou art so far before,
That swiftest wing of recompense is slow
To overtake thee. Would thou hadst less deserved,
That the proportion° both of thanks and payment
20 Might have been mine! Only I have left to say,
More is thy due than more than all can pay.

Macbeth. The service and the loyalty I owe,
In doing it, pays itself.° Your Highness' part
Is to receive our duties: and our duties
25 Are to your throne and state children and servants;
Which do but what they should, by doing every
    thing
Safe toward° your love and honor.

King.   Welcome hither.
I have begun to plant thee, and will labor
To make thee full of growing. Noble Banquo,
30 That hast no less deserved, nor must be known
No less to have done so, let me enfold thee
And hold thee to my heart.

Banquo.   There if I grow,
The harvest is your own.

King.   My plenteous joys,
Wanton° in fullness, seek to hide themselves
35 In drops of sorrow. Sons, kinsmen, thanes,
And you whose places are the nearest, know,
We will establish our estate° upon
Our eldest, Malcolm, whom we name hereafter

---

19 *proportion* preponderance   23 *pays itself* is its own reward   27 *Safe
toward* safeguarding (?)   34 *Wanton* unrestrained   37 *establish our
estate* settle the succession

The Prince of Cumberland: which honor must
Not unaccompanied invest him only,   40
But signs of nobleness, like stars, shall shine
On all deservers. From hence to Inverness,
And bind us further to you.

Macbeth. The rest is labor, which is not used for you.°
I'll be myself the harbinger, and make joyful   45
The hearing of my wife with your approach;
So, humbly take my leave.

King.   My worthy Cawdor!

Macbeth. [*Aside*] The Prince of Cumberland! That
    is a step
On which I must fall down, or else o'erleap,
For in my way it lies. Stars, hide your fires;   50
Let not light see my black and deep desires:
The eye wink at the hand;° yet let that be
Which the eye fears, when it is done, to see.

                                        Exit.

King. True, worthy Banquo; he is full so valiant,
And in his commendations° I am fed;   55
It is a banquet to me. Let's after him,
Whose care is gone before to bid us welcome.
It is a peerless kinsman.   *Flourish. Exeunt.*

Scene V.   [*Inverness. Macbeth's castle.*]

Enter Macbeth's wife, alone, with a letter.

Lady Macbeth. [*Reads*] "They met me in the day
    of success; and I have learned by the perfect'st

44 *The rest . . . you* i.e., repose is laborious when not employed for
you   52 *wink at the hand* i.e., be blind to the hand's deed   55 *his commendations* commendations of him

report they have more in them than mortal knowledge. When I burned in desire to question them
further, they made themselves air, into which they
vanished. Whiles I stood rapt in the wonder of it,
came missives° from the King, who all-hailed me
'Thane of Cawdor'; by which title, before, these
weïrd sisters saluted me, and referred me to the
coming on of time, with 'Hail, King that shalt
be!' This have I thought good to deliver thee,° my
dearest partner of greatness, that thou mightst not
lose the dues of rejoicing, by being ignorant of
what greatness is promised thee. Lay it to thy heart,
and farewell."

Glamis thou art, and Cawdor, and shalt be
What thou art promised. Yet do I fear thy nature;
It is too full o' th' milk of human kindness°
To catch the nearest way. Thou wouldst be great,
Art not without ambition, but without
The illness° should attend it. What thou wouldst
    highly,
That wouldst thou holily; wouldst not play false,
And yet wouldst wrongly win. Thou'dst have,
    great Glamis,
That which cries "Thus thou must do" if thou have
    it;
And that which rather thou dost fear to do
Than wishest should be undone. Hie thee hither,
That I may pour my spirits in thine ear,
And chastise with the valor of my tongue
All that impedes thee from the golden round°
Which fate and metaphysical° aid doth seem
To have thee crowned withal.°

Enter Messenger.

I.v.   7 *missives* messengers   11 *deliver thee* report to you   18 *milk of human kindness* i.e., gentle quality of human nature   21 *illness* wickedness   29 *round* crown   30 *metaphysical* supernatural   31 *withal* with

                      What is your tidings?

Messenger. The King comes here tonight.

Lady Macbeth.   Thou'rt mad to say it!
Is not thy master with him, who, were 't so,
Would have informed for preparation?

Messenger. So please you, it is true. Our thane is
    coming.   35
One of my fellows had the speed of him,°
Who, almost dead for breath, had scarcely more
Than would make up his message.

Lady Macbeth.   Give him tending;
He brings great news.   *Exit Messenger.*
                 The raven himself is hoarse
That croaks the fatal entrance of Duncan   40
Under my battlements. Come, you spirits
That tend on mortal° thoughts, unsex me here,
And fill me, from the crown to the toe, top-full
Of direst cruelty! Make thick my blood,
Stop up th' access and passage to remorse,°   45
That no compunctious visitings of nature°
Shake my fell° purpose, nor keep peace between
Th' effect° and it! Come to my woman's breasts,
And take my milk for° gall, you murd'ring ministers,°
Wherever in your sightless° substances   50
You wait on° nature's mischief! Come, thick night,
And pall° thee in the dunnest° smoke of hell,
That my keen knife see not the wound it makes,
Nor heaven peep through the blanket of the dark,
To cry "Hold, hold!"

Enter Macbeth.

            Great Glamis! Worthy Cawdor!   55
Greater than both, by the all-hail hereafter!°

---

36 *had the speed of him* outdistanced him   42 *mortal* deadly   45 *remorse* compassion   46 *compunctious visitings of nature* natural feelings of compassion   47 *fell* savage   48 *effect* fulfillment   49 *for* in ex-
change for   49 *ministers* agents   50 *sightless* invisible   51 *wait on* assist
52 *pall* enshroud   52 *dunnest* darkest   56 *all-hail hereafter* the third
all-hail (?) the all-hail of the future(?)

Thy letters have transported me beyond
This ignorant° present, and I feel now
The future in the instant.°

Macbeth.   My dearest love,
Duncan comes here tonight.

60 *Lady Macbeth.*   And when goes hence?

Macbeth. Tomorrow, as he purposes.

Lady Macbeth.   O, never
Shall sun that morrow see!
Your face, my Thane, is as a book where men
May read strange matters. To beguile the time,°
65 Look like the time; bear welcome in your eye,
Your hand, your tongue: look like th' innocent
        flower,
But be the serpent under 't. He that's coming
Must be provided for: and you shall put
This night's great business into my dispatch;°
70 Which shall to all our nights and days to come
Give solely sovereign sway and masterdom.

Macbeth. We will speak further.

Lady Macbeth.   Only look up clear.°
To alter favor ever is to fear.°
Leave all the rest to me.   *Exeunt.*

---

58 *ignorant* unknowing   59 *instant* present   64 *To beguile the time* i.e.,
to deceive people of the day   69 *dispatch* management   72 *look up clear*
appear undisturbed   73 *To alter . . . fear* to show a disturbed face is
dangerous

Scene VI.   [*Before Macbeth's castle.*]

Hautboys° and torches. Enter King [Duncan],
Malcolm, Donalbain, Banquo, Lennox, Macduff,
Ross, Angus, and Attendants.

King. This castle hath a pleasant seat;° the air
  Nimbly and sweetly recommends itself
  Unto our gentle° senses.

Banquo.   This guest of summer,
  The temple-haunting martlet,° does approve°
  By his loved mansionry° that the heaven's breath   *5*
  Smells wooingly here. No jutty,° frieze,
  Buttress, nor coign of vantage,° but this bird
  Hath made his pendent bed and procreant° cradle.
  Where they most breed and haunt,° I have observed
  The air is delicate.

Enter Lady [Macbeth].

King.   See, see, our honored hostess!   *10*
  The love that follows us sometime is our trouble,
  Which still we thank as love.° Herein I teach you
  How you shall bid God 'ield° us for your pains
  And thank us for your trouble.

Lady Macbeth.   All our service
  In every point twice done, and then done double,   *15*
  Were poor and single business° to contend
  Against those honors deep and broad wherewith

I.vi.s.d. *Hautboys* oboes ¹ *seat* site ³ *gentle* soothed ⁴ *temple-haunt-ing martlet* martin (swift) nesting in churches ⁴ *approve* prove ⁵ *mansionry* nests ⁶ *jutty* projection ⁷ *coign of vantage* advantageous corner ⁸ *procreant* breeding ⁹ *haunt* visit ¹¹⁻¹² *The love . . . love* the love offered me sometimes inconveniences me, but still I value it as love ¹³ *'ield* reward ¹⁶ *single business* feeble service

Your Majesty loads our house: for those of old,
And the late dignities heaped up to them,
We rest your hermits.°

20 *King.*   Where's the Thane of Cawdor?
We coursed° him at the heels, and had a purpose
To be his purveyor:° but he rides well,
And his great love, sharp as his spur, hath holp°
     him
To his home before us. Fair and noble hostess,
We are your guest tonight.

23 *Lady Macbeth.*   Your servants ever
Have theirs, themselves, and what is theirs, in
     compt,°
To make their audit at your Highness' pleasure,
Still° to return your own.

King.   Give me your hand.
Conduct me to mine host: we love him highly,
30 And shall continue our graces towards him.
By your leave, hostess.   *Exeunt.*

Scene VII.   [*Macbeth's castle.*]

Hautboys. Torches. Enter a Sewer,° and diverse
Servants with dishes and service over the stage.
Then enter Macbeth.

Macbeth. If it were done° when 'tis done, then 'twere
     well
It were done quickly. If th' assassination

---

20 *your hermits* dependents bound to pray for you   21 *coursed* pursued
22 *purveyor* advance-supply officer   23 *holp* helped   26 *Have theirs . . .
compt* have their dependents, themselves, and their possessions in trust
28 *Still* always   I.vii.s.d. *Sewer* chief butler   1 *done* over and done
with

Could trammel up° the consequence, and catch,
With his surcease,° success;° that but this blow
Might be the be-all and the end-all—here,   5
But here, upon this bank and shoal of time,
We'd jump° the life to come. But in these cases
We still° have judgment here; that we but teach
Bloody instructions, which, being taught, return
To plague th' inventor: this even-handed° justice   10
Commends° th' ingredients of our poisoned
   chalice
To our own lips. He's here in double trust:
First, as I am his kinsman and his subject,
Strong both against the deed; then, as his host,
Who should against his murderer shut the door,   15
Not bear the knife myself. Besides, this Duncan
Hath borne his faculties° so meek, hath been
So clear° in his great office, that his virtues
Will plead like angels trumpet-tongued against
The deep damnation of his taking-off;   20
And pity, like a naked newborn babe,
Striding° the blast, or heaven's cherubin horsed
Upon the sightless couriers° of the air,
Shall blow the horrid deed in every eye,
That° tears shall drown the wind. I have no spur   25
To prick the sides of my intent, but only
Vaulting ambition, which o'erleaps itself
And falls on th' other——

                    Enter Lady [*Macbeth*].

                                        How now! What news?

Lady Macbeth. He has almost supped. Why have you
   left the chamber?

3 *trammel up* catch in a net   4 *his surcease* Duncan's death(?) the
consequence's cessation(?)   4 *success* what follows   7 *jump* risk   8 *still*
always   10 *even-handed* impartial   11 *Commends* offers   17 *faculties*
powers   18 *clear* spotless   22 *Striding* bestriding   23 *sightless couriers*
invisible coursers (i.e., the winds)   25 *That* so that

Macbeth. Hath he asked for me?

30 *Lady Macbeth.*   Know you not he has?

Macbeth. We will proceed no further in this business:
 He hath honored me of late, and I have bought°
 Golden opinions from all sorts of people,
 Which would be worn now in their newest gloss,
 Not cast aside so soon.

35 *Lady Macbeth.*   Was the hope drunk
 Wherein you dressed yourself? Hath it slept since?
 And wakes it now, to look so green° and pale
 At what it did so freely? From this time
 Such I account thy love. Art thou afeard
40   To be the same in thine own act and valor
 As thou art in desire? Wouldst thou have that
 Which thou esteem'st the ornament of life,
 And live a coward in thine own esteem,
 Letting "I dare not" wait upon° "I would,"
 Like the poor cat° i' th' adage?

45 *Macbeth.*   Prithee, peace!
 I dare do all that may become a man;
 Who dares do more is none.

Lady Macbeth.   What beast was 't then
 That made you break° this enterprise to me?
 When you durst do it, then you were a man;
50   And to be more than what you were, you would
 Be so much more the man. Nor time nor place
 Did then adhere,° and yet you would make both.
 They have made themselves, and that their° fitness
  now
 Does unmake you. I have given suck, and know
55   How tender 'tis to love the babe that milks me:
 I would, while it was smiling in my face,
 Have plucked my nipple from his boneless gums,

---

32 *bought* acquired 37 *green* sickly 44 *wait upon* follow 45 *cat* (who
wants fish but fears to wet its paws) 48 *break* broach 52 *adhere* suit
53 *that their* their very

And dashed the brains out, had I so sworn as you
Have done to this.

Macbeth.   If we should fail?

Lady Macbeth.   We fail?
But° screw your courage to the sticking-place,°   60
And we'll not fail. When Duncan is asleep—
Whereto the rather shall his day's hard journey
Soundly invite him—his two chamberlains
Will I with wine and wassail° so convince,°
That memory, the warder° of the brain,   65
Shall be a fume, and the receipt of reason
A limbeck only:° when in swinish sleep
Their drenchèd natures lies° as in a death,
What cannot you and I perform upon
Th' unguarded Duncan, what not put upon   70
His spongy° officers, who shall bear the guilt
Of our great quell?°

Macbeth.   Bring forth men-children only;
For thy undaunted mettle° should compose
Nothing but males. Will it not be received,
When we have marked with blood those sleepy two   75
Of his own chamber, and used their very daggers,
That they have done 't?

Lady Macbeth.   Who dares receive it other,°
As we shall make our griefs and clamor roar
Upon his death?

Macbeth.   I am settled, and bend up
Each corporal agent to this terrible feat.   80
Away, and mock the time° with fairest show:
False face must hide what the false heart doth know.

                                        Exeunt.

---

60 *But* only   60 *sticking place* notch (holding the bowstring of a taut
crossbow)   64 *wassail* carousing   64 *convince* overpower   65 *warder*
guard   66-67 *receipt . . . only* i.e., the receptacle   (*receipt*), which
should collect the distillate of thought—reason—will be a mere vessel
(*limbeck*) of undistilled liquids   68 *lies* lie   71 *spongy* sodden   72 *quell*
killing   73 *mettle* substance   77 *other* otherwise   81 *mock the time* beguile the world

ACT II

Scene I. [*Inverness. Court of Macbeth's castle.*]

Enter Banquo, and Fleance, with a torch before him.

Banquo. How goes the night, boy?

Fleance. The moon is down; I have not heard the
clock.

Banquo. And she goes down at twelve.

Fleance.   I take't, 'tis later, sir.

Banquo. Hold, take my sword. There's husbandry° in
heaven.
5   Their candles are all out. Take thee that too.
A heavy summons° lies like lead upon me,
And yet I would not sleep. Merciful powers,
Restrain in me the cursèd thoughts that nature
Gives way to in repose!

Enter Macbeth, and a Servant with a torch.

                         Give me my sword!
10   Who's there?

Macbeth. A friend.

Banquo. What, sir, not yet at rest? The King's a-bed:
He hath been in unusual pleasure, and
Sent forth great largess to your offices:°
15   This diamond he greets your wife withal,
By the name of most kind hostess; and shut up°
In measureless content.

II.i. 4 *husbandry* frugality   6 *summons* call (to sleep)   14 *largess to your offices* gifts to your servants' quarters   16 *shut up* concluded

Macbeth.   Being unprepared,
Our will became the servant to defect,°
Which else should free have wrought.

Banquo.   All's well.
I dreamt last night of the three weïrd sisters: 20
To you they have showed some truth.

Macbeth.   I think not of them.
Yet, when we can entreat an hour to serve,
We would spend it in some words upon that
    business,
If you would grant the time.

Banquo.   At your kind'st leisure.

Macbeth. If you shall cleave to my consent, when
    'tis,°   25
It shall make honor for you.

Banquo.   So° I lose none
In seeking to augment it, but still keep
My bosom franchised° and allegiance clear,°
I shall be counseled.

Macbeth.   Good repose the while!

Banquo. Thanks, sir. The like to you!   30

                    Exit Banquo [with Fleance].

Macbeth. Go bid thy mistress, when my drink is ready,
She strike upon the bell. Get thee to bed.

                              Exit [Servant].

Is this a dagger which I see before me,
The handle toward my hand? Come, let me clutch
    thee.
I have thee not, and yet I see thee still.   35
Art thou not, fatal vision, sensible°
To feeling as to sight, or art thou but
A dagger of the mind, a false creation,

---

18 *Our . . . defect* our good will was hampered by our deficient preparations   25 *cleave . . . 'tis* join my cause, when the time comes
26 *So* provided that   28 *franchised* free (from guilt)   28 *clear* spotless
86 *sensible* perceptible

Proceeding from the heat-oppressèd brain?
40 I see thee yet, in form as palpable
As this which now I draw.
Thou marshal'st me the way that I was going;
And such an instrument I was to use.
Mine eyes are made the fools o' th' other senses,
45 Or else worth all the rest. I see thee still;
And on thy blade and dudgeon° gouts° of blood,
Which was not so before. There's no such thing.
It is the bloody business which informs°
Thus to mine eyes. Now o'er the one half-world
50 Nature seems dead, and wicked dreams abuse°
The curtained sleep; witchcraft celebrates
Pale Hecate's offerings;° and withered murder,
Alarumed° by his sentinel, the wolf,
Whose howl's his watch, thus with his stealthy pace,
55 With Tarquin's° ravishing strides, towards his design
Moves like a ghost. Thou sure and firm-set earth,
Hear not my steps, which way they walk, for fear
Thy very stones prate of my whereabout,
And take the present horror from the time,
Which now suits with it.° Whiles I threat, he
60   lives:
Words to the heat of deeds too cold breath gives.

A bell rings.

I go, and it is done: the bell invites me.
Hear it not, Duncan, for it is a knell
That summons thee to heaven, or to hell.

                                    Exit.

---

46 *dudgeon* wooden hilt 46 *gouts* large drops 48 *informs* gives shape
(?) 50 *abuse* deceive 52 *Hecate's offerings* offerings to Hecate (goddess of sorcery) 53 *Alarumed* called to action 55 *Tarquin* (Roman
tyrant who ravished Lucrece) 59-60 *take . . . it* remove (by noise) the
horrible silence attendant on this moment and suitable to it (?)

Scene II.　[*Macbeth's Castle.*]

Enter Lady [*Macbeth*].

Lady Macbeth. That which hath made them drunk hath made me bold;

What hath quenched them hath given me fire. Hark! Peace!

It was the owl that shrieked, the fatal bellman,

Which gives the stern'st good-night.° He is about it.

The doors are open, and the surfeited grooms　　　　　*5*

Do mock their charge with snores. I have drugged their possets,°

That death and nature° do contend about them,

Whether they live or die.

Macbeth.　　　　　[*Within*] Who's there? What, ho?

Lady Macbeth. Alack, I am afraid they have awaked

And 'tis not done! Th' attempt and not the deed　　*10*

Confounds° us. Hark! I laid their daggers ready;

He could not miss 'em. Had he not resembled

My father as he slept, I had done 't.

Enter Macbeth.

My husband!

Macbeth. I have done the deed. Didst thou not hear a noise?

Lady Macbeth. I heard the owl scream and the crickets cry.　　　　　*15*

Did not you speak?

Macbeth.　　　　　When?

II.ii.³⁻⁴ *bellman . . . good-night* i.e., the owl's call, portending death, is like the town crier's call to a condemned man　⁶ *possets* (bedtime drinks)　⁷ *nature* natural vitality　¹¹ *Confounds* ruins

Lady Macbeth.   Now.

Macbeth.   As I descended?

Lady Macbeth. Ay.

Macbeth. Hark!
Who lies i' th' second chamber?

Lady Macbeth.   Donalbain.

20 *Macbeth.* This is a sorry° sight.

Lady Macbeth. A foolish thought, to say a sorry sight.

Macbeth. There's one did laugh in 's sleep, and one
    cried "Murder!"
That they did wake each other. I stood and heard
    them.
But they did say their prayers, and addressed them
Again to sleep.

25 *Lady Macbeth.*   There are two lodged together.

Macbeth. One cried "God bless us!" and "Amen" the
    other,
As they had seen me with these hangman's° hands:
List'ning their fear, I could not say "Amen,"
When they did say "God bless us!"

Lady Macbeth.   Consider it not so deeply.

Macbeth. But wherefore could not I pronounce
30   "Amen"?
I had most need of blessing, and "Amen"
Stuck in my throat.

Lady Macbeth.   These deeds must not be thought
After these ways; so, it will make us mad.

Macbeth. Methought I heard a voice cry "Sleep no
    more!
35   Macbeth does murder sleep"—the innocent sleep,
Sleep that knits up the raveled sleave° of care,

---

20 *sorry* miserable   27 *hangman's* executioner's (i.e., bloody)   36 *knits
up the raveled sleave* straightens out the tangled skein

The death of each day's life, sore labor's bath,
Balm of hurt minds, great nature's second course,°
Chief nourisher in life's feast——

Lady Macbeth.   What do you mean?

Macbeth. Still it cried "Sleep no more!" to all the
   house: 40
"Glamis hath murdered sleep, and therefore
   Cawdor
Shall sleep no more: Macbeth shall sleep no more."

Lady Macbeth. Who was it that thus cried? Why,
   worthy Thane,
You do unbend° your noble strength, to think
So brainsickly of things. Go get some water,   45
And wash this filthy witness° from your hand.
Why did you bring these daggers from the place?
They must lie there: go carry them, and smear
The sleepy grooms with blood.

Macbeth.   I'll go no more.
I am afraid to think what I have done;   50
Look on 't again I dare not.

Lady Macbeth.   Infirm of purpose!
Give me the daggers. The sleeping and the dead
Are but as pictures. 'Tis the eye of childhood
That fears a painted° devil. If he do bleed,
I'll gild° the faces of the grooms withal,   55
For it must seem their guilt.

                 Exit. Knock within.

Macbeth.   Whence is that knocking?
How is 't with me, when every noise appalls me?
What hands are here? Ha! They pluck out mine
   eyes!
Will all great Neptune's ocean wash this blood
Clean from my hand? No; this my hand will rather   60

---

38 *second course* i.e., sleep (the less substantial first course is food)
44 *unbend* relax **46** *witness* evidence **54** *painted* depicted **55** *gild* paint

The multitudinous seas incarnadine,°
Making the green one red.°

Enter Lady [Macbeth].

Lady Macbeth. My hands are of your color, but I
    shame
    To wear a heart so white. (*Knock.*) I hear a
    knocking
65 At the south entry. Retire we to our chamber.
    A little water clears us of this deed:
    How easy is it then! Your constancy
    Hath left you unattended.° (*Knock.*) Hark! more
    knocking.
    Get on your nightgown,° lest occasion call us
70 And show us to be watchers.° Be not lost
    So poorly° in your thoughts.

Macbeth. To know my deed, 'twere best not know
    myself. (*Knock.*)
    Wake Duncan with thy knocking! I would thou
    couldst!   *Exeunt.*

Scene III.   [*Macbeth's Castle.*]

Enter a Porter. Knocking within.

Porter. Here's a knocking indeed! If a man were
    porter of hell gate, he should have old° turning the
    key. (*Knock.*) Knock, knock, knock! Who's there,

---

61 *incarnadine* redden   62 *the green one red* (perhaps "the green one"
means "the ocean," but perhaps "one" here means "totally," "uniformly")   67-68 *Your . . . unattended* your firmness has deserted you
69 *nightgown* dressing-gown   70 *watchers* i.e., up late   71 *poorly* weakly
II.iii. 2 *should have old* would certainly have plenty of

i' th' name of Beelzebub? Here's a farmer, that
hanged himself on th' expectation of plenty.° Come   5
in time! Have napkins enow° about you; here you'll
sweat for 't. (*Knock.*) Knock, knock! Who's there,
in th' other devil's name? Faith, here's an equivocator,° that could swear in both the scales against
either scale; who committed treason enough for   10
God's sake, yet could not equivocate to heaven. O,
come in, equivocator. (*Knock.*) Knock, knock,
knock! Who's there? Faith, here's an English tailor
come hither for stealing out of a French hose:°
come in, tailor. Here you may roast your goose.°   15
(*Knock.*) Knock, knock; never at quiet! What are
you? But this place is too cold for hell. I'll devil-
porter it no further. I had thought to have let in
some of all professions that go the primrose way
to th' everlasting bonfire. (*Knock.*) Anon, anon!   20
[*Opens an entrance.*] I pray you, remember the
porter.

Enter Macduff and Lennox.

Macduff. Was it so late, friend, ere you went to bed,
   That you do lie so late?

Porter. Faith, sir, we were carousing till the second   25
   cock:° and drink, sir, is a great provoker of three
   things.

Macduff. What three things does drink especially pro-
   voke?

Porter. Marry, sir, nose-painting, sleep, and urine.   30
   Lechery, sir, it provokes and unprovokes; it provokes the desire, but it takes away the performance: therefore much drink may be said to be an
   equivocator with lechery: it makes him and it mars

4-5 *farmer . . . plenty* (the farmer hoarded so he could later sell high,
but when it looked as though there would be a crop surplus he hanged
himself) 6 *enow* enough 8-9 *equivocator* i.e., Jesuit (who allegedly
employed deceptive speech to further God's ends) 14 *French hose* tight-
fitting hose 15 *goose* pressing iron 25-26 *second cock* (about 3 a.m.)

35　　him; it sets him on and it takes him off; it persuades him and disheartens him; makes him stand
to and not stand to; in conclusion, equivocates
him in a sleep, and giving him the lie, leaves him.

Macduff. I believe drink gave thee the lie° last night.

40　*Porter.* That it did, sir, i' the very throat on me: but
I requited him for his lie, and, I think, being too
strong for him, though he took up my legs sometime, yet I make a shift to cast° him.

Macduff. Is thy master stirring?

Enter Macbeth.

45　　Our knocking has awaked him; here he comes.

Lennox. Good morrow, noble sir.

Macbeth.　　　　　　　　　　Good morrow, both.

Macduff. Is the king stirring, worthy Thane?

Macbeth.　　　　　　　　　　　　Not yet.

Macduff. He did command me to call timely° on him:
I have almost slipped° the hour.

Macbeth.　　　　　　　　I'll bring you to him.

50　*Macduff.* I know this is a joyful trouble to you;
But yet 'tis one.

Macbeth. The labor we delight in physics pain.°
This is the door.

Macduff.　　　　　　I'll make so bold to call,
For 'tis my limited service.°

Exit Macduff.

Lennox. Goes the king hence today?

53　*Macbeth.*　　　　　　　He does: he did appoint so.

---

89 *gave thee the lie* called you a liar (with a pun on "stretched you
out")　43 *cast* (with a pun on "cast," meaning "vomit")　48 *timely*
early　49 *slipped* let slip　52 *The labor . . . pain* labor that gives us
pleasure cures discomfort　54 *limited service* appointed duty

Lennox. The night has been unruly. Where we lay,
  Our chimneys were blown down, and, as they say,
  Lamentings heard i' th' air, strange screams of
    death,
  And prophesying with accents terrible
  Of dire combustion° and confused events   60
  New hatched to th' woeful time: the obscure bird°
  Clamored the livelong night. Some say, the earth
  Was feverous and did shake.

Macbeth.   'Twas a rough night.

Lennox. My young remembrance cannot parallel
  A fellow to it.   65

Enter Macduff.

Macduff. O horror, horror, horror! Tongue nor heart
  Cannot conceive nor name thee.

Macbeth and Lennox.   What's the matter?

Macduff. Confusion° now hath made his masterpiece.
  Most sacrilegious murder hath broke ope
  The Lord's anointed temple, and stole thence   70
  The life o' th' building.

Macbeth.   What is 't you say? The life?

Lennox. Mean you his Majesty?

Macduff. Approach the chamber, and destroy your
    sight
  With a new Gorgon:° do not bid me speak;
  See, and then speak yourselves. Awake, awake!   75

Exeunt Macbeth and Lennox.

  Ring the alarum bell. Murder and Treason!
  Banquo and Donalbain! Malcolm! Awake!
  Shake off this downy sleep, death's counterfeit,°
  And look on death itself! Up, up, and see
  The great doom's image!° Malcolm! Banquo!   80

60 *combustion* tumult   61 *obscure bird* bird of darkness, i.e., the owl
68 *Confusion* destruction   74 *Gorgon* (creature capable of turning be-
holders to stone)   78 *counterfeit* imitation   80 *great doom's image* likeness of Judgment Day

As from your graves rise up, and walk like sprites,°
To countenance° this horror. Ring the bell.

Bell rings. Enter Lady [Macbeth].

Lady Macbeth. What's the business,
That such a hideous trumpet calls to parley
The sleepers of the house? Speak, speak!

85 Macduff.   O gentle lady,
'Tis not for you to hear what I can speak:
The repetition,° in a woman's ear,
Would murder as it fell.

Enter Banquo.

                        O Banquo, Banquo!
Our royal master's murdered.

Lady Macbeth.   Woe, alas!
What, in our house?

90 Banquo.   Too cruel anywhere.
Dear Duff, I prithee, contradict thyself,
And say it is not so.

Enter Macbeth, Lennox, and Ross.

Macbeth. Had I but died an hour before this chance,
I had lived a blessèd time; for from this instant
95 There's nothing serious in mortality:°
All is but toys.° Renown and grace is dead,
The wine of life is drawn, and the mere lees°
Is left this vault° to brag of.

Enter Malcolm and Donalbain.

Donalbain. What is amiss?

Macbeth.   You are, and do not know 't.
100 The spring, the head, the fountain of your blood
Is stopped; the very source of it is stopped.

Macduff. Your royal father's murdered.

---

81 *sprites* spirits   82 *countenance* be in keeping with   87 *repetition* report   95 *serious in mortality* worthwhile in mortal life   96 *toys* trifles
97 *lees* dregs   98 *vault* (1) wine vault (2) earth, with the sky as roof
(?)

Malcolm   O, by whom?

Lennox. Those of his chamber, as it seemed, had
    done 't:
  Their hands and faces were all badged° with blood;
  So were their daggers, which unwiped we found   *105*
  Upon their pillows. They stared, and were
    distracted.
  No man's life was to be trusted with them.

Macbeth. O, yet I do repent me of my fury,
  That I did kill them.

Macduff.   Wherefore did you so?

Macbeth. Who can be wise, amazed,° temp'rate and
    furious,   *110*
  Loyal and neutral, in a moment? No man.
  The expedition° of my violent love
  Outrun the pauser, reason. Here lay Duncan,
  His silver skin laced with his golden blood,
  And his gashed stabs looked like a breach in nature *113*
  For ruin's wasteful entrance: there, the murderers,
  Steeped in the colors of their trade, their daggers
  Unmannerly breeched with gore.° Who could
    refrain,°
  That had a heart to love, and in that heart
  Courage to make 's love known?

Lady Macbeth.   Help me hence, ho! *120*

Macduff. Look to° the lady.

Malcolm. [*Aside to Donalbain*] Why do we hold
    our tongues,
  That most may claim this argument for ours?°

Donalbain. [*Aside to Malcolm*] What should be
    spoken here,
  Where our fate, hid in an auger-hole,°

104 *badged* marked   110 *amazed* bewildered   112 *expedition* h a s t e
118 *Unmannerly breeched with gore* covered with unseemly breeches of
blood   118 *refrain* check oneself   121 *Look to* look after   123 *That
most . . . ours?* who are the most concerned with this topic   124 *auger-
hole* i.e., unsuspected place

123   May rush, and seize us? Let's away:
           Our tears are not yet brewed.

Malcolm. [*Aside to Donalbain*] Nor our strong
           sorrow
           Upon the foot of motion.°
Banquo.   Look to the lady.

                        [*Lady Macbeth is carried out.*]

           And when we have our naked frailties hid,°
           That suffer in exposure, let us meet
130   And question° this most bloody piece of work,
           To know it further. Fears and scruples° shake us.
           In the great hand of God I stand, and thence
           Against the undivulged pretense° I fight
           Of treasonous malice.

Macduff.   And so do I.

All.   So all.

135 *Macbeth.* Let's briefly° put on manly readiness,
           And meet i' th' hall together.

All.   Well contented.

                        Exeunt [*all but Malcolm and Donalbain*].

Malcolm. What will you do? Let's not consort with
           them.
           To show an unfelt sorrow is an office°
           Which the false man does easy. I'll to England.

140 *Donalbain.* To Ireland, I; our separated fortune
           Shall keep us both the safer. Where we are
           There's daggers in men's smiles; the near in blood,
           The nearer bloody.

Malcolm.   This murderous shaft that's shot
           Hath not yet lighted, and our safest way

126-27 *Our tears . . . motion* i.e., we have not yet had time for tears
nor to express our sorrows in action (?)   128 *naked frailties hid* poor
bodies clothed   130 *question* discuss   131*scruples* suspicions   133 *un-
divulged pretense* hidden purpose   135 *briefly* quickly   139 *office* function

Is to avoid the aim. Therefore to horse;   145
And let us not be dainty of° leave-taking,
But shift away. There's warrant° in that theft
Which steals itself° when there's no mercy left.

Exeunt.

Scene IV.   [*Outside Macbeth's castle.*]

Enter Ross with an Old Man.

Old Man. Threescore and ten I can remember well:
Within the volume of which time I have seen
Hours dreadful and things strange, but this sore°
    night
Hath trifled former knowings.°

Ross.   Ha, good father,
Thou seest the heavens, as troubled with man's act,   5
Threatens his bloody stage. By th' clock 'tis day,
And yet dark night strangles the traveling lamp:°
Is 't night's predominance,° or the day's shame,
That darkness does the face of earth entomb,
When living light should kiss it?

Old Man.   'Tis unnatural,   10
Even like the deed that's done. On Tuesday last
A falcon, tow'ring in her pride of place,°
Was by a mousing° owl hawked at and killed.

Ross. And Duncan's horses—a thing most strange
        and certain—
Beauteous and swift, the minions° of their race,   15

146 *dainty of* fussy about   147 *warrant* justification   148 *steals itself*
steals oneself away   II.iv.   3 *sore* grievous   4 *trifled former knowings*
made trifles of former experiences   7 *traveling lamp* i.e., the sun   8 *predominance* astrological supremacy   12 *tow'ring . . . place* soaring at
her summit   13 *mousing* i.e., normally mouse-eating   15 *minions* darlings

Turned wild in nature, broke their stalls, flung out,°
Contending 'gainst obedience, as they would make
War with mankind.

Old Man.   'Tis said they eat° each other.

Ross. They did so, to th' amazement of mine eyes,
That looked upon 't.

Enter Macduff.

20   Here comes the good Macduff.
How goes the world, sir, now?

Macduff.   Why, see you not?

Ross. Is 't known who did this more than bloody deed?

Macduff. Those that Macbeth hath slain.

Ross.   Alas, the day!
What good could they pretend?°

Macduff.   They were suborned:°
25   Malcolm and Donalbain, the king's two sons,
Are stol'n away and fled, which puts upon them
Suspicion of the deed.

Ross.   'Gainst nature still.
Thriftless° ambition, that will ravin up°
Thine own life's means! Then 'tis most like
30   The sovereignty will fall upon Macbeth.

Macduff. He is already named,° and gone to Scone
To be invested.°

Ross.   Where is Duncan's body?

Macduff. Carried to Colmekill,
The sacred storehouse of his predecessors
And guardian of their bones.

35   *Ross.*   Will you to Scone?

Macduff. No, cousin, I'll to Fife.

16 *flung out* lunged wildly   18 *eat* ate   24 *pretend* hope for   24 *sub-*
orned bribed   28 *Thriftless* wasteful   28 *ravin up* greedily devour
31 *named* elected   32 *invested* installed as king

Ross.   Well, I will thither.

Macduff. Well, may you see things well done there.
    Adieu,
  Lest our old robes sit easier than our new!

Ross. Farewell, father.

Old Man. God's benison° go with you, and with those   40
  That would make good of bad, and friends of foes!

                                   Exeunt omnes.

---

40 *benison* blessing

ACT III

Scene I. [*Forres. The palace.*]

Enter Banquo.

Banquo. Thou hast it now: King, Cawdor, Glamis, all,
As the weïrd women promised, and I fear
Thou play'dst most foully for 't. Yet it was said
It should not stand° in thy posterity,
5 But that myself should be the root and father
Of many kings. If there come truth from them—
As upon thee, Macbeth, their speeches shine—
Why, by the verities on thee made good,
May they not be my oracles as well
10 And set me up in hope? But hush, no more!

*Sennet° sounded. Enter Macbeth as King, Lady
[Macbeth], Lennox, Ross, Lords, and Attendants*

Macbeth. Here's our chief guest.

Lady Macbeth.   If he had been forgotten,
It had been as a gap in our great feast,
And all-thing° unbecoming.

Macbeth. Tonight we hold a solemn° supper, sir,
And I'll request your presence.

15 *Banquo.*   Let your Highness
Command upon me, to the which my duties

III.i 4 *stand* continue s.d. *Sennet* trumpet call 13 *all-thing* altogether
14 *solemn* ceremonious

74

Are with a most indissoluble tie
For ever knit.

Macbeth. Ride you this afternoon?

Banquo.   Ay, my good lord.

Macbeth. We should have else desired your good advice 20
  (Which still° hath been both grave and
       prosperous°)
  In this day's council; but we'll take tomorrow.
  Is 't far you ride?

Banquo. As far, my lord, as will fill up the time
  'Twixt this and supper. Go not my horse the
       better,°   25
  I must become a borrower of the night
  For a dark hour or twain.

Macbeth.   Fail not our feast.

Banquo. My lord, I will not.

Macbeth. We hear our bloody cousins are bestowed°
  In England and in Ireland, not confessing   30
  Their cruel parricide, filling their hearers
  With strange invention.° But of that tomorrow,
  When therewithal we shall have cause of state
  Craving us jointly.° Hie you to horse. Adieu,
  Till you return at night. Goes Fleance with you?   35

Banquo. Ay, my good lord: our time does call upon 's.

Macbeth. I wish your horses swift and sure of foot,
  And so I do commend you to their backs.
  Farewell.   *Exit Banquo.*
  Let every man be master of his time   40
  Till seven at night. To make society
  The sweeter welcome, we will keep ourself

---

21 *still* always 21 *grave and prosperous* weighty and profitable 25*Go
. . . better* unless my horse goes better than I expect 29 *are bestowed*
have taken refuge 32 *invention* lies 33-34 *cause . . . jointly* matters of
state demanding our joint attention

Till supper-time alone. While° then, God be with
you!

Exeunt Lords [and all but Macbeth and a Servant].

Sirrah,° a word with you: attend° those men
45   Our pleasure?

Attendant. They are, my lord, without° the palace
gate.

Macbeth. Bring them before us.   *Exit Servant.*
To be thus is nothing, but° to be safely thus—
Our fears in° Banquo stick deep,
50   And in his royalty of nature reigns that
Which would° be feared. 'Tis much he dares;
And, to° that dauntless temper° of his mind,
He hath a wisdom that doth guide his valor
To act in safety. There is none but he
55   Whose being I do fear: and under him
My genius is rebuked,° as it is said
Mark Antony's was by Cæsar. He chid the sisters,
When first they put the name of King upon me,
And bade them speak to him; then prophetlike
60   They hailed him father to a line of kings.
Upon my head they placed a fruitless crown
And put a barren scepter in my gripe,°
Thence to be wrenched with an unlineal hand,
No son of mine succeeding. If 't be so,
65   For Banquo's issue have I filed° my mind;
For them the gracious Duncan have I murdered;
Put rancors° in the vessel of my peace
Only for them, and mine eternal jewel°
Given to the common enemy of man,°
70   To make them kings, the seeds of Banquo kings!

---

48 *While* until   44 *Sirrah* (common address to an inferior)   44 *attend*
await   46 *without* outside   48 *but* unless   49*in* about   51 *would* must
52 *to* added to   52 *temper* quality   56 *genius is rebuked* guardian spirit
is cowed   62 *gripe* grasp   65 *filed* defiled   67 *rancors* bitter enmities
68 *eternal jewel* i.e., soul   69 *common enemy of man* i.e., the Devil

Rather than so, come, fate, into the list,°
And champion me to th' utterance!° Who's there?

Enter Servant and Two Murderers.

Now go to the door, and stay there till we call.

Exit Servant.

Was it not yesterday we spoke together?

Murderers. It was, so please your Highness.

Macbeth   Well then, now   75
Have you considered of my speeches? Know
That it was he in the times past, which held you
So under fortune,° which you thought had been
Our innocent self: this I made good to you
In our last conference; passed in probation° with   80
        you,
How you were born in hand,° how crossed;° the
        instruments,°
Who wrought with them, and all things else that
        might
To half a soul° and to a notion° crazed
Say "Thus did Banquo."

First Murderer.   You made it known to us.

Macbeth. I did so; and went further, which is now   85
Our point of second meeting. Do you find
Your patience so predominant in your nature,
That you can let this go? Are you so gospeled,°
To pray for this good man and for his issue,
Whose heavy hand hath bowed you to the grave   90
And beggared yours for ever?

First Murderer.   We are men, my liege.

Macbeth. Ay, in the catalogue ye go for° men;

---

71 *list* lists 72 *champion me to th' utterance* fight against me to the
death 77-78 *held . . . fortune* kept you from good fortune (?) 80 *passed
in probation* reviewed the proofs 81 *borne in hand* deceived 81 *crossed*
thwarted 81 *instruments* tools 83 *half a soul* a halfwit 83 *notion* mind
88 *gospeled* i.e., made meek by the gospel 92 *go for* pass as

As hounds and greyhounds, mongrels, spaniels,
    curs,
Shoughs, water-rugs° and demi-wolves, are clept°
95 All by the name of dogs: the valued file°
Distinguishes the swift, the slow, the subtle,
The housekeeper,° the hunter, every one
According to the gift which bounteous nature
Hath in him closed,° whereby he does receive
100 Particular addition, from the bill°
That writes them all alike: and so of men.
Now if you have a station in the file,
Not i' th' worst rank of manhood, say 't,
And I will put that business in your bosoms
105 Whose execution takes your enemy off,
Grapples you to the heart and love of us,
Who wear our health but sickly in his life,°
Which in his death were perfect.

Second Murderer.   I am one, my liege,
Whom the vile blows and buffets of the world
110 Hath so incensed that I am reckless what
I do to spite the world.

First Murderer.   And I another
So weary with disasters, tugged with fortune,
That I would set° my life on any chance,
To mend it or be rid on 't.

Macbeth.   Both of you
Know Banquo was your enemy.

115 *Both Murderers.*   True, my lord.

Macbeth. So is he mine, and in such bloody distance°
That every minute of his being thrusts
Against my near'st of life:° and though I could

---

94 *Shoughs, water-rugs* shaggy dogs, long-haired water dogs 94 *clept*
called 95 *valued file* classification by valuable traits 97 *housekeeper*
watchdog 99 *closed* enclosed 100 *Particular addition, from the bill*
special distinction in opposition to the list 107 *wear . . . life* have
only imperfect health while he lives 118 *set* risk 116 *distance* quarrel
118 *near'st of life* most vital spot

With barefaced power sweep him from my sight
And bid my will avouch° it, yet I must not,   *120*
For° certain friends that are both his and mine,
Whose loves I may not drop, but wail his fall°
Who I myself struck down: and thence it is
That I to your assistance do make love,
Masking the business from the common eye   *125*
For sundry weighty reasons.

Second Murderer.   We shall, my lord,
    Perform what you command us.

First Murderer.   Though our lives——

Macbeth. Your spirits shine through you. Within this
        hour at most
    I will advise you where to plant yourselves,
    Acquaint you with the perfect spy° o' th' time,   *130*
    The moment on 't;° for 't must be done tonight,
    And something° from the palace; always thought°
    That I require a clearness:° and with him—
    To leave no rubs° nor botches in the work—
    Fleance his son, that keeps him company,   *135*
    Whose absence is no less material to me
    Than is his father's, must embrace the fate
    Of that dark hour. Resolve yourselves apart:°
    I'll come to you anon.

Murderers.   We are resolved, my lord.

Macbeth. I'll call upon you straight.° Abide within.   *140*
    It is concluded: Banquo, thy soul's flight,
    If it find heaven, must find it out tonight.   *Exeunt.*

---

120 *avouch* justify   **121** *For* because of   **122** *wail his fall* bewail his death
130 *perfect spy* exact information (?) (*spy* literally means "observation";
apparently Macbeth already has the Third Murderer in mind)   **131** *on 't*
of it   **132** *something* some distance   **132** *thought* remembered   **133** *clearness* freedom from suspicion   **134** *rubs* flaws   **138** *Resolve yourselves apart* decide by yourself   **140** *straight* immediately

Scene II.   [*The palace.*]

Enter Macbeth's Lady and a Servant.

Lady Macbeth. Is Banquo gone from court?

Servant. Ay, madam, but returns again tonight.

Lady Macbeth. Say to the King, I would attend his
   leisure
For a few words.

Servant.   Madam, I will.   *Exit.*

Lady Macbeth.   Nought's had, all's spent,
5 Where our desire is got without content:
'Tis safer to be that which we destroy
Than by destruction dwell in doubtful joy.

Enter Macbeth.

How now, my lord! Why do you keep alone,
Of sorriest° fancies your companions making,
Using those thoughts which should indeed have
10   died
With them they think on? Things without° all
   remedy
Should be without regard: what's done is done.

Macbeth. We have scorched° the snake, not killed it:
She'll close° and be herself, whilst our poor malice°
15 Remains in danger of her former tooth.
But let the frame of things disjoint,° both the
   worlds° suffer,
Ere we will eat our meal in fear, and sleep
In the affliction of these terrible dreams

III.ii.   9 *sorriest* most despicable   11 *without* beyond   13 *scorched*
slashed, scored   14 *close* heal   14 *poor malice* feeble enmity   16 *frame
of things disjoint* universe collapse   16 *both the worlds* heaven and
earth (?)

That shake us nightly: better be with the dead,
Whom we, to gain our peace, have sent to peace,   20
Than on the torture° of the mind to lie
In restless ecstasy.° Duncan is in his grave;
After life's fitful fever he sleeps well.
Treason has done his° worst: nor steel, nor poison,
Malice domestic,° foreign levy, nothing,   25
Can touch him further.

Lady Macbeth.   Come on.
Gentle my lord, sleek° o'er your rugged° looks;
Be bright and jovial among your guests tonight.

Macbeth. So shall I, love; and so, I pray, be you:
Let your remembrance apply to Banquo;°   30
Present him eminence,° both with eye and tongue:
Unsafe the while, that we must lave°
Our honors in these flattering streams
And make our faces vizards° to our hearts,
Disguising what they are.

Lady Macbeth.   You must leave this.   33

Macbeth. O, full of scorpions is my mind, dear wife!
Thou know'st that Banquo, and his Fleance, lives.

Lady Macbeth. But in them nature's copy's° not eterne.

Macbeth. There's comfort yet; they are assailable.
Then be thou jocund. Ere the bat hath flown   40
His cloistered flight, ere to black Hecate's summons
The shard-borne° beetle with his drowsy hums
Hath rung night's yawning peal, there shall be done
A deed of dreadful note.

Lady Macbeth.   What's to be done?

---

21 *torture* i.e., rack **22** *ecstasy* frenzy **24** *his* its **25** *Malice domestic* civil war **27** *sleek* smooth **27** *rugged* furrowed **30** *Let . . . Banquo* focus your thoughts on Banquo **31** *Present him eminence* honor him **32** *Unsafe . . . lave* i.e., you and I are unsafe because we must dip **34** *vizards* masks **38** *nature's copy* nature's lease (?) imitation (i.e., a son) made by nature (?) **42** *shard-borne* borne on scaly wings (?) dung-bred (?)

Macbeth. Be innocent of the knowledge, dearest
45   chuck,°
          Till thou applaud the deed. Come, seeling° night,
          Scarf up° the tender eye of pitiful day,
          And with thy bloody and invisible hand
          Cancel and tear to pieces that great bond°
50   Which keeps me pale! Light thickens, and the crow
          Makes wing to th' rooky° wood.
          Good things of day begin to droop and drowse,
          Whiles night's black agents to their preys do rouse.
          Thou marvel'st at my words: but hold thee still;
55   Things bad begun make strong themselves by ill:
          So, prithee, go with me.   *Exeunt.*

Scene III.   [*Near the palace.*]

Enter Three Murderers.

First Murderer. But who did bid thee join with us?

Third Murderer.   Macbeth.

Second Murderer. He needs not our mistrust; since he
          delivers
          Our offices and what we have to do
          To the direction just.°

First Murderer.   Then stand with us.
5   The west yet glimmers with some streaks of day.
          Now spurs the lated° traveler apace
          To gain the timely inn, and near approaches
          The subject of our watch.

---

45 *chuck* chick (a term of endearment) 46 *seeling* eye-closing 47 *Scarf up* blindfold 49 *bond* i.e., between Banquo and fate (?) Banquo's lease on life (?) Macbeth's link to humanity (?) 51 *rooky* full of rooks III.iii. 2-4 *He needs . . . just* we need not mistrust him (i.e., the Third Murderer) since he describes our duties according to our exact directions 6 *lated* belated

Third Murderer.   Hark! I hear horses.

Banquo. (*Within*) Give us a light there, ho!

Second Murderer.   Then 'tis he. The rest   10
   That are within the note of expectation°
   Already are i' th' court.

First Murderer.   His horses go about.

Third Murderer. Almost a mile: but he does usually—
   So all men do—from hence to th' palace gate
   Make it their walk.

       Enter Banquo and Fleance, with a torch.

Second Murderer. A light, a light!

Third Murderer.   'Tis he.

First Murderer.   Stand to 't.   15

Banquo. It will be rain tonight.

First Murderer.   Let it come down.

        [*They set upon Banquo.*]

Banquo. O, treachery! Fly, good Fleance, fly, fly, fly!

                    [*Exit Fleance.*]

   Thou mayst revenge. O slave! [*Dies.*]

Third Murderer. Who did strike out the light?

First Murderer.   Was 't not the way?°

Third Murderer. There's but one down; the son is fled.   20

Second Murderer. We have lost best half of our affair.

First Murderer. Well, let's away and say how much is
     done.   *Exeunt.*

---

10 *within the note of expectation* on the list of expected guests   19 *way*
i.e., thing to do

Scene IV. [*The palace.*]

Banquet prepared. Enter Macbeth, Lady [Macbeth], Ross, Lennox, Lords, and Attendants.

Macbeth. You know your own degrees;° sit down:
    At first and last, the hearty welcome.

Lords. Thanks to your Majesty.

Macbeth. Ourself will mingle with society°
5   And play the humble host.
    Our hostess keeps her state,° but in best time
    We will require° her welcome.

Lady Macbeth. Pronounce it for me, sir, to all our
      friends,
    For my heart speaks they are welcome.

Enter First Murderer.

Macbeth. See, they encounter° thee with their hearts'
10   thanks.
    Both sides are even: here I'll sit i' th' midst:
    Be large in mirth; anon we'll drink a measure°
    The table round. [*Goes to Murderer*] There's
      blood upon thy face.

Murderer. 'Tis Banquo's then.

15 *Macbeth.* 'Tis better thee without than he within.°
    Is he dispatched?

Murderer. My lord, his throat is cut; that I did for
      him.

Macbeth. Thou art the best o' th' cutthroats.

III.iv. 1 *degrees* ranks   4 *society* the company   6 *keeps her state* remains seated in her chair of state   7 *require* request   10 *encounter* meet
12 *measure* goblet   15 *thee without than he within* outside you than inside him

Yet he's good that did the like for Fleance;
If thou didst it, thou art the nonpareil.   20

Murderer. Most royal sir, Fleance is 'scaped.

Macbeth. [*Aside*] Then comes my fit again: I had
    else been perfect,
Whole as the marble, founded° as the rock,
As broad and general as the casing° air:
But now I am cabined, cribbed,° confined, bound in   25
To saucy° doubts and fears.——But Banquo's safe?

Murderer. Ay, my good lord: safe in a ditch he bides,
With twenty trenchèd° gashes on his head,
The least a death to nature.

Macbeth.   Thanks for that.
[*Aside*] There the grown serpent lies; the worm°
    that's fled   30
Hath nature that in time will venom breed,
No teeth for th' present. Get thee gone. Tomorrow
We'll hear ourselves° again.   *Exit Murderer.*

Lady Macbeth.   My royal lord,
You do not give the cheer.° The feast is sold
That is not often vouched, while 'tis a-making,   35
'Tis given with welcome. To feed were best at
    home;°
From thence, the sauce to meat° is ceremony;
Meeting were bare without it.

            Enter the Ghost of Banquo, and sits in
                    Macbeth's place.

Macbeth.   Sweet remembrancer!°
Now good digestion wait on appetite,
And health on both!

23 *founded* firmly based 24 *broad . . . casing* unconfined as the surrounding 25 *cribbed* penned up 26 *saucy* insolent 28 *trenchèd* trench-
like 30 *worm* serpent 33 *hear ourselves* talk it over 34 *the cheer* a
sense of cordiality 34-36 *The feast . . . home* i.e., the feast seems sold
(not given) during which the host fails to welcome the guests. Mere eat-
ing is best done at home 37 *meat* food 38 *remembrancer* reminder

40 *Lennox.*   May 't please your Highness sit.

Macbeth. Here had we now our country's honor
 roofed,°
 Were the graced person of our Banquo present—
 Who may I rather challenge for unkindness
 Than pity for mischance!°

Ross.   His absence, sir,
 Lays blame upon his promise. Please 't your
45 Highness
 To grace us with your royal company?

Macbeth. The table's full.

Lennox.   Here is a place reserved, sir.

Macbeth. Where?

Lennox. Here, my good lord. What is 't that moves
 your Highness?

Macbeth. Which of you have done this?

50 *Lords.*   What, my good lord?

Macbeth. Thou canst not say I did it. Never shake
 Thy gory locks at me.

Ross. Gentlemen, rise, his Highness is not well.

Lady Macbeth. Sit, worthy friends. My lord is often
 thus,
55 And hath been from his youth. Pray you, keep seat.
 The fit is momentary; upon a thought°
 He will again be well. If much you note him,
 You shall offend him and extend his passion.°
 Feed, and regard him not.—Are you a man?

60 *Macbeth.* Ay, and a bold one, that dare look on that
 Which might appall the devil.

Lady Macbeth.   O proper stuff!
 This is the very painting of your fear.
 This is the air-drawn dagger which, you said,

---

41 *our country's honor roofed* our nobility under one roof   43-44 *Who
. . . mischance* whom I hope I may reprove because he is unkind rather
than pity because he has encountered an accident   56 *upon a thought*
as quick as thought   58 *extend his passion* lengthen his fit

Led you to Duncan. O, these flaws° and starts,
Impostors to° true fear, would well become   65
A woman's story at a winter's fire,
Authorized° by her grandam. Shame itself!
Why do you make such faces? When all's done,
You look but on a stool.

Macbeth.   Prithee, see there!
Behold! Look! Lo! How say you?   70
Why, what care I? If thou canst nod, speak too.
If charnel houses° and our graves must send
Those that we bury back, our monuments
Shall be the maws of kites.°   [Exit Ghost.]

Lady Macbeth.   What, quite unmanned in folly?

Macbeth. If I stand here, I saw him.

Lady Macbeth.   Fie, for shame!   73

Macbeth. Blood hath been shed ere now, i' th' olden
     time,
Ere humane statute purged the gentle weal;°
Ay, and since too, murders have been performed
Too terrible for the ear. The times has been
That, when the brains were out, the man would die,   80
And there an end; but now they rise again,
With twenty mortal murders on their crowns,°
And push us from our stools. This is more strange
Than such a murder is.

Lady Macbeth.   My worthy lord,
Your noble friends do lack you.

Macbeth.   I do forget.   85
Do not muse at me, my most worthy friends;
I have a strange infirmity, which is nothing
To those that know me. Come, love and health to
     all!

---

64 *flaws* gusts, outbursts   65 *to* compared with   67 *Authorized* vouched
for   72 *charnel houses* vaults containing bones   73-74 *our . . . kites*
our tombs shall be the bellies of rapacious birds   77 *purged the gentle
weal* i.e., cleansed the state and made it gentle   82 *mortal murders on
their crowns* deadly wounds on their heads

Then I'll sit down. Give me some wine, fill full.

Enter Ghost.

90   I drink to th' general joy o' th' whole table,
And to our dear friend Banquo, whom we miss;
Would he were here! To all and him we thirst,°
And all to all.°

Lords.   Our duties, and the pledge.

Macbeth. Avaunt! and quit my sight! Let the earth hide
thee!
95   Thy bones are marrowless, thy blood is cold;
Thou hast no speculation° in those eyes
Which thou dost glare with.

Lady Macbeth.   Think of this, good peers,
But as a thing of custom; 'tis no other.
Only it spoils the pleasure of the time.

100   *Macbeth.* What man dare, I dare.
Approach thou like the rugged Russian bear,
The armed rhinoceros, or th' Hyrcan° tiger;
Take any shape but that, and my firm nerves°
Shall never tremble. Or be alive again,
105   And dare me to the desert° with thy sword.
If trembling I inhabit then, protest me
The baby of a girl.° Hence, horrible shadow!
Unreal mock'ry, hence!   *[Exit Ghost.]*
               Why, so: being gone,
I am a man again. Pray you, sit still.

Lady Macbeth. You have displaced the mirth, broke the
110   good meeting,
With most admired° disorder.

Macbeth.   Can such things be,
And overcome us° like a summer's cloud,

92 *thirst* desire to drink 93 *all to all* everything to everybody (?) let
everybody drink to everybody (?) 96 *speculation* sight 102 *Hyrcan* of
Hyrcania (near the Caspian Sea) 103 *nerves* sinews 105 *the desert* a
lonely place 106-07 *If . . . girl* if then I tremble, proclaim me a baby
girl 111 *admired* amazing 112 *overcome us* come over us

Without our special wonder? You make me strange
Even to the disposition that I owe,°
When now I think you can behold such sights,   *115*
And keep the natural ruby of your cheeks,
When mine is blanched with fear.

Ross.   What sights, my lord?

Lady Macbeth. I pray you, speak not: he grows worse
and worse;
Question enrages him: at once, good night.
Stand not upon the order of your going,°   *120*
But go at once.

Lennox.   Good night; and better health
Attend his Majesty!

Lady Macbeth.   A kind good night to all!

                              Exeunt Lords.

Macbeth. It will have blood, they say: blood will have
blood.
Stones have been known to move and trees to
speak;
Augures and understood relations° have   *125*
By maggot-pies and choughs and rooks brought
forth°
The secret'st man of blood. What is the night?°

Lady Macbeth. Almost at odds° with morning, which is
which.

Macbeth. How say'st thou, that Macduff denies his
person
At our great bidding?

Lady Macbeth.   Did you send to him, sir?   *130*

Macbeth. I hear it by the way,° but I will send:

---

²¹³⁻¹⁴ *You . . . owe* i.e., you make me wonder what my nature is
¹²⁰ *Stand . . . going* do not insist on departing in your order of rank
¹²⁵ *Augures and understood relations* auguries and comprehended reports   ¹²⁶ *By . . . forth* by magpies, choughs, and rooks (telltale
birds) revealed   ¹²⁷ *What is the night* what time of night is it
¹²⁸ *at odds* striving   ¹³¹ *by the way* incidentally

There's not a one of them but in his house
I keep a servant fee'd.° I will tomorrow,
And betimes° I will, to the weïrd sisters:
135   More shall they speak, for now I am bent° to know
By the worst means the worst. For mine own good
All causes° shall give way. I am in blood
Stepped in so far that, should I wade no more,
Returning were as tedious as go o'er.
140   Strange things I have in head that will to hand,
Which must be acted ere they may be scanned.°

Lady Macbeth. You lack the season of all natures,°
      sleep.

Macbeth. Come, we'll to sleep. My strange and self-
      abuse°
Is the initiate fear that wants hard use.°
143   We are yet but young in deed.   *Exeunt.*

Scene V.   [*A Witches' haunt.*]

*Thunder. Enter the Three Witches, meeting
Hecate.*

First Witch. Why, how now, Hecate! you look
      angerly.

Hecate. Have I not reason, beldams° as you are,
      Saucy and overbold? How did you dare
      To trade and traffic with Macbeth
5   In riddles and affairs of death;

---

133 *fee'd* i.e., paid to spy 134 *betimes* quickly 135 *bent* determined
137 *causes* considerations 141 *may be scanned* can be examined
142 *season of all natures* seasoning (preservative) of all living creatures
143 *My strange and self-abuse* my strange delusion 144 *initiate . . .
use* beginner's fear that lacks hardening practice III.v. 2 *beldams* hags

And I, the mistress of your charms,
The close contriver° of all harms,
Was never called to bear my part,
Or show the glory of our art?
And, which is worse, all you have done   10
Hath been but for a wayward son,
Spiteful and wrathful; who, as others do,
Loves for his own ends, not for you.
But make amends now: get you gone,
And at the pit of Acheron°   15
Meet me i' th' morning: thither he
Will come to know his destiny.
Your vessels and your spells provide,
Your charms and everything beside.
I am for th' air; this night I'll spend   20
Unto a dismal and a fatal end:
Great business must be wrought ere noon.
Upon the corner of the moon
There hangs a vap'rous drop profound;°
I'll catch it ere it come to ground: 25
And that distilled by magic sleights°
Shall raise such artificial sprites°
As by the strength of their illusion
Shall draw him on to his confusion.°
He shall spurn fate, scorn death, and bear   30
His hopes 'bove wisdom, grace, and fear:
And you all know security°
Is mortals' chiefest enemy.

Music and a song.

Hark! I am called; my little spirit, see,
Sits in a foggy cloud and stays for me.   [*Exit.*]   35
    Sing within, "Come away, come away," &c.

First Witch. Come, let's make haste; she'll soon be
    back again.   *Exeunt.*

---

7 *close contriver* secret inventor   15 *Acheron* (river of Hades)   24 *profound* heavy   26 *sleights* arts   27 *artificial sprites* spirits created by magic arts (?) artful (cunning) spirits (?)   29 *confusion* ruin   32 *security* overconfidence

Scene VI.   [*The palace.*]

Enter Lennox and another Lord.

Lennox. My former speeches have but hit your
    thoughts,°
    Which can interpret farther. Only I say
    Things have been strangely borne.° The gracious
    Duncan
    Was pitied of Macbeth: marry, he was dead.
5   And the right-valiant Banquo walked too late;
    Whom, you may say, if 't please you, Fleance
    killed,
    For Fleance fled. Men must not walk too late.
    Who cannot want the thought,° how monstrous
    It was for Malcolm and for Donalbain
10   To kill their gracious father? Damnèd fact!°
    How it did grieve Macbeth! Did he not straight,
    In pious rage, the two delinquents tear,
    That were the slaves of drink and thralls° of sleep?
    Was not that nobly done? Ay, and wisely too;
15   For 'twould have angered any heart alive
    To hear the men deny 't. So that I say
    He has borne° all things well: and I do think
    That, had he Duncan's sons under his key—
    As, an 't° please heaven, he shall not—they should
    find
20   What 'twere to kill a father. So should Fleance.
    But, peace! for from broad words,° and 'cause he
    failed
    His presence at the tyrant's feast, I hear,

III.vi. 1 *My . . . thoughts* i.e., my recent words have only coincided
with what you have in your mind 8 *borne* managed 8 *cannot want
the thought* can fail to think 10 *fact* evil deed 13 *thralls* slaves
17 *borne* managed 19 *an 't* if it 21 *for from broad words* because of
frank talk

Macduff lives in disgrace. Sir, can you tell
Where he bestows himself?

Lord.   The son of Duncan,
  From whom this tyrant holds the due of birth,°   25
  Lives in the English court, and is received
  Of the most pious Edward° with such grace
  That the malevolence of fortune nothing
  Takes from his high respect.° Thither Macduff
  Is gone to pray the holy King, upon his aid°   30
  To wake Northumberland° and warlike Siward;
  That by the help of these, with Him above
  To ratify the work, we may again
  Give to our tables meat, sleep to our nights,
  Free from our feasts and banquets bloody knives,   35
  Do faithful homage and receive free° honors:
  All which we pine for now. And this report
  Hath so exasperate the King that he
  Prepares for some attempt of war.

Lennox.   Sent he to Macduff?

Lord. He did: and with an absolute "Sir, not I,"   40
  The cloudy° messenger turns me his back,
  And hums, as who should say "You'll rue the time
  That clogs° me with this answer."

Lennox.   And that well might
  Advise him to a caution, t' hold what distance
  His wisdom can provide. Some holy angel   45
  Fly to the court of England and unfold
  His message ere he come, that a swift blessing
  May soon return to this our suffering country
  Under a hand accursed!

Lord.   I'll send my prayers with him.

                             Exeunt.

25 *due of birth* birthright   27 *Edward* Edward the Confessor (reigned
1042–1066)   28-29 *nothing . . . respect* does not diminish the high respect in which he is held   30 *upon his aid* to aid him (Malcolm)
31 *To wake Northumberland* i.e., to arouse the people in an English
county near Scotland   36 *free* freely granted   41 *cloudy* disturbed
43 *clogs* burdens

ACT IV

Scene I. [*A Witches' haunt.*]

Thunder. Enter the Three Witches.

First Witch. Thrice the brinded° cat hath mewed.

Second Witch. Thrice and once the hedge-pig°
    whined.

Third Witch. Harpier° cries. 'Tis time, 'tis time.

First Witch. Round about the caldron go:
5   In the poisoned entrails throw.
    Toad, that under cold stone
    Days and nights has thirty-one
    Swelt'red venom sleeping got,°
    Boil thou first i' th' charmèd pot.

10 *All.* Double, double, toil and trouble;
    Fire burn and caldron bubble.

Second Witch. Fillet° of a fenny° snake,
    In the caldron boil and bake;
    Eye of newt and toe of frog,
15   Wool of bat and tongue of dog,
    Adder's fork° and blindworm's° sting,
    Lizard's leg and howlet's° wing,

IV.i. 1 *brinded* brindled 2 *hedge-pig* hedgehog 8 *Harpier* (an attendant spirit, like Graymalkin and Paddock in I.i) 8 *Swelt'red venom sleeping got* venom sweated out while sleeping 12 *Fillet* slice 12 *fenny* from a swamp 16 *fork* forked tongue 16 *blindworm* (a legless lizard) 17 *howlet* owlet

For a charm of pow'rful trouble,
Like a hell-broth boil and bubble.

All. Double, double, toil and trouble;   20
Fire burn and caldron bubble.

Third Witch. Scale of dragon, tooth of wolf,
Witch's mummy,° maw and gulf°
Of the ravined° salt-sea shark,
Root of hemlock digged i' th' dark,   25
Liver of blaspheming Jew,
Gall of goat, and slips of yew
Slivered in the moon's eclipse,
Nose of Turk and Tartar's lips,
Finger of birth-strangled babe   30
Ditch-delivered by a drab,°
Make the gruel thick and slab:°
Add thereto a tiger's chaudron,°
For th' ingredience of our caldron.

All. Double, double, toil and trouble;   35
Fire burn and caldron bubble.

Second Witch. Cool it with a baboon's blood,
Then the charm is firm and good.

> *Enter Hecate and the other Three Witches.*

Hecate. O, well done! I commend your pains;
And every one shall share i' th' gains: 40
And now about the caldron sing,
Like elves and fairies in a ring,
Enchanting all that you put in.

> *Music and a song:* "Black Spirits," &c.

> [*Exeunt Hecate and the other Three Witches.*]

Second Witch. By the pricking of my thumbs,
Something wicked this way comes: 45
Open, locks,
Whoever knocks!

---

²³ *Witch's mummy* mummified flesh of a witch   ²³ *maw and gulf*
stomach and gullet   ²⁴ *ravined* ravenous   ³¹ *Ditch-delivered by a drab*
born in a ditch of a harlot   ³² *slab* viscous   ³³ *chaudron* entrails

Enter Macbeth.

Macbeth. How now, you secret, black, and midnight
     hags!
  What is 't you do?

All.   A deed without a name.

50 *Macbeth.* I conjure you, by that which you profess,
      Howe'er you come to know it, answer me:
      Though you untie the winds and let them fight
      Against the churches; though the yesty° waves
      Confound° and swallow navigation up;
      Though bladed corn be lodged° and trees blown
55   down;
      Though castles topple on their warders' heads;
      Though palaces and pyramids do slope°
      Their heads to their foundations; though the treas-
        ure
      Of nature's germens° tumble all together,
60   Even till destruction sicken,° answer me
      To what I ask you.

First Witch.   Speak.

Second Witch.   Demand.

Third Witch.   We'll answer.

First Witch. Say, if th' hadst rather hear it from our
      mouths,
    Or from our masters?

Macbeth.   Call 'em, let me see 'em.

First Witch. Pour in sow's blood, that hath eaten
65   Her nine farrow;° grease that's sweaten°
      From the murderer's gibbet throw
      Into the flame.

All.   Come, high or low,
    Thyself and office° deftly show!

---

53 *yesty* foamy **54** *Confound* destroy **55** *bladed corn be lodged* grain
in the ear be beaten down **57** *slope* bend **59** *nature's germens* seeds
of all life **60** *sicken* i.e., sicken at its own work **65** *farrow* young pigs
65 *sweaten* sweated **68** *office* function

Thunder. First Apparition: an Armed Head.

Macbeth. Tell me, thou unknown power——

First Witch.   He knows thy thought:
Hear his speech, but say thou nought.   70

First Apparition. Macbeth! Macbeth! Macbeth! Beware
    Macduff!
Beware the Thane of Fife. Dismiss me: enough.

                                        He descends.

Macbeth. Whate'er thou art, for thy good caution
    thanks:
Thou hast harped° my fear aright. But one word
    more——

First Witch. He will not be commanded. Here's an-
    other,   75
More potent than the first.

    Thunder. Second Apparition: a Bloody Child.

Second Apparition. Macbeth! Macbeth! Macbeth!

Macbeth. Had I three ears, I'd hear thee.

Second Apparition. Be bloody, bold, and resolute!
    Laugh to scorn
The pow'r of man, for none of woman born   80
Shall harm Macbeth.   *Descends.*

Macbeth. Then live, Macduff: what need I fear of
    thee?
But yet I'll make assurance double sure,
And take a bond of fate.° Thou shalt not live;
That I may tell pale-hearted fear it lies,   85
And sleep in spite of thunder.

    *Thunder. Third Apparition: a Child Crowned,
        with a tree in his hand.*

---

⁷⁴ *harped* hit upon, struck the note of ⁸⁴ *take a bond of fate* get a
guarantee from fate (i.e., he will kill Macduff and thus will compel
fate to keep its word)

                                    What is this,
        That rises like the issue° of a king,
        And wears upon his baby-brow the round
        And top of sovereignty?°

All.   Listen, but speak not to 't.

Third Apparition. Be lion-mettled, proud, and take
90   no care
        Who chafes, who frets, or where conspirers are:
        Macbeth shall never vanquished be until
        Great Birnam Wood to high Dunsinane Hill
        Shall come against him.   *Descends.*

Macbeth.   That will never be.
95   Who can impress° the forest, bid the tree
        Unfix his earth-bound root? Sweet bodements,°
          good!
        Rebellious dead,° rise never, till the Wood
        Of Birnam rise, and our high-placed Macbeth
        Shall live the lease of nature,° pay his breath
100   To time and mortal custom.° Yet my heart
        Throbs to know one thing. Tell me, if your art
        Can tell so much: shall Banquo's issue ever
        Reign in this kingdom?

All.   Seek to know no more.

Macbeth. I will be satisfied.° Deny me this,
105   And an eternal curse fall on you! Let me know.
        Why sinks that caldron? And what noise° is this?

                        Hautboys.

First Witch. Show!

Second Witch. Show!

Third Witch. Show!

87 *issue* offspring   88-89 *round/And top of sovereignty* i.e., crown
95 *impress* conscript   96 *bodements* prophecies   97 *Rebellious dead*
(perhaps a reference to Banquo; but perhaps a misprint for "rebellion's
head")   99 *lease of nature* natural lifespan   100 *mortal custom* natural
death   104 *satisfied* i.e., fully informed   106 *noise* music

All. Show his eyes, and grieve his heart;   110
 Come like shadows, so depart!

 *A show of eight Kings and Banquo, last [King]
        with a glass° in his hand.*

Macbeth. Thou art too like the spirit of Banquo.
    Down!
 Thy crown does sear mine eyelids. And thy hair,
 Thou other gold-bound brow, is like the first.
 A third is like the former. Filthy hags!   115
 Why do you show me this? A fourth! Start,° eyes!
 What, will the line stretch out to th' crack of
    doom?°
 Another yet! A seventh! I'll see no more.
 And yet the eighth appears, who bears a glass
 Which shows me many more; and some I see   120
 That twofold balls and treble scepters° carry:
 Horrible sight! Now I see 'tis true;
 For the blood-boltered° Banquo smiles upon me,
 And points at them for his. What, is this so?

First Witch. Ay, sir, all this is so. But why   125
 Stands Macbeth thus amazedly?
 Come, sisters, cheer we up his sprites,°
 And show the best of our delights:
 I'll charm the air to give a sound,
 While you perform your antic round,°   130
 That this great king may kindly say
 Our duties did his welcome pay.

    Music. The Witches dance, and vanish.

Macbeth. Where are they? Gone? Let this pernicious
    hour
 Stand aye accursèd in the calendar!
 Come in, without there!

III.s.d. *glass* mirror   ¹¹⁶ *Start* i.e., from the sockets   ¹¹⁷ *crack of doom*
blast (of a trumpet?) at doomsday   ¹²¹ *twofold balls and treble
scepters* (coronation emblems)   ¹²³ *blood-boltered* matted with blood
¹²⁷ *sprites* spirits   ¹³⁰ *antic round* grotesque circular dance

Enter Lennox.

135 *Lennox.*   What's your Grace's will?

Macbeth. Saw you the weïrd sisters?

Lennox.   No, my lord.

Macbeth. Came they not by you?

Lennox.   No indeed, my lord.

Macbeth. Infected be the air whereon they ride,
    And damned all those that trust them! I did hear
140 The galloping of horse.° Who was 't came by?

Lennox. 'Tis two or three, my lord, that bring you
        word
    Macduff is fled to England.

Macbeth.   Fled to England?

Lennox. Ay, my good lord.

Macbeth. [*Aside*] Time, thou anticipat'st° my
        dread exploits.
145 The flighty purpose never is o'ertook
    Unless the deed go with it.° From this moment
    The very firstlings of my heart° shall be
    The firstlings of my hand. And even now,
    To crown my thoughts with acts, be it thought and
        done:
150 The castle of Macduff I will surprise;°
    Seize upon Fife; give to th' edge o' th' sword
    His wife, his babes, and all unfortunate souls
    That trace him in his line.° No boasting like a fool;
    This deed I'll do before this purpose cool:
155 But no more sights!——Where are these gentlemen?
    Come, bring me where they are.   *Exeunt.*

---

140 *horse* horses (or "horsemen")   144 *anticipat'st* foretold   145-46 *The
flighty . . . it* the fleeting plan is never fulfilled unless an action ac-
companies it   147 *firstlings of my heart* i.e., first thoughts, impulses
150 *surprise* attack suddenly   153 *trace him in his line* are of his lineage

Scene II.   [*Macduff's castle.*]

Enter Macduff's wife, her Son, and Ross.

Lady Macduff. What had he done, to make him fly the
  land?

Ross. You must have patience, madam.

Lady Macduff.   He had none:
  His flight was madness. When our actions do not,
  Our fears do make us traitors.

Ross.   You know not
  Whether it was his wisdom or his fear.   5

Lady Macduff. Wisdom! To leave his wife, to leave his
    babes,
  His mansion and his titles,° in a place
  From whence himself does fly? He loves us not;
  He wants the natural touch:° for the poor wren,
  The most diminutive of birds, will fight,   10
  Her young ones in her nest, against the owl.
  All is the fear and nothing is the love;
  As little is the wisdom, where the flight
  So runs against all reason.

Ross.   My dearest coz,°
  I pray you, school° yourself. But, for your husband,   15
  He is noble, wise, judicious, and best knows
  The fits o' th' season.° I dare not speak much
    further:
  But cruel are the times, when we are traitors
  And do not know ourselves; when we hold rumor
  From what we fear,° yet know not what we fear,   20

IV.ii.   **7** *titles* possessions   **9** *wants the natural touch* i.e., lacks natural
affection for his wife and children   **14** *coz* cousin   **15** *school* control
17 *fits o' th' season* disorders of the time   **19-20** *hold rumor/From what
we fear* believe rumors because we fear

But float upon a wild and violent sea
Each way and move. I take my leave of you.
Shall not be long but I'll be here again.
Things at the worst will cease,° or else climb up-
    ward
25 To what they were before. My pretty cousin,
Blessing upon you!

Lady Macduff. Fathered he is, and yet he's fatherless.

Ross. I am so much a fool, should I stay longer,
It would be my disgrace° and your discomfort.
I take my leave at once.   *Exit Ross.*

30 *Lady Macduff.*   Sirrah,° your father's dead:
And what will you do now? How will you live?

Son. As birds do, mother.

Lady Macduff.   What, with worms and flies?

Son. With what I get, I mean; and so do they.

Lady Macduff. Poor bird! thou'dst never fear the net
    nor lime,°
35 The pitfall nor the gin.°

Son. Why should I, mother? Poor birds they are not
    set for.
My father is not dead, for all your saying.

Lady Macduff. Yes, he is dead: how wilt thou do for a
    father?

Son. Nay, how will you do for a husband?

Lady Macduff. Why, I can buy me twenty at any
40   market.

Son. Then you'll buy 'em to sell° again.

Lady Macduff. Thou speak'st with all thy wit, and yet,
    i' faith,
With wit enough for thee.°

24 *cease* i.e., cease worsening   29 *It would be my disgrace* i.e., I would
weep   30 *Sirrah* (here an affectionate address to a child)   34 *lime* bird-
lime (smeared on branches to catch birds)   35 *gin* trap   41 *sell* betray
43 *for thee* i.e., for a child

Son. Was my father a traitor, mother?

Lady Macduff. Ay, that he was.   45

Son. What is a traitor?

Lady Macduff. Why, one that swears and lies.°

Son. And be all traitors that do so?

Lady Macduff. Every one that does so is a traitor, and must be hanged.

Son. And must they all be hanged that swear and lie? 50

Lady Macduff. Every one.

Son. Who must hang them?

Lady Macduff. Why, the honest men.

Son. Then the liars and swearers are fools; for there are liars and swearers enow° to beat the honest 55 men and hang up them.

Lady Macduff. Now, God help thee, poor monkey! But how wilt thou do for a father?

Son. If he were dead, you'd weep for him. If you would not, it were a good sign that I should quickly 60 have a new father.

Lady Macduff. Poor prattler, how thou talk'st!

Enter a Messenger.

Messenger. Bless you, fair dame! I am not to you known,
Though in your state of honor I am perfect.°
I doubt° some danger does approach you nearly: 65
If you will take a homely° man's advice,
Be not found here; hence, with your little ones.
To fright you thus, methinks I am too savage;
To do worse to you were fell° cruelty,
Which is too nigh your person. Heaven preserve you! 70

---

⁴⁷ *swears and lies* i.e., takes an oath and breaks it ⁵⁵ *enow* enough
⁶⁴ *in . . . perfect* I am fully informed of your honorable rank ⁶⁵ *doubt* fear ⁶⁶ *homely* plain ⁶⁹ *fell* fierce

I dare abide no longer.   *Exit Messenger.*

Lady Macduff.   Whither should I fly?
  I have done no harm. But I remember now
  I am in this earthly world, where to do harm
  Is often laudable, to do good sometime
75 Accounted dangerous folly. Why then, alas,
  Do I put up that womanly defense,
  To say I have done no harm?—What are these faces?

                Enter Murderers.

Murderer. Where is your husband?

Lady Macduff. I hope, in no place so unsanctified
  Where such as thou mayst find him.

80 *Murderer.*   He's a traitor.

Son. Thou li'st, thou shag-eared° villain!

Murderer.   What, you egg!

            [*Stabbing him.*]

  Young fry° of treachery!

Son.   He has killed me, mother:
  Run away, I pray you!

                [*Dies.*]
            *Exit [Lady Macduff], crying "Murder!" [fol-
                lowed by Murderers].*

Scene III.   [*England. Before the King's palace.*]

        Enter Malcolm and Macduff.

Malcolm. Let us seek out some desolate shade, and
    there
  Weep our sad bosoms empty.

---

81 *shag-eared* hairy-eared (?), with shaggy hair hanging over the ears
(?) 82 *fry* spawn

Macduff.   Let us rather
Hold fast the mortal° sword, and like good men
Bestride our down-fall'n birthdom.° Each new
    morn
New widows howl, new orphans cry, new sorrows   5
Strike heaven on the face, that° it resounds
As if it felt with Scotland and yelled out
Like syllable of dolor.°

Malcolm.   What I believe, I'll wail;
What know, believe; and what I can redress,
As I shall find the time to friend,° I will.   10
What you have spoke, it may be so perchance.
This tyrant, whose sole° name blisters our tongues,
Was once thought honest:° you have loved him
    well;
He hath not touched you yet. I am young; but
    something
You may deserve of him through me;° and wisdom°   15
To offer up a weak, poor, innocent lamb
T' appease an angry god.

Macduff. I am not treacherous.

Malcolm.   But Macbeth is.
A good and virtuous nature may recoil
In° an imperial charge. But I shall crave your
    pardon;   20
That which you are, my thoughts cannot
    transpose:°
Angels are bright still, though the brightest° fell:
Though all things foul would wear° the brows of
    grace,
Yet grace must still look so.°

IV.iii. 3 *mortal* deadly   4 *Bestride our down-fall'n birthdom* protectively
stand over our native land   6 *that* so that   8 *Like syllable of dolor*
similar sound of grief   40 *to friend* friendly, propitious   12 *sole* very
13 *honest* good   15 *deserve of him through me* i.e., earn by betraying
me to Macbeth   15 *wisdom* it may be wise   19-20 *recoil/In* give way
under   21 *transpose* transform   22 *the brightest* i.e., Lucifer   23 *would
wear* desire to wear   24 *so* i.e., like itself

Macduff.   I have lost my hopes.

Malcolm. Perchance even there where I did find my
25   doubts.
    Why in that rawness° left you wife and child,
    Those precious motives, those strong knots of
      love,
    Without leave-taking? I pray you,
    Let not my jealousies° be your dishonors,
30   But mine own safeties. You may be rightly just°
    Whatever I shall think.

Macduff.   Bleed, bleed, poor country:
    Great tyranny, lay thou thy basis° sure,
    For goodness dare not check° thee: wear thou thy
      wrongs;
    The title is affeered.° Fare thee well, lord:
35   I would not be the villain that thou think'st
    For the whole space that's in the tyrant's grasp
    And the rich East to boot.

Malcolm.   Be not offended:
    I speak not as in absolute fear of you.
    I think our country sinks beneath the yoke;
40   It weeps, it bleeds, and each new day a gash
    Is added to her wounds. I think withal°
    There would be hands uplifted in my right;°
    And here from gracious England° have I offer
    Of goodly thousands: but, for° all this,
45   When I shall tread upon the tyrant's head,
    Or wear it on my sword, yet my poor country
    Shall have more vices than it had before,
    More suffer, and more sundry ways than ever,
    By him that shall succeed.

Macduff.   What should he be?

50 *Malcolm.* It is myself I mean, in whom I know

---

26 *rawness* unprotected condition   29 *jealousies* suspicions   30 *rightly just*
perfectly honorable   32 *basis* foundation   33 *check* restrain   34 *affeered*
legally confirmed   41 *withal* moreover   42 *in my right* on behalf of my
claim   43 *England* i.e., the King of England   44 *for* despite

All the particulars° of vice so grafted°
That, when they shall be opened,° black Macbeth
Will seem as pure as snow, and the poor state
Esteem him as a lamb, being compared
With my confineless harms.°

Macduff.   Not in the legions   55
Of horrid hell can come a devil more damned
In evils to top Macbeth.

Malcolm.   I grant him bloody,
Luxurious,° avaricious, false, deceitful,
Sudden,° malicious, smacking of every sin
That has a name: but there's no bottom, none,   60
In my voluptuousness:° your wives, your daughters,
Your matrons and your maids, could not fill up
The cistern of my lust, and my desire
All continent° impediments would o'erbear,
That did oppose my will. Better Macbeth   65
Than such an one to reign.

Macduff.   Boundless intemperance
In nature° is a tyranny; it hath been
Th' untimely emptying of the happy throne,
And fall of many kings. But fear not yet
To take upon you what is yours: you may   70
Convey° your pleasures in a spacious plenty,
And yet seem cold, the time° you may so hoodwink.
We have willing dames enough. There cannot be
That vulture in you, to devour so many
As will to greatness dedicate themselves,   75
Finding it so inclined.

Malcolm.   With this there grows
In my most ill-composed affection° such

---

⁵¹ *particulars* special kinds ⁵¹ *grafted* engrafted ⁵² *opened* in bloom,
i.e., revealed ⁵⁵ *confineless harms* unbounded evils ⁵⁸ *Luxurious* lech-
erous ⁵⁹ *Sudden* violent ⁶¹ *voluptuousness* lust ⁶⁴ *continent* restraining
⁶⁷ *In nature* in man's nature ⁷¹ *Convey* secretly manage ⁷² *time* age,
i.e., people ⁷⁷ *ill-composed affection* evilly compounded character

A stanchless° avarice that, were I King,
I should cut off the nobles for their lands,
80   Desire his jewels and this other's house:
And my more-having would be as a sauce
To make me hunger more, that I should forge
Quarrels unjust against the good and loyal,
Destroying them for wealth.

Macduff.   This avarice
85   Sticks deeper, grows with more pernicious root
Than summer-seeming° lust, and it hath been
The sword of our slain kings.° Yet do not fear.
Scotland hath foisons to fill up your will
Of your mere own.° All these are portable,°
90   With other graces weighed.

Malcolm. But I have none: the king-becoming graces,
As justice, verity, temp'rance, stableness,
Bounty, perseverance, mercy, lowliness,
Devotion, patience, courage, fortitude,
95   I have no relish of° them, but abound
In the division of each several crime,°
Acting it many ways. Nay, had I pow'r, I should
Pour the sweet milk of concord into hell,
Uproar° the universal peace, confound
All unity on earth.

100 *Macduff.*   O Scotland, Scotland!

Malcolm. If such a one be fit to govern, speak:
I am as I have spoken.

Macduff.   Fit to govern!
No, not to live. O nation miserable!
With an untitled tyrant bloody-sceptered,
105 When shalt thou see thy wholesome days again,

---

78 *stanchless* never-ending 86 *summer-seeming* befitting summer, i.e.,
youthful (?) transitory (?) 87 *sword of our slain kings* i.e., the cause
of death to our kings 88-89 *foisons . . . own* enough abundance of
your own to satisfy your covetousness 89 *portable* bearable 95 *relish
of* taste for (?) trace of (?) 96 *division of each several crime* varia-
tions of each kind of crime 99 *Uproar* put into a tumult

Since that the truest issue of thy throne
By his own interdiction° stands accursed,
And does blaspheme his breed?° Thy royal father
Was a most sainted king: the queen that bore thee,
Oft'ner upon her knees than on her feet,   *110*
Died° every day she lived. Fare thee well!
These evils thou repeat'st upon thyself
Hath banished me from Scotland. O my breast,
Thy hope ends here!

Malcolm.   Macduff, this noble passion,
Child of integrity, hath from my soul   *115*
Wiped the black scruples,° reconciled my thoughts
To thy good truth and honor. Devilish Macbeth
By many of these trains° hath sought to win me
Into his power; and modest wisdom° plucks me
From over-credulous haste: but God above   *120*
Deal between thee and me! For even now
I put myself to° thy direction, and
Unspeak mine own detraction; here abjure
The taints and blames I laid upon myself,
For° strangers to my nature. I am yet   *125*
Unknown to woman, never was forsworn,
Scarcely have coveted what was mine own,
At no time broke my faith, would not betray
The devil to his fellow, and delight
No less in truth than life. My first false speaking   *130*
Was this upon myself. What I am truly,
Is thine and my poor country's to command:
Whither indeed, before thy here-approach,
Old Siward, with ten thousand warlike men,
Already at a point,° was setting forth.   *135*
Now we'll together, and the chance of goodness
Be like our warranted quarrel!° Why are you
        silent?

---

107 *interdiction* curse, exclusion   108 *breed* ancestry   111 *Died* i.e., prepared for heaven   116 *scruples* suspicions   118 *trains* plots   119 *modest
wisdom* i.e., prudence   122 *to* under   125 *For* as   135 *at a point* prepared
136-37 *the chance . . . quarrel* i.e., may our chance of success equal the
justice of our cause

Macduff. Such welcome and unwelcome things at once
'Tis hard to reconcile.

Enter a Doctor.

Malcolm. Well, more anon. Comes the King forth, I
140   pray you?

Doctor. Ay, sir. There are a crew of wretched souls
That stay° his cure: their malady convinces
The great assay of art;° but at his touch,
Such sanctity hath heaven given his hand,
They presently amend.°

145 *Malcolm.*   I thank you, doctor.

Exit [Doctor].

Macduff. What's the disease he means?

Malcolm.   'Tis called the evil:°
A most miraculous work in this good King,
Which often since my here-remain in England
I have seen him do. How he solicits heaven,
150   Himself best knows: but strangely-visited° people,
All swoll'n and ulcerous, pitiful to the eye,
The mere° despair of surgery, he cures,
Hanging a golden stamp° about their necks,
Put on with holy prayers: and 'tis spoken,
155   To the succeeding royalty he leaves
The healing benediction. With this strange virtue°
He hath a heavenly gift of prophecy,
And sundry blessings hang about his throne
That speak° him full of grace.

Enter Ross.

Macduff.   See, who comes here?

160 *Malcolm.* My countryman; but yet I know him not.

---

142 *stay* await   142-43 *convinces/The great assay of art* i.e., defies the
efforts of medical science   145 *presently amend* immediately recover
146 *evil* (scrofula, called "the king's evil" because it could allegedly be
cured by the king's touch)   150 *strangely-visited* · oddly afflicted
152 *mere* utter   153 *stamp* coin   156 *virtue* power   159 *speak* proclaim

Macduff. My ever gentle° cousin, welcome hither.

Malcolm. I know him now: good God, betimes°
   remove
The means that makes us strangers!

Ross.   Sir, amen.

Macduff. Stands Scotland where it did?

Ross.   Alas, poor country!
Almost afraid to know itself! It cannot   165
Be called our mother but our grave, where nothing°
But who knows nothing is once seen to smile;
Where sighs and groans, and shrieks that rent the
   air,
Are made, not marked;° where violent sorrow seems
A modern ecstasy.° The dead man's knell   170
Is there scarce asked for who, and good men's lives
Expire before the flowers in their caps,
Dying or ere they sicken.

Macduff.   O, relation
Too nice,° and yet too true!

Malcolm.   What's the newest grief?

Ross. That of an hour's age doth hiss the speaker;°   175
Each minute teems° a new one.

Macduff.   How does my wife?

Ross. Why, well.

Macduff.   And all my children?

Ross.   Well too.

Macduff. The tyrant has not battered at their peace?

Ross. No; they were well at peace when I did leave
   'em.

---

161 *gentle* noble   162 *betimes* quickly   166 *nothing* no one   169 *marked*
noticed   170 *modern ecstasy* i.e., ordinary emotion   173-74 *relation/Too
nice* tale too accurate   175 *That . . . speaker* i.e., the report of the
grief of an hour ago is hissed as stale news   176 *teems* gives birth to

180 *Macduff.* Be not a niggard of your speech: how goes 't?

   Ross. When I came hither to transport the tidings,
     Which I have heavily° borne, there ran a rumor
     Of many worthy fellows that were out;°
     Which was to my belief witnessed° the rather,
185   For that I saw the tyrant's power° afoot.
     Now is the time of help. Your eye in Scotland
     Would create soldiers, make our women fight,
     To doff their dire distresses.

   Malcolm.   Be 't their comfort
     We are coming thither. Gracious England hath
190   Lent us good Siward and ten thousand men;
     An older and a better soldier none
     That Christendom gives out.°

   Ross.   Would I could answer
     This comfort with the like! But I have words
     That would° be howled out in the desert air,
     Where hearing should not latch° them.

195 *Macduff.*   What concern they?
     The general cause or is it a fee-grief
     Due to some single breast?°

   Ross.   No mind that's honest
     But in it shares some woe, though the main part
     Pertains to you alone.

   Macduff.   If it be mine,
200   Keep it not from me, quickly let me have it.

   Ross. Let not your ears despise my tongue for ever,
     Which shall possess them with the heaviest sound
     That ever yet they heard.

   Macduff.   Humh! I guess at it.

   Ross. Your castle is surprised;° your wife and babes

---

182 *heavily* sadly   183 *out* i.e., up in arms   184 *witnessed* attested
185 *power* army   192 *gives out* reports   194 *would* should   195 *latch*
catch   196-97 *fee-grief/Due to some single breast* i.e., a personal grief
belonging to an individual   204 *surprised* suddenly attacked

Savagely slaughtered. To relate the manner,   205
Were, on the quarry° of these murdered deer,
To add the death of you.

Malcolm.   Merciful heaven!
What, man! Ne'er pull your hat upon your brows;
Give sorrow words. The grief that does not speak
Whispers the o'er-fraught heart,° and bids it break.   210

Macduff. My children too?

Ross.   Wife, children, servants, all
That could be found.

Macduff.   And I must be from thence!
My wife killed too?

Ross.   I have said.

Malcolm.   Be comforted.
Let's make us med'cines of our great revenge,
To cure this deadly grief.   215

Macduff. He has no children. All my pretty ones?
Did you say all? O hell-kite!° All?
What, all my pretty chickens and their dam
At one fell swoop?

Malcolm. Dispute° it like a man.

Macduff.   I shall do so;   220
But I must also feel it as a man.
I cannot but remember such things were,
That were most precious to me. Did heaven look on,
And would not take their part? Sinful Macduff,
They were all struck for thee! Naught° that I am,   225
Not for their own demerits but for mine
Fell slaughter on their souls. Heaven rest them now!

Malcolm. Be this the whetstone of your sword. Let
      grief
Convert to anger; blunt not the heart, enrage it.

---

206 *quarry* heap of slaughtered game   210 *Whispers the o'er-fraught heart*
whispers to the overburdened heart   217 *hell-kite* hellish bird of prey
220 *Dispute* counter   225 *Naught* wicked

230   *Macduff.* O, I could play the woman with mine eyes,
        And braggart with my tongue! But, gentle heavens,
        Cut short all intermission;° front to front°
        Bring thou this fiend of Scotland and myself;
        Within my sword's length set him. If he 'scape,
        Heaven forgive him too!

235   *Malcolm.*   This time goes manly.
        Come, go we to the King. Our power is ready;
        Our lack is nothing but our leave.° Macbeth
        Is ripe for shaking, and the pow'rs above
        Put on their instruments.° Receive what cheer you
          may.
240   The night is long that never finds the day.   *Exeunt.*

---

232 *intermission* interval   232 *front to front* forehead to forehead i.e.,
face to face   237 *Our lack is nothing but our leave* i.e., we need only
to take our leave   239 *Put on their instruments* arm themselves (?)
urge us, their agents, onward (?)

ACT V

Scene I. [*Dunsinane. In the castle.*]

*Enter a Doctor of Physic and a
Waiting-Gentlewoman.*

Doctor. I have two nights watched with you, but can
perceive no truth in your report. When was it she
last walked?

Gentlewoman. Since his Majesty went into the field, I
have seen her rise from her bed, throw her night- 5
gown upon her, unlock her closet,° take forth
paper, fold it, write upon 't, read it, afterwards seal
it, and again return to bed; yet all this while in a
most fast sleep.

Doctor. A great perturbation in nature, to receive at 10
once the benefit of sleep and do the effects of
watching!° In this slumb'ry agitation, besides her
walking and other actual performances,° what, at
any time, have you heard her say?

Gentlewoman. That, sir, which I will not report after 15
her.

Doctor. You may to me, and 'tis most meet° you
should.

Gentlewoman. Neither to you nor anyone, having no
witness to confirm my speech. 20

Enter Lady [Macbeth], with a taper.

V.i.   6 *closet* chest   11-12 *effects of watching* deeds of one awake
13 *actual performance* deeds   17 *meet* suitable

Lo you, here she comes! This is her very guise,° and, upon my life, fast asleep! Observe her; stand close.°

Doctor. How came she by that light?

25 *Gentlewoman.* Why, it stood by her. She has light by her continually. 'Tis her command.

Doctor. You see, her eyes are open.

Gentlewoman. Ay, but their sense° are shut.

Doctor. What is it she does now? Look, how she rubs
30 her hands.

Gentlewoman. It is an accustomed action with her, to seem thus washing her hands: I have known her continue in this a quarter of an hour.

Lady Macbeth. Yet here's a spot.

35 *Doctor.* Hark! she speaks. I will set down what comes from her, to satisfy° my remembrance the more strongly.

Lady Macbeth. Out, damned spot! Out, I say! One: two: why, then 'tis time to do 't. Hell is murky.
40 Fie, my lord, fie! A soldier, and afeard? What need we fear who knows it, when none can call our pow'r to accompt?° Yet who would have thought the old man to have had so much blood in him?

Doctor. Do you mark that?

45 *Lady Macbeth.* The Thane of Fife had a wife. Where is she now? What, will these hands ne'er be clean? No more o' that, my lord, no more o' that! You mar all with this starting.

Doctor. Go to,° go to! You have known what you
50 should not.

Gentlewoman. She has spoke what she should not, I

---

21 *guise* custom   23 *close* hidden   28 *sense* i.e., powers of sight   86 *satis-fy* confirm   42 *to accompt* into account   49 *Go to* (an exclamation)

am sure of that. Heaven knows what she has known.

Lady Macbeth. Here's the smell of the blood still. All
the perfumes of Arabia will not sweeten this little
hand. Oh, oh, oh!   55

Doctor. What a sigh is there! The heart is sorely
charged.°

Gentlewoman. I would not have such a heart in my
bosom for the dignity° of the whole body.

Doctor. Well, well, well——   60

Gentlewoman. Pray God it be, sir.

Doctor. This disease is beyond my practice.° Yet I
have known those which have walked in their sleep
who have died holily in their beds.

Lady Macbeth. Wash your hands; put on your night-   65
gown; look not so pale! I tell you yet again, Banquo's buried. He cannot come out on 's° grave.

Doctor. Even so?

Lady Macbeth. To bed, to bed! There's knocking at
the gate. Come, come, come, come, give me your   70
hand! What's done cannot be undone. To bed, to
bed, to bed!   *Exit Lady* [*Macbeth*].

Doctor. Will she go now to bed?

Gentlewoman. Directly.

Doctor. Foul whisp'rings are abroad. Unnatural deeds   75
Do breed unnatural troubles. Infected minds
To their deaf pillows will discharge their secrets.
More needs she the divine than the physician.
God, God forgive us all! Look after her;
Remove from her the means of all annoyance,°   80
And still° keep eyes upon her. So good night.

---

⁵⁷ *charged* burdened ⁵⁹ *dignity* worth, rank ⁶² *practice* professional
skill ⁶⁷ *on 's* of his ⁸⁰ *annoyance* injury ⁸¹ *still* continuously

My mind she has mated° and amazed my sight:
I think, but dare not speak.

Gentlewoman.   Good night, good doctor.

                                        Exeunt.

Scene II.   [*The country near Dunsinane.*]

Drum and colors. Enter Menteith, Caithness,
Angus, Lennox, Soldiers.

Menteith. The English pow'r° is near, led on by
        Malcolm,
    His uncle Siward and the good Macduff.
    Revenges burn in them; for their dear° causes
    Would to the bleeding and the grim alarm
    Excite the mortified man.°

5 *Angus.*   Near Birnam Wood
    Shall we well meet them; that way are they coming.

Caithness. Who knows if Donalbain be with his
        brother?

Lennox. For certain, sir, he is not. I have a file°
    Of all the gentry: there is Siward's son,
10   And many unrough° youths that even now
    Protest° their first of manhood.

Menteith.   What does the tyrant?

Caithness. Great Dunsinane he strongly fortifies.
    Some say he's mad; others, that lesser hate him,
    Do call it valiant fury: but, for certain,

---

82 *mated* baffled V.ii. 1 *pow'r* army 3 *dear* heartfelt 4-5 *Would . . .*
man i.e., would incite a dead man (or "a paralyzed man") to join the
bloody and grim call to battle 8 *file* list 10 *unrough* i.e., beardless
11 *Protest* assert

He cannot buckle his distempered° cause   15
Within the belt of rule.°

Angus.   Now does he feel
His secret murders sticking on his hands;
Now minutely revolts upbraid° his faith-breach.
Those he commands move only in command,
Nothing in love. Now does he feel his title   20
Hang loose about him, like a giant's robe
Upon a dwarfish thief.

Menteith.   Who then shall blame
His pestered° senses to recoil and start,
When all that is within him does condemn
Itself for being there?

Caithness.   Well, march we on,   25
To give obedience where 'tis truly owed.
Meet we the med'cine° of the sickly weal,°
And with him pour we, in our country's purge,
Each drop of us.°

Lennox.   Or so much as it needs
To dew° the sovereign° flower and drown the
    weeds.   30
Make we our march towards Birnam.

                    Exeunt, marching.

Scene III.   [*Dunsinane. In the castle.*]

Enter Macbeth, Doctor, and Attendants.

Macbeth. Bring me no more reports; let them fly all!
Till Birnam Wood remove to Dunsinane
I cannot taint° with fear. What's the boy Malcolm?

---

15 *distempered* swollen by dropsy 16 *rule* self-control 18 *minutely
revolts upbraid* rebellions every minute rebuke 23 *pestered* tormented
27 *med'cine* i.e., Malcolm 27 *weal* commonwealth 29 *Each drop of
us* i.e., every last drop of our blood (?) 30 *dew* bedew, water (and
thus make grow) 30 *sovereign* (1) royal (2) remedial V.iii. 3 *taint*
become infected

Was he not born of woman? The spirits that know
All mortal consequences° have pronounced me
5   thus:
"Fear not, Macbeth; no man that's born of woman
Shall e'er have power upon thee." Then fly, false thanes,
And mingle with the English epicures.
The mind I sway° by and the heart I bear
10   Shall never sag with doubt nor shake with fear.

Enter Servant.

The devil damn thee black, thou cream-faced loon!°
Where got'st thou that goose look?

Servant. There is ten thousand——

Macbeth.   Geese, villain?

Servant.   Soldiers, sir.

Macbeth. Go prick thy face and over-red° thy fear,
15   Thou lily-livered boy. What soldiers, patch?°
Death of° thy soul! Those linen° cheeks of thine
Are counselors to fear. What soldiers, whey-face?

Servant. The English force, so please you.

Macbeth. Take thy face hence.   [*Exit Servant.*]
                     Seyton!—I am sick at heart,
20   When I behold—Seyton, I say!—This push°
Will cheer me ever, or disseat° me now.
I have lived long enough. My way of life
Is fall'n into the sear,° the yellow leaf,
And that which should accompany old age,
25   As honor, love, obedience, troops of friends,
I must not look to have; but, in their stead,
Curses not loud but deep, mouth-honor, breath,
Which the poor heart would fain deny, and dare not.
Seyton!

---

5 *mortal consequences* future human events   9 *sway* move   11 *loon* fool   14 *over-red* cover with red   15 *patch* fool   16 *of* upon   16 *linen* i.e., pale   20 *push* effort   21 *disseat* i.e., unthrone (with wordplay on "cheer," pronounced "chair")   23 *sear* withered

Enter Seyton.

Seyton. What's your gracious pleasure?

Macbeth.   What news more?   30

Seyton. All is confirmed, my lord, which was reported.

Macbeth. I'll fight, till from my bones my flesh be
    hacked.
  Give me my armor.

Seyton.   'Tis not needed yet.

Macbeth. I'll put it on.
  Send out moe° horses, skirr° the country round.   35
  Hang those that talk of fear. Give me mine armor.
  How does your patient, doctor?

Doctor.   Not so sick, my lord,
  As she is troubled with thick-coming fancies
  That keep her from her rest.

Macbeth.   Cure her of that.
  Canst thou not minister to a mind diseased,   40
  Pluck from the memory a rooted sorrow,
  Raze out° the written troubles of the brain,
  And with some sweet oblivious° antidote
  Cleanse the stuffed bosom of that perilous stuff
  Which weighs upon the heart?

Doctor.   Therein the patient   45
  Must minister to himself.

Macbeth. Throw physic° to the dogs, I'll none of it.
  Come, put mine armor on. Give me my staff.
  Seyton, send out.——Doctor, the thanes fly from
    me.——
  Come, sir, dispatch.° If thou couldst, doctor, cast   50
  The water° of my land, find her disease
  And purge it to a sound and pristine health,
  I would applaud thee to the very echo,

---

35 *moe* more 35 *skirr* scour 42 *Raze out* erase 43 *oblivious* causing
forgetfulness 47 *physic* medical science 50 *dispatch* hurry 50-51 *cast/
The water* analyze the urine

That should applaud again.——Pull 't off, I say.——
55   What rhubarb, senna, or what purgative drug,
    Would scour these English hence? Hear'st thou of
      them?

Doctor. Ay, my good lord; your royal preparation
    Makes us hear something.

Macbeth.   Bring it° after me.
    I will not be afraid of death and bane°
60   Till Birnam Forest come to Dunsinane.

Doctor. [*Aside*] Were I from Dunsinane away
      and clear,
    Profit again should hardly draw me here.   *Exeunt.*

Scene IV.   [*Country near Birnam Wood.*]

*Drum and colors. Enter Malcolm, Siward, Mac-
duff, Siward's Son, Menteith, Caithness, Angus,
and Soldiers, marching.*

Malcolm. Cousins, I hope the days are near at hand
    That chambers will be safe.°

Menteith.   We doubt it nothing.°

Siward. What wood is this before us?

Menteith.   The Wood of Birnam.

Malcolm. Let every soldier hew him down a bough
5   And bear 't before him. Thereby shall we shadow
    The numbers of our host, and make discovery°
    Err in report of us.

Soldiers.   It shall be done.

---

58 *it* i.e., the armor   59 *bane* destruction   V.iv.   2 *That chambers will
be safe* i.e., that a man will be safe in his bedroom   2 *nothing* not at
all   6 *discovery* reconnaisance

Siward. We learn no other but° the confident tyrant
  Keeps still in Dunsinane, and will endure°
  Our setting down before 't.

Malcolm.   'Tis his main hope,   10
  For where there is advantage to be given°
  Both more and less° have given him the revolt,
  And none serve with him but constrainèd things
  Whose hearts are absent too.

Macduff.   Let our just censures
  Attend the true event,° and put we on   15
  Industrious soldiership.

Siward.   The time approaches,
  That will with due decision make us know
  What we shall say we have and what we owe.°
  Thoughts speculative their unsure hopes relate,
  But certain issue strokes must arbitrate:°   20
  Towards which advance the war.°

                              Exeunt, marching.

Scene V.   [*Dunsinane. Within the castle.*]

*Enter Macbeth, Seyton, and Soldiers, with drum
                and colors.*

Macbeth. Hang out our banners on the outward walls.
  The cry is still "They come!" Our castle's strength
  Will laugh a siege to scorn. Here let them lie
  Till famine and the ague° eat them up.
  Were they not forced° with those that should be
    ours,   5

8 *no other but* nothing but that   9 *endure* allow   11 *advantage to
be given* afforded an opportunity   12 *more and less* high and low
14-15 *just censures/Attend the true event* true judgment await the actual
outcome   18 *owe* own (the contrast is between "what we shall say we
have" and "what we shall really have")   20 *certain issue strokes must
arbitrate* the definite outcome must be decided by battle   21 *war* army
V.v.   4 *ague* fever   5 *forced* reinforced

We might have met them dareful,° beard to beard,
And beat them backward home.

A cry within of women.

What is that noise?

Seyton. It is the cry of women, my good lord. [*Exit.*]

Macbeth. I have almost forgot the taste of fears:
10   The time has been, my senses would have cooled
To hear a night-shriek, and my fell° of hair
Would at a dismal treatise° rouse and stir
As life were in 't. I have supped full with horrors.
Direness, familiar to my slaughterous thoughts,
Cannot once start° me.

[*Enter Seyton.*]

15   Wherefore was that cry?

Seyton. The Queen, my lord, is dead.

Macbeth. She should° have died hereafter;
There would have been a time for such a word.°
Tomorrow, and tomorrow, and tomorrow
20   Creeps in this petty pace from day to day,
To the last syllable of recorded time;
And all our yesterdays have lighted fools
The way to dusty death. Out, out, brief candle!
Life's but a walking shadow, a poor player
25   That struts and frets his hour upon the stage
And then is heard no more. It is a tale
Told by an idiot, full of sound and fury
Signifying nothing.

Enter a Messenger.

Thou com'st to use thy tongue; thy story quickly!

30 *Messenger.* Gracious my lord,
I should report that which I say I saw,
But know not how to do 't.

Macbeth.   Well, say, sir.

---

6 *met them dareful* i.e., met them in the battlefield boldly   11 *fell* pelt
12 *treatise* story   15 *start* startle   17 *should* inevitably would (?)
18 *word* message

Messenger. As I did stand my watch upon the hill,
  I looked toward Birnam, and anon, methought,
  The wood began to move.

Macbeth.   Liar and slave!   35

Messenger. Let me endure your wrath, if 't be not so.
  Within this three mile may you see it coming;
  I say a moving grove.

Macbeth.   If thou speak'st false,
  Upon the next tree shalt thou hang alive,
  Till famine cling° thee. If thy speech be sooth,°   40
  I care not if thou dost for me as much.
  I pull in resolution,° and begin
  To doubt° th' equivocation of the fiend
  That lies like truth: "Fear not, till Birnam Wood
  Do come to Dunsinane!" And now a wood   45
  Comes toward Dunsinane. Arm, arm, and out!
  If this which he avouches° does appear,
  There is nor flying hence nor tarrying here.
  I 'gin to be aweary of the sun,
  And wish th' estate° o' th' world were now undone.   50
  Ring the alarum bell! Blow wind, come wrack!
  At least we'll die with harness° on our back.

                                      Exeunt.

Scene VI.   [*Dunsinane. Before the castle.*]

  *Drum and colors. Enter Malcolm, Siward,
    Macduff, and their army, with boughs.*

Malcolm. Now near enough. Your leavy° screens
    throw down,
  And show like those you are. You, worthy uncle,

40 *cling* wither 40 *sooth* truth 42 *pull in resolution* restrain confidence
43 *doubt* suspect 47 *avouches* asserts 50 *th' estate* the orderly condition 52 *harness* armor V.vi. 1 *leavy* leafy

    Shall, with my cousin, your right noble son,
    Lead our first battle.° Worthy Macduff and we°
5   Shall take upon 's what else remains to do,
    According to our order.°

Siward.   Fare you well.
    Do we° but find the tyrant's power° tonight,
    Let us be beaten, if we cannot fight.

Macduff. Make all our trumpets speak; give them all
        breath,
10 Those clamorous harbingers of blood and death.

                    Exeunt. Alarums continued.

        Scene VII.   [*Another part of the field.*]

                Enter Macbeth.

Macbeth. They have tied me to a stake; I cannot fly,
    But bearlike I must fight the course.° What's he
    That was not born of woman? Such a one
    Am I to fear, or none.

                Enter Young Siward.

Young Siward. What is thy name?

5   *Macbeth.*   Thou'lt be afraid to hear it.

Young Siward. No; though thou call'st thyself a hotter
        name
    Than any is in hell.

Macbeth.   My name's Macbeth.

---

4 *battle* battalion   4 *we* (Malcolm uses the royal "we")   6 *order* plan
7 *Do we* if we do   7 *power* forces   V.vii. 2 *course* bout, round (he has
in mind an attack of dogs or men upon a bear chained to a stake)

Young Siward. The devil himself could not pronounce
      a title
   More hateful to mine ear.

Macbeth.   No, nor more fearful.

Young Siward. Thou liest, abhorrèd tyrant; with my
      sword   10
   I'll prove the lie thou speak'st.

> *Fight, and Young Siward slain.*

Macbeth.   Thou wast born of woman.
   But swords I smile at, weapons laugh to scorn,
   Brandished by man that's of a woman born.

                                               Exit.

> *Alarums. Enter Macduff.*

Macduff. That way the noise is. Tyrant, show thy face!
   If thou be'st slain and with no stroke of mine,   15
   My wife and children's ghosts will haunt me still.
   I cannot strike at wretched kerns,° whose arms
   Are hired to bear their staves.° Either thou,
      Macbeth,
   Or else my sword, with an unbattered edge,
   I sheathe again undeeded.° There thou shouldst
      be;   20
   By this great clatter, one of greatest note
   Seems bruited.° Let me find him, Fortune!
   And more I beg not.   *Exit. Alarums.*

> *Enter Malcolm and Siward.*

Siward. This way, my lord. The castle's gently
      rend'red:°
   The tyrant's people on both sides do fight;   25
   The noble thanes do bravely in the war;
   The day almost itself professes° yours,
   And little is to do.

---

17 *kerns* foot soldiers (contemptuous) 18 *staves* spears 20 *undeeded*
i.e., having done nothing 22 *bruited* reported 24 *gently rend'red* surrendered without a struggle 27 *itself professes* declares itself

Malcolm.   We have met with foes
That strike beside us.°

Siward.   Enter, sir, the castle.

Exeunt. Alarum.

[Scene VIII.   *Another part of the field.*]

Enter Macbeth.

Macbeth. Why should I play the Roman fool, and die
On mine own sword? Whiles I see lives,° the gashes
Do better upon them.

Enter Macduff.

Macduff.   Turn, hell-hound, turn!

Macbeth. Of all men else I have avoided thee.
5   But get thee back! My soul is too much charged°
With blood of thine already.

Macduff.   I have no words:
My voice is in my sword, thou bloodier villain
Than terms can give thee out!°

Fight. Alarum.

Macbeth.   Thou losest labor:
As easy mayst thou the intrenchant° air
10   With thy keen sword impress° as make me bleed:
Let fall thy blade on vulnerable crests;
I bear a charmèd life, which must not yield
To one of woman born.

29 *beside us* i.e., deliberately miss us (?) as our comrades (?) V.viii.
2 *Whiles I see lives* so long as I see living men   5 *charged* burdened
8 *terms can give thee out* words can describe you   9 *intrenchant*
incapable of being cut   10 *impress* make an impression on

Macduff.   Despair° thy charm,
And let the angel° whom thou still hast served
Tell thee, Macduff was from his mother's womb   *15*
Untimely ripped.

Macbeth. Accursèd be that tongue that tells me so,
For it hath cowed my better part of man!°
And be these juggling fiends no more believed,
That palter° with us in a double sense;   *20*
That keep the word of promise to our ear,
And break it to our hope. I'll not fight with thee.

Macduff. Then yield thee, coward,
And live to be the show and gaze o' th' time:°
We'll have thee, as our rarer monsters° are,   *25*
Painted upon a pole,° and underwrit,
"Here may you see the tyrant."

Macbeth.   I will not yield,
To kiss the ground before young Malcolm's feet,
And to be baited° with the rabble's curse.
Though Birnam Wood be come to Dunsinane,   *30*
And thou opposed, being of no woman born,
Yet I will try the last. Before my body
I throw my warlike shield. Lay on, Macduff;
And damned be him that first cries "Hold,
     enough!"   *Exeunt, fighting. Alarums.*

[*Re-*]*enter fighting, and Macbeth slain.* [*Exit
Macduff, with Macbeth.*] *Retreat and flour-
ish.*° *Enter, with drum and colors, Malcolm,
Siward, Ross, Thanes, and Soldiers.*

Malcolm. I would the friends we miss were safe
     arrived.   *35*

Siward. Some must go off;° and yet, by these I see,
So great a day as this is cheaply bought.

---

¹³ *Despair* despair of   ¹⁴ *angel* i.e., fallen angel, fiend   ¹⁸ *better part
of man* manly spirit   ²⁰ *palter* equivocate   ²⁴ *gaze o' th' time* spectacle
of the age   ²⁵ *monsters* freaks   ²⁶ *Painted upon a pole* i.e., pictured
on a banner set by a showman's booth   ²⁹ *baited* assailed (like a bear
by dogs)   ³⁴ s.d. *Retreat and flourish* trumpet call to withdraw, and
fanfare   ³⁶ *go off* die (theatrical metaphor)

Malcolm. Macduff is missing, and your noble son.

Ross. Your son, my lord, has paid a soldier's debt:
40   He only lived but till he was a man;
      The which no sooner had his prowess confirmed
      In the unshrinking station° where he fought,
      But like a man he died.

Siward.   Then he is dead?

Ross. Ay, and brought off the field. Your cause of
          sorrow
45   Must not be measured by his worth, for then
      It hath no end.

Siward.   Had he his hurts before?

Ross. Ay, on the front.

Siward.   Why then, God's soldier be he!
      Had I as many sons as I have hairs,
      I would not wish them to a fairer death:
      And so his knell is knolled.

50 *Malcolm.*   He's worth more sorrow,
      And that I'll spend for him.

Siward.   He's worth no more:
      They say he parted well and paid his score:°
      And so God be with him! Here comes newer
          comfort.

          Enter Macduff, with Macbeth's head.

Macduff. Hail, King! for so thou art: behold, where
          stands
55   Th' usurper's cursèd head. The time is free.°
      I see thee compassed° with thy kingdom's pearl,
      That speak my salutation in their minds,
      Whose voices I desire aloud with mine:
      Hail, King of Scotland!

All.   Hail, King of Scotland!

---

42 *unshrinking station* i.e., place at which he stood firmly   52 *parted well and paid his score* departed well and settled his account   55 *The time is free* the world is liberated   56 *compassed* surrounded

Flourish.

Malcolm. We shall not spend a large expense of time   60
    Before we reckon with your several loves,°
    And make us even with you. My thanes and
      kinsmen,
    Henceforth be earls, the first that ever Scotland
    In such an honor named. What's more to do,
    Which would be planted newly with the time°—   65
    As calling home our exiled friends abroad
    That fled the snares of watchful tyranny,
    Producing forth the cruel ministers°
    Of this dead butcher and his fiendlike queen,
    Who, as 'tis thought, by self and violent° hands   70
    Took off her life—this, and what needful else
    That calls upon us,° by the grace of Grace
    We will perform in measure, time, and place:°
    So thanks to all at once and to each one,
    Whom we invite to see us crowned at Scone.   75

Flourish. Exeunt Omnes.

FINIS

---

⁶¹ *reckon with your several loves* reward the devotion of each of you
⁶⁴⁻⁶⁵ *What's more . . . time* i.e., what else must be done which should
be newly established in this age ⁶⁸ *ministers* agents ⁷⁰ *self and violent* her own violent ⁷² *calls upon us* demands my attention ⁷³ *in
measure, time and place* fittingly, at the appropriate time and place

Textual Note

Macbeth, never printed during Shakespeare's lifetime, was first printed in the Folio of 1623. The play is remarkably short, and it may be that there has been some cutting. That in I.v Lady Macbeth apparently proposes to kill Duncan, and that later in the play Macbeth kills him, is scarcely evidence that a scene had been lost, but the inconsistent stage directions concerning Macbeth's death (one calls for him to be slain on stage, another suggests he is both slain and decapitated off stage) indicate some sort of revision. Nevertheless, when one reads the account of Macbeth in Holinshed (Shakespeare's source) one does not feel that the play as it has come down to us omits anything of significance. If, as seems likely, the play was presented at court, its brevity may well be due to King James's known aversion to long plays. On the other hand, it is generally believed that Hecate is a non-Shakespearean addition to the play (she dominates III.v and has a few lines in IV.i), but the evidence is not conclusive, although the passages (along with IV.i.125-32) sound un-Shakespearean.

The present division into acts and scenes is that of the Folio except for V.viii, a division added by the Globe editors. The present edition silently modernizes spelling and punctuation, regularizes speech prefixes, and translates into English the Folio's Latin designations of act and scene. Other departures from the Folio are listed

below. The reading of the present text is given first, in
italics, and then the reading of the Folio (F) in roman.

I.i.9 *Second Witch . . . Anon* [F attributes to "All," as part of the
ensuing speech]

I.ii.13 *gallowglasses* gallowgrosses   14 *quarrel* Quarry   26 *thunders break* Thunders   33-34 *Dismayed . . . Banquo* [one line in
F] 33-35 *Dismayed . . . lion* [three lines in F, ending: Banquoh,
Eagles, Lyon]   42 *But . . . faint* [F gives to previous line]   46
So . . . look [F gives to next line]   59 *Sweno . . . king* [F gives
to previous line]

I.iii.5 *Give . . . I* [F prints as a separate line]

32 *weïrd* weyward [also at I.v.9; II.i.20; "weyard" at III.i.2;
III.iv.134; IV.i.136]   39 *Forres* Soris   78 *Speak . . . you* [F
prints as a separate line]   81-82 *Into . . . stayed* [three lines in
F, ending: corporall, Winde, stay'd]   98 *Came* can   108 *why
. . . me* [F gives to next line]   111-14 *Which . . . not* [five lines
in F, ending: loose, Norway, helpe, labour'd, not]   131 *If ill*
[F gives to next line]   140-42 *Shakes . . . not* [F's lines end:
Man, surmise, not]   143 *If . . . crown me* [two lines in F, ending: King, crown me]   149-53 *Give . . . time* [seven lines in F,
ending: fauour, forgotten, registred, Leafe, them, vpon, time]
156 *Till . . . friends* [two lines in F, ending: enough, friends]

I.iv.1 *Are not* Or not [given in F to next line]   2-8 *My . . . died*
[seven lines in F, ending: back, die, hee, Pardon, Repentance,
him, dy'de]   23-27 *In . . . honor* [six lines in F, ending: selfe,
Duties, State, should, Loue, Honor]

I.v.23-24 *And yet . . . have it* [three lines in F, ending: winne,
cryes, haue it]

I.vi.1 *the air* [F gives to next line]   4 *martlet* Barlet   9 *most*
must   17-20 *Against . . . hermits* [F's lines end: broad, House,
Dignities, Ermites]

I. vii.6 *shoal* Schoole [variant spelling]   47 *do* no   58 *as you*
[F gives to next line]

II.i.4 *Hold . . . heaven* [two lines in F, ending: Sword, Heauen]
7-9 *And . . . repose* [F's endings: sleepe, thoughts, repose]   13-17
He . . . content [F's endings: Pleasure, Offices, withall, Hostesse,
content]   25 *when 'tis* [F gives to next line]   55 *strides* sides
56 *sure* sowre   57 *way they* they may

II.ii.2-6 *What . . . possets* [6 lines in F, ending: fire, shriek'd, good-night, open, charge, Possets] 13 s.d. *Enter Macbeth* [F places after "die" in 1.8] 14 *I . . . noise* [two lines in F, ending: deed, noyse] 18-19 *Hark . . . chamber* [one line in F] 22-25 *There's . . . sleep* [F's endings: sleepe, other, Prayers, sleepe] 32 *Stuck . . . throat* [F gives to previous line] 64-65 *To wear . . . chamber* [three lines in F, ending: white, entry, Chamber] 68 *Hath . . . knocking* [two lines in F, ending: vnattended, knocking] 72-73 *To . . . couldst* [four lines in F, ending: deed, my selfe, knocking, could'st. The s.d. "Knock" appears after "deed"]

II.iii.25-27 *Faith . . . things* [two lines of verse in F, the second beginning "And"] 44 s.d. *Enter Macbeth* [F places after 1.43] 53-54 *I'll . . . service* [one line of prose in F] 56-63 *The night . . . shake* [10 lines in F, ending: vnruly, downe, Ayre, Death, terrible, Euents, time, Night, feuorous, shake] 66 *Tongue nor heart* [F gives to next line] 88-89 *O . . . murdered* [one line in F] 137-43 *What . . . bloody* [nine lines in F, ending: doe, them, Office, easie, England, I, safer, Smiles, bloody]

II.iv.14 *And . . . horses* [F prints as a separate line] 17 *make* [F gives to next line] 19 *They . . . so* [F prints as a separate line]

III.i.34-35 *Craving . . . with you* [three lines in F, ending: Horse, Night, you] 42-43 *The sweeter . . . you* [three lines in F, ending: welcome, alone, you] 72 *Who's there* [F prints as a separate line] 75-82 *Well . . . might* [ten lines in F, ending: then, speeches, past, fortune, selfe, conference, with you, crost, them, might] 85-91 *I . . . ever* [nine lines in F, ending: so, now, meeting, predominant, goe, man, hand, begger'd, euer] 111 *I do* [F gives to previous line] 114-15 *Both . . . enemy* [one line in F] 128 *Your . . . most* [two lines in F, ending: you, most]

III.ii.16 *But . . . suffer* [two lines in F, ending: dis-ioynt, suffer] 22 *Duncan . . . grave* [F prints as a separate line] 43 *there . . . done* [F gives to next line] 50 *and . . . crow* [F gives to next line]

III.iii.9 *The rest* [F gives to next line] 17 *O . . . fly, fly, fly* [two lines in F, the first ending: Trecherie] 21 *We . . . affair* [two lines in F, ending: lost, Affaire]

III.iv.21-22 *Most . . . perfect* [four lines in F, ending: Sir, scap'd, againe, perfect] 49 *Here . . . Highness* [two lines in F, ending: Lord, Highness] 110 *broke . . . meeting* [F gives to next line]

122 s.d. *Exeunt* Exit   123 *blood will have blood* [F prints as a
separate line]   145 *in deed* indeed

III.v.36 *back again* [F prints as a separate line]

III.vi.1 *My . . . thoughts* [two lines in F, ending: Speeches,
Thoughts]   24 *son* Sonnes   38 *the* their

IV.i.46-47 *Open . . . knocks* [one line in F]   59 *germens* Ger-
maine   71 *Beware Macduff* [F prints as a separate line]   79
Laugh to scorn [F prints as a separate line]   86 *What is this*
[F gives to next line]   93 *Dunsinane* Dunsmane   98 *Birnam*
Byrnan [this F spelling, or with *i* for *y* or with a final *e*, occurs
at V.ii.5, 31; V.iii.2, 60; V.iv.3; V.v.34, 44; V.viii.30]   119 *eighth*
eight   133 *Let . . . hour* [F prints as a separate line]

IV.ii.27 *Fathered . . . fatherless* [two lines in F, ending: is,
Father-lesse] IV.ii.34 *Poor bird* [F prints as a separate line]   36-
43 *Why . . . for thee* [ten lines in F, ending: Mother, for, saying,
is dead, Father, Husband, Market, againe, wit, thee]   48-49
Every . . . hanged [two lines of verse in F, ending: Traitor,
hang'd]   57-58 [two lines of verse in F, ending: Monkie, Father]
77 *What . . . faces* [F prints as a separate line]

IV.iii.4 *down-fall'n* downfall   15 *deserve* discerne   25 *where
. . . doubts* [F prints as a separate line]   102 *Fit to govern* [F
gives to next line]   107 *accursed* accust   133 *thy* they   140 *I
pray you* [F prints as a separate line]   173 *O relation* [F gives
to next line]   211-12 *Wife . . . found* [one line in F]   212-13
And . . . too [one line in F]

V.iii.39 *Cure her* Cure   55 *senna* Cyme

V.vi.1 *Your . . . down* [F prints as a separate line]

V.viii.54 *behold . . . stands* [F prints as a separate line]

The Source of *Macbeth*

The selections given below, from the second edition (1587) of Raphael Holinshed's *Chronicles of England, Scotland, and Ireland,* are the materials that furnished Shakespeare his plot. A study of Holinshed's account of Macbeth's usurpation, and of Donwald's murder of King Duff (which Shakespeare in part transferred to the story of Macbeth), may help a reader to see Shakespeare's play more clearly, for what he added he must have felt necessary, and what he omitted he must have felt undesirable. Some of the changes are examined by E. E. Stoll in an essay printed in this volume, but, excellent as his essay is, he has not said the last word on the relation of the play to the historical account. It should be mentioned that scholars have occasionally suggested Shakespeare may have supplemented Holinshed with other accounts, but there is no evidence that he certainly did so. But of course other books gave him hints for phrases. For example, the Porter's comment on those who "go the primrose way to th' everlasting bonfire" (II.iii) is indebted to the Bible's mention of "the wide gate and broad way that leadeth to destruction; and many there be which go in thereat." But Holinshed alone seems to have provided Shakespeare with the raw material of the story of Macbeth. Presumably Shakespeare read Holinshed's narrative of Macbeth, and in browsing through the adjacent material he hit on the idea of revising this narrative in the light of Donwald's murder of King Duff. Relevant selec-

tions from these two portions of Holinshed's chronicle of
Scotland are printed below, followed by a brief selection
(relevant to V.viii.39-53) from the chronicle of England
telling of Old Siward's response to the news of his son's
death. The spelling, except for many proper nouns, has
been modernized.

Selections from Raphael Holinshed
Chronicles of England, Scotland, and Ireland

[Donwald] conceived such an inward malice towards the king (though he showed it not outwardly at
the first) that the same continued still boiling in his
stomach, and ceased not, till through setting on of his
wife, and in revenge of such unthankfulness, he found
means to murder the king within the foresaid castle of
Fores where he used to sojourn. For the king being in
that country, was accustomed to lie most commonly
within the same castle, having a special trust in Donwald,
as a man whom he never suspected.

But Donwald, not forgetting the reproach which his
lineage had sustained by the execution of those his kinsmen, whom the king for a spectacle to the people had
caused to be hanged, could not but show manifest tokens
of great grief at home amongst his family: which his
wife perceiving, ceased not to travel with him, till she
understood what the cause was of his displeasure. Which
at length when she had learned by his own relation, she
as one that bare no less malice in her heart towards the
king, for the like cause on her behalf, than her husband did for his friends, counseled him (sith the king
oftentimes used to lodge in his house without any guard
about him, other than the garrison of the castle, which
was wholly at his commandment) to make him away, and

showed him the means whereby he might soonest accomplish it.

Donwald thus being the more kindled in wrath by the words of his wife, determined to follow her advice in the execution of so heinous an act. Whereupon devising with himself for a while, which way he might best accomplish his cursed intent, at length got opportunity, and sped his purpose as followeth. It chanced that the king upon the day before he purposed to depart forth of the castle, was long in his oratory at his prayers, and there continued till it was late in the night. At the last, coming forth, he called such afore him as had faithfully served him in pursuit and apprehension of the rebels, and giving them hearty thanks, he bestowed sundry honorable gifts amongst them, of the which number Donwald was one, as he that had been ever accounted a most faithful servant to the king.

At length, having talked with them a long time, he got him into his privy chamber, only with two of his chamberlains, who having brought him to bed, came forth again, and then fell to banqueting with Donwald and his wife, who had prepared diverse delicate dishes, and sundry sorts of drinks for their rear supper or collation, whereat they sat up so long, till they had charged their stomachs with such full gorges, that their heads were no sooner got to the pillow, but asleep they were so fast, that a man might have removed the chamber over them, sooner than to have awaked them out of their drunken sleep.

Then Donwald, though he abhorred the act greatly in heart, yet through instigation of his wife he called four of his servants unto him (whom he had made privy to his wicked intent before, and framed to his purpose with large gifts) and now declaring unto them, after what sort they should work the feat, they gladly obeyed his instructions, & speedily going about the murder, they enter the chamber (in which the king lay a little before cocks crow, where they secretly cut his throat as he lay sleeping, without any buskling at all: and immediately by

a postern gate they carried forth the dead body into the fields. . . .

Donwald, about the time that the murder was in doing, got him amongst them that kept the watch, and so continued in company with them all the residue of the night. But in the morning when the noise was raised in the king's chamber how the king was slain, his body conveyed away, and the bed all berayed with blood; he with the watch ran thither, as though he had known nothing of the matter, and breaking into the chamber, and finding cakes of blood in the bed, and on the floor about the sides of it, he forthwith slew the chamberlains, as guilty of that heinous murder, and then like a mad man running to and fro, he ransacked every corner within the castle, as though it had been to have seen if he might have found either the body, or any of the murderers hid in any privy place: but at length coming to the postern gate, and finding it open, he burdened the chamberlains, whom he had slain, with all the fault, they having the keys of the gates committed to their keeping all the night, and therefore it could not be otherwise (said he) but that they were of counsel in the committing of that most detestable murder.

Finally, such was his overearnest diligence in the severe inquisition and trial of the offenders herein, that some of the lords began to mislike the matter, and to smell forth shrewd tokens, that he should not be altogether clear himself. But for so much as they were in that country, where he had the whole rule, what by reason of his friends and authority together, they doubted to utter what they thought, till time and place should better serve thereunto, and hereupon got them away every man to his home. For the space of six months together, after this heinous murder thus committed, there appeared no sun by day, nor moon by night in any part of the realm, but still was the sky covered with continual clouds, and sometimes such outrageous winds arose, with lightnings and tempests, that the people were in great fear of present destruction. . . .

Monstrous sights also that were seen within the Scottish

kingdom that year were these: horses in Louthian, being of singular beauty and swiftness, did eat their own flesh, and would in no wise taste any other meat. In Angus there was a gentlewoman brought forth a child without eyes, nose, hand, or foot. There was a sparhawk also strangled by an owl. Neither was it any less wonder that the sun, as before is said, was continually covered with clouds for six months' space. But all men understood that the abominable murder of King Duffe was the cause hereof. . . .

Thus might he seem happy to all men, having the love both of his lords and commons: but yet to himself he seemed most unhappy, as he that could not but still live in continual fear, lest his wicked practice concerning the death of Malcolme Duffe should come to light and knowledge of the world. For so cometh it to pass, that such as are pricked in conscience for any secret offense committed, have ever an unquiet mind. And (as the fame goeth) it chanced that a voice was heard as he was in bed in the night time to take his rest, uttering unto him these or the like words in effect: "Think not Kenneth that the wicked slaughter of Malcolme Duffe by thee contrived, is kept secret from the knowledge of the eternal God: thou art he that didst conspire the innocent's death, enterprising by traitorous means to do that to thy neighbor, which thou wouldst have revenged by cruel punishment in any of thy subjects, if it had been offered to thyself. It shall therefore come to pass, that both thou thyself, and thy issue, through the just vengeance of almighty God, shall suffer worthy punishment, to the infamy of thy house and family for evermore. For even at this present are there in hand secret practices to dispatch both thee and thy issue out of the way, that other may enjoy this kingdom which thou dost endeavor to assure unto thine issue."

The king, with this voice being stricken into great dread and terror, passed that night without any sleep coming in his eyes.

[*Macbeth's History*]

Doada was married unto Sinell the Thane of Glammis, by whom she had issue one Makbeth a valiant gentleman, and one that if he had not been somewhat cruel of nature, might have been thought most worthy the government of a realm. On the other part, Duncane was so soft and gentle of nature, that the people wished the inclinations and manners of these two cousins to have been so tempered and interchangeably bestowed betwixt them, that where the one had too much of clemency, and the other of cruelty, the mean virtue betwixt these two extremities might have reigned by indifferent partition in them both, so should Duncane have proved a worthy king, and Makbeth an excellent captain. The beginning of Duncane's reign was very quiet and peaceable, without any notable trouble; but after it was perceived how negligent he was in punishing offenders, many misruled persons took occasion thereof to trouble the peace and quiet state of the commonwealth, by seditious commotions which first had their beginnings in this wise.

Banquho the Thane of Lochquhaber, of whom the house of the Stewarts is descended, the which by order of lineage hath now for a long time enjoyed the crown of Scotland, even till these our days . . . gathered the finances due to the king. . . .

Then doubting not but for such contemptuous demeanor against the king's regal authority, they should be invaded with all the power the king could make, Makdowald one of great estimation among them, making first a confederacy with his nearest friends and kinsmen, took upon him to be chief captain of all such rebels as would stand against the king, in maintenance of their grievous offenses lately committed against him. . . . He used also such subtle persuasions and forged allurements, that in a small time he had gotten together a mighty power of men: for out of the western Isles there came unto him a great multitude of people . . . and out of Ire-

land . . . no small number of *Kerns and Galloglasses*. . . .

At length Makbeth speaking much against the king's softness, and overmuch slackness in punishing offenders, . . . he promised notwithstanding, if the charge were committed unto him and unto Banquho, so to order the matter, that the rebels should be shortly vanquished & quite put down, and that not so much as one of them should be found to make resistance within the country.

And even so it came to pass: for being sent forth with a new power, at his entering into Lochquhaber, the fame of his coming put the enemies in such fear, that a great number of them stole secretly away from their captain Makdowald, who nevertheless enforced thereto, gave battle unto Makbeth, with the residue which remained with him: but being overcome, and fleeing for refuge into a castle (within the which his wife & children were enclosed) at length when he saw how he could neither defend the hold any longer against his enemies, nor yet upon surrender be suffered to depart with life saved, he first slew his wife and children, and lastly himself, lest if he had yielded simply, he should have been executed in most cruel wise for an example to other. Makbeth entering into the castle by the gates, as then set open, found the carcass of Makdowald lying dead there amongst the residue of the slain bodies, which when he beheld, remitting no piece of his cruel nature with that pitiful sight, he caused the head to be cut off, and set upon a pole's end, and so sent it as present to the king, who as then lay at Bertha. The headless trunk he commanded to be hung up upon a high pair of gallows. . . . Thus was justice and law restored again to the old accustomed course, by the diligent means of Makbeth. Immediately whereupon word came that Sueno king of Norway was arrived in Fife with a puissant army, to subdue the whole realm of Scotland.

. . . Makbeth and Banquho were sent with the king's authority, who having with them a convenient power, encountered the enemies, slew part of them, and chased the other to their ships. They that escaped and got once to their ships, obtained of Makbeth for a great sum of gold, that such of their friends as were slain at this last bicker-

ing, might be buried in Saint Colme's Inch. . . .

And these were the wars that Duncane had with foreign enemies, in the seventh year of his reign. Shortly after happened a strange and uncouth wonder, which afterward was the cause of much trouble in the realm of Scotland, as ye shall after hear. It fortuned as Makbeth and Banquho journeyed towards Fores, where the king then lay, they went sporting by the way together without other company, save only themselves, passing through the woods and fields, when suddenly in the midst of a land, there met them three women in strange and wild apparel, resembling creatures of elder world, whom when they attentively beheld, wondering much at the sight, the first of them spoke and said: "All hail Makbeth, Thane of Glammis" (for he had lately entered into that dignity and office by the death of his father Sinell). The second of them said: "Hail Makbeth, Thane of Cawder." But the third said: "All hail Makbeth that hereafter shalt be king of Scotland."

Then Banquho: "What manner of women (saith he) are you, that seem so little favorable unto me, whereas to my fellow here, besides high offices, ye assign also the kingdom, appointing forth nothing for me at all?" "Yes (saith the first of them) we promise greater benefits unto thee, than unto him, for he shall reign indeed, but with an unlucky end: neither shall he leave any issue behind him to succeed in his place, where contrarily thou indeed shalt not reign at all, but of thee those shall be born which shall govern the Scottish kingdom by long order of continual descent." Herewith the foresaid women vanished immediately out of their sight. This was reputed at the first but some vain fantastical illusion by Mackbeth and Banquho, insomuch that Banquho would call Mackbeth in jest, king of Scotland; and Mackbeth again would call him in sport likewise, the father of many kings. But afterwards the common opinion was, that these women were either the weird sisters, that is (as ye would say) the goddesses of destiny, or else some nymphs or fairies, endued with knowledge of prophecy by their necromantical science, because everything came to pass as they had spoken. For shortly after, the Thane of Cawder being condemned at Fores of treason against the king committed; his lands, livings, and offices were given of the king's liberality to Mackbeth.

The same night after, at supper, Banquho jested with him and said: "Now Mackbeth thou hast obtained those things which the two former sisters prophesied, there remaineth only for thee to purchase that which the third said should come to pass." Whereupon Mackbeth revolving the thing in his mind, began even then to devise how he might attain to the kingdom: but yet he thought with himself that he must tarry a time, which should advance him thereto (by the divine providence) as it had come to pass in his former preferment. But shortly after it chanced that King Duncane, having two sons by his wife which was the daughter of Siward Earl of Northumberland, he made the elder of them called Malcolme Prince of Cumberland, as it were thereby to appoint him his successor in the kingdom, immediately after his decease. Mackbeth sore troubled herewith, for that he saw by this means his hope sore hindered (where, by the old laws of the realm, the ordinance was, that if he that should succeed were not of able age to take the charge upon himself, he that was next of blood unto him should be admitted) he began to take counsel how he might usurp the kingdom by force, having a just quarrel so to do (as he took the matter) for that Duncane did what in him lay to defraud him of all manner of title and claim, which he might in time to come, pretend unto the crown.

The words of the three weird sisters also (of whom before ye have heard) greatly encouraged him hereunto, but specially his wife lay sore upon him to attempt the thing, as she that was very ambitious, burning in unquenchable desire to bear the name of a queen. At length therefore, communicating his purposed intent with his trusty friends, amongst whom Banquho was the chiefest, upon confidence of their promised aid, he slew the king at Enverns, or (as some say) at Botgosuane, in the sixth year of his reign. Then having a company about him of such as he had made privy to his enterprise, he caused himself to be proclaimed king, and forthwith went into Scone, where (by common consent) he received the investure of the kingdom according to the accustomed manner. The body of Duncane was first conveyed unto Elgine, & there buried in kingly wise; but afterwards it was removed and conveyed unto Colmekill, and there laid in a sepulcher amongst his predecessors, in the year after the birth of our Savior, 1046.

Malcolme Cammore and Donald Bane the sons of King Duncane, for fear of their lives (which they might well know that Mackbeth would seek to bring to end for his more sure confirmation in the estate) fled into Cumberland, where Malcolme remained, till time that Saint Edward the son of Ethelred recovered the dominion of England from the Danish power, the which Edward received Malcolme by way of most friendly entertainment: but Donald passed over into Ireland, where he was tenderly cherished by the king of that land. Mackbeth, after the departure thus of Duncane's sons, used great liberality towards the nobles of the realm, thereby to win their favor, and when he saw that no man went about to trouble him, he set his whole intention to maintain justice, and to punish all enormities and abuses, which had chanced through the feeble and slothful administration of Duncane. . . . He made many wholesome laws and statutes for the public weal of his subjects. [There follows a list of good laws.]

These and the like commendable laws Makbeth caused to be put as then in use, governing the realm for the space of ten years in equal justice. But this was but a counterfeit zeal of equity showed by him, partly against his natural inclination to purchase thereby the favor of the people. Shortly after, he began to show what he was, instead of equity practicing cruelty. For the prick of conscience (as it chanceth ever in tyrants, and such as attain to any estate by unrighteous means) caused him ever to fear, lest he should be served of the same cup, as he had ministered to his predecessor. The words also of the three weird sisters, would not out of his mind, which as they promised him the kingdom, so likewise did they promise it at the same time unto the posterity of Banquho. He willed therefore the same Banquho with his son named Fleance, to come to a supper that he had prepared for them, which was indeed, as he had devised, present death at the hands of certain murderers, whom he hired to execute that deed, appointing them to meet with the same Banquho and his son without the palace, as they returned to their lodgings, and there to slay them, so that he would not have his house slandered, but that in time to come he might clear himself, if anything were laid to his charge upon any suspicion that might arise.

It chanced yet by the benefit of the dark night, that though the father were slain, the son yet by the help of almighty God reserving him to better fortune, escaped that danger: and afterwards having some inkling (by the admonition of some friends which he had in the court) how his life was sought no less than his father's, who was slain not by chance-medley (as by the handling of the matter Makbeth would have had it to appear) but even upon a prepensed device: whereupon to avoid further peril he fled into Wales. . . .

But to return unto Makbeth, in continuing the history, and to begin where I left, ye shall understand that, after the contrived slaughter of Banquho, nothing prospered with the foresaid Makbeth: for in manner every man began to doubt his own life, and durst unneth appear in the king's presence; and even as there were many that stood in fear of him, so likewise stood he in fear of many, in such sort that he began to make those away by one surmised cavillation or other, whom he thought most able to work him any displeasure.

At length he found such sweetness by putting his nobles thus to death, that his earnest thirst after blood in this behalf might in no wise be satisfied: for ye must consider he won double profit (as he thought) hereby: for first they were rid out of the way whom he feared, and then again his coffers were enriched by their goods which were forfeited to his use, whereby he might better maintain a guard of armed men about him to defend his person from injury of them whom he had in any suspicion. Further, to the end he might the more cruelly oppress his subjects with all tyrantlike wrongs, he builded a strong castle on the top of a high hill called Dunsinane, situate in Gowrie, ten miles from Perth, on such a proud height, that, standing there aloft, a man might behold well near all the countries of Angus, Fife, Stermond, and Ernedale, as it were lying underneath him. This castle, then, being founded on the top of that high hill, put the realm to great charges before it was finished, for all the stuff necessary to the building could not be brought up without much toil and business. But Makbeth, being once determined to have the work go forward, caused the thanes of each shire within the realm, to come and help towards that building, each man his course about.

At the last, when the turn fell unto Makduffe, Thane of Fife, to build his part, he sent workmen with all needful provision, and commanded them to show such diligence in every behalf, that no occasion might be given for the king to find fault with him, in that he came not himself as other had done, which he refused to do, for doubt lest the king, bearing him (as he partly understood) no great good will, would lay violent hands upon him, as he had done upon diverse other. Shortly after, Makbeth coming to behold how the work went forward, and because he found not Makduffe there, he was sore offended, and said: "I perceive this man will never obey my commandments, till he be ridden with a snaffle; but I shall provide well enough for him." . . .

Neither could he afterwards abide to look upon the said Makduffe, either for that he thought his puissance overgreat; either else for that he had learned of certain wizards, in whose words he put great confidence (for that the prophecy had happened so right, which the three fairies or weird sisters had declared unto him) how that he ought to take heed of Makduffe, who in time to come should seek to destroy him.

And surely hereupon had he put Makduffe to death, but that a certain witch, whom he had in great trust, had told that he should never be slain with man born of any woman, nor vanquished till the wood of Bernane came to the castle of Dunsinane. By this prophecy Makbeth put all fear out of his heart, supposing he might do what he would, without any fear to be punished for the same, for by the one prophecy he believed it was unpossible for any man to vanquish him, and by the other unpossible to slay him. This vain hope caused him to do many outrageous things, to the grievous oppression of his subjects. At length Makduffe, to avoid peril of life, purposed with himself to pass into England, to procure Malcolme Cammore to claim the crown of Scotland. But this was not so secretly devised by Makduffe, but that Makbeth had knowledge given him thereof: for kings (as is said) have sharp sight like unto Lynx, and long ears like unto Midas. For Makbeth had in every nobleman's house one sly fellow or other in fee with him, to reveal all that was said or done within the same, by which sleight he oppressed the most part of the nobles of his realm.

Immediately then, being advertised whereabout Makduffe went, he came hastily with a great power into Fife, and forthwith besieged the castle where Makduffe dwelled, trusting to have found him therein. They that kept the house, without any resistance opened the gates, and suffered him to enter, mistrusting none evil. But nevertheless Makbeth most cruelly caused the wife and children of Makduffe, with all other whom he found in that castle, to be slain. Also he confiscated the goods of Makduffe, proclaimed him traitor, and confined him out of all the parts of his realm; but Makduffe was already escaped out of danger, and gotten into England unto Malcolme Cammore, to try what purchase he might make by means of his support, to revenge the slaughter so cruelly executed on his wife, his children, and other friends. At his coming unto Malcolme, he declared into what great misery the estate of Scotland was brought, by the detestable cruelties exercised by the tyrant Makbeth, having committed many horrible slaughters and murders, both as well of the nobles as commons, for the which he was hated right mortally of all his liege people, desiring nothing more than to be delivered of that intolerable and most heavy yoke of thralldom, which they sustained at such a caitiff's hands.

Malcome hearing Makduffe's words, which he uttered in very lamentable sort, for mere compassion and very ruth that pierced his sorrowful heart, bewailing the miserable state of his country, he fetched a deep sigh; which Makduffe perceiving, began to fall most earnestly in hand with him, to enterprise the delivering of the Scottish people out of the hands of so cruel and bloody a tyrant, as Makbeth by too many plain experiments did show himself to be: which was an easy matter for him to bring to pass, considering not only the good title he had, but also the earnest desire of the people to have some occasion ministered, whereby they might be revenged of those notable injuries, which they daily sustained by the outrageous cruelty of Makbeth's misgovernance. Though Malcolme was very sorrowful for the oppression of his countrymen the Scots, in manner as Makduffe had declared; yet doubting whether he were come as one that meant unfeignedly as he spoke, or else as sent from Makbeth to betray him, he thought to have some further trial, and thereupon dissembling his mind at the first, he answered as followeth.

"I am truly very sorry for the misery chanced to my country of Scotland, but though I have never so great affection to relieve the same, yet by reason of certain incurable vices, which reign in me, I am nothing meet thereto. First, such immoderate lust and voluptuous sensuality (the abominable fountain of all vices) followeth me, that if I were made king of Scots, I should seek to deflower your maids and matrons, in such wise that mine intemperancy should be more importable unto you than the bloody tyranny of Makbeth now is." Hereunto Makduffe answered: "This surely is a very evil fault, for many noble princes and kings have lost both lives and kingdoms for the same; nevertheless there are women enow in Scotland, and therefore follow my counsel. Make thyself king, and I shall convey the matter so wisely, that thou shalt be so satisfied at thy pleasure in such secret wise, that no man shall be aware thereof."

Then said Malcolme, "I am also the most avaricious creature on the earth, so that if I were king, I should seek so many ways to get lands and goods, that I would slay the most part of all the nobles of Scotland by surmised accusations, to the end I might enjoy their lands, goods, and possessions; and therefore to show you what mischief may ensue on you through mine unsatiable covetousness, I will rehearse unto you a fable. There was a fox having a sore place on him overset with a swarm of flies, that continually sucked out her blood: and when one that came by and saw this manner, demanded whether she would have the flies driven beside her, she answered no: for if these flies that are already full, and by reason thereof suck not very eagerly, should be chased away, other that are empty and fellie and hungered, should light in their places, and suck out the residue of my blood far more to my grievance than these, which now being satisfied do not much annoy me. Therefore," saith Malcolme, "suffer me to remain where I am, lest if I attain to the regiment of your realm, mine unquenchable avarice may prove such; that ye would think the displeasures which now grieve you, should seem easy in respect of the unmeasurable outrage, which might ensue through my coming amongst you."

Makduffe to this made answer, how it was a far worse fault than the other: "for avarice is the root of all mischief, and for that crime the most part of our kings have been slain and brought to their final end. Yet notwithstanding follow my counsel, and take upon thee the crown. There is gold and riches enough in Scotland to satisfy thy greedy desire." Then said Malcolme again, "I am furthermore inclined to dissimulation, telling of leasings, and all other kinds of deceit, so that I naturally rejoice in nothing so much, as to betray & deceive such as put any trust or confidence in my words. Then sith there is nothing that more becometh a prince than constancy, verity, truth, and justice, with the other laudable fellowship of those fair and noble virtues which are comprehended only in soothfastness, and that lying utterly overthroweth the same; you see how unable I am to govern any province or region: and therefore sith you have remedies to cloak and hide all the rest of my other vices, I pray you find shift to cloak this vice amongst the residue."

Then said Makduffe: "This yet is the worst of all, and there I leave thee, and therefore say: Oh ye unhappy and miserable Scottishmen, which are thus scourged with so many and sundry calamities, each one above other! Ye have one cursed and wicked tyrant that now reigneth over you, without any right or title, oppressing you with his most bloody cruelty. This other that hath the right to the crown, is so replete with the inconstant behavior and manifest vices of Englishmen, that he is nothing worthy to enjoy it: for by his own confession he is not only avaricious, and given to unsatiable lust, but so false a traitor withal, that no trust is to be had unto any word he speaketh. Adieu Scotland, for now I account myself a banished man forever, without comfort or consolation": and with those words the brackish tears trickled down his cheeks very abundantly.

At the last, when he was ready to depart, Malcolme took him by the sleeve, and said: "Be of good comfort Makduffe, for I have none of these vices before remembered, but have jested with thee in this manner, only to prove thy mind: for diverse times heretofore hath Makbeth sought by this manner of means to bring me into his hands, but the more slow I have showed myself to condescend to thy motion and request, the more diligence shall I use in accomplishing the same." Incontinently hereupon they embraced each other, and promising to be faithful the one to the other, they fell in consultation how they might best provide for all their business, to bring the same to good effect. Soon after, Makduffe repairing to the borders of Scotland, addressed his letters with secret dispatch unto the nobles of the realm, declaring how Malcolme was confederate with him, to come hastily into Scotland to claim the crown, and therefore he required them, sith he was right inheritor thereto, to assist him with their powers to recover the same out of the hands of the wrongful usurper.

In the meantime, Malcolme purchased such favor at King Edward's hands, that old Siward Earl of Northumberland was appointed with ten thousand men to go with him into Scotland, to support him in this enterprise, for recovery of his right. After these news were spread abroad in Scotland, the nobles drew into two several factions, the one taking part with Makbeth, and the other with Malcolme. Hereupon ensued oftentimes sundry bickerings, & diverse light skirmishes: for those that were of Malcolme's side, would not jeopard to join with their enemies in a pight field, till his coming out of England to their support. But after that Makbeth perceived his enemy's power to increase, by such aid as came to them forth of England with his adversary Malcolme, he recoiled back into Fife, there purposing to abide in camp fortified, at the castle of Dunsinane, and to fight with his enemies, if they meant to pursue him; howbeit some of his friends advised him, that it should be best for him, either to make some agreement with Malcolme, or else to flee with all speed into the Isles, and to take his treasure with him, to the end he might wage sundry great princes of the realm to take his part, & retain strangers, in whom he might better trust than in his own subjects, which stole daily from him: but he had such confidence in his prophecies, that he believed he should never be vanquished, till Birnane wood were brought to Dunsinane; nor yet to be slain with any man, that should be or was born of any woman.

Malcolme following hastily after Makbeth, came the night before the battle unto Birnane wood, and when his army had rested a while there to refresh them, he commanded every man to get a bough of some tree or other of that wood in his hand, as big as he might bear, and to march forth therewith in such wise, that on the next morrow they might come closely and without sight in this manner within view of his enemies. On the morrow when Makbeth beheld them coming in this sort, he first marveled what the matter meant, but in the end remembered himself that the prophecy which he had heard long before that time, of the coming of Birnane wood to Dunsinane castle, was likely to be now fulfilled. Nevertheless, he brought his men in order of battle, and exhorted them to do valiantly, howbeit his enemies had scarcely cast from them their boughs, when Makbeth perceiving their numbers, betook him straight to flight, whom Makduffe pursued with great hatred even till he came unto Lunfannaine, where Makbeth perceiving that Makduffe was hard at his back, leaped beside his horse, saying: "Thou traitor, what meaneth it that thou shouldest thus in vain follow me that am not appointed to be slain by any creature that is born of a woman, come on therefore, and receive thy reward which thou hast deserved for thy pains," and therewithal he lifted up his sword thinking to have slain him.

But Makduffe quickly avoiding from his horse, ere he came at him, answered (with his naked sword in his hand) saying: "It is true Makbeth, and now shall thine insatiable cruelty have an end, for I am even he that thy wizards have told thee of, who was never born of my mother, but ripped out of her womb": therewithal he stepped unto him, and slew him in the place. Then cutting his head from his shoulders, he set it upon a pole, and brought it unto Malcolme. This was the end of Makbeth, after he had reigned 17 years over the Scottishmen. In the beginning of his reign he accomplished many worthy acts, very profitable to the commonwealth (as ye have heard), but afterward by illusion of the devil, he defamed the same with most terrible cruelty. He was slain in the year of the incarnation 1057, and in the 16 year of King Edward's reign over the Englishmen.

Malcolme Cammore thus recovering the realm (as ye have heard) by support of King Edward, in the 16 year of the same Edward's reign, he was crowned at Scone, the 25 day of April, in the year of our Lord 1057. Immediately after his coronation he called a parliament at Forfair, in the which he rewarded them with lands and livings that had assisted him against Makbeth, advancing

them to fees and offices as he saw cause, & commanded
that specially those, that bare the surname of any offices
or lands, should have and enjoy the same. He created
many earls, lords, barons, and knights. Many of them,
that before were thanes, were at this time made earls,
as Fife, Menteth . . . Leuenox . . . Cathnes, Rosse, and
Angus. These were the first earls that have been heard
of amongst the Scottishmen as their histories do make
mention. Many new surnames were taken up at this time
amongst them, as Cauder . . . Seiton . . . with many
other that had possessions given them, which gave names
to the owners for the time. . . .

[*Siward and his Son*]

About the thirteenth year of King Edward his reign (as
some write) or rather about the nineteenth or twentieth
year, as should appear by the Scottish writers, Siward
the noble Earl of Northumberland with a great power of
horsemen went into Scotland, and in battle put to flight
Mackbeth that had usurped the crown of Scotland, and,
that done, placed Malcolme surnamed Camoir, the son
of Duncane, sometime king of Scotland, in the government of that realm, who afterward slew the said Mackbeth, and then reigned in quiet. . . .

It is recorded also, that, in the foresaid battle, in
which Earl Siward vanquished the Scots, one of Siward's
sons chanced to be slain, whereof although the father had
good cause to be sorrowful, yet, when he heard that he
died of a wound which he had received in fighting stoutly,
in the forepart of his body, and that with his face towards the enemy, he greatly rejoiced thereat, to hear
that he died so manfully. But here is to be noted, that not
now, but a little before (as *Henry Hunt* saith) that Earl
Siward went into Scotland himself in person, he sent his
son with an army to conquer the land, whose hap was
there to be slain: and when his father heard the news,
he demanded whether he received the wound whereof he
died, in the forepart of the body, or in the hinder part:

and when it was told him that he received it in the forepart: "I rejoice (saith he) even with all my heart, for
I would not wish either to my son nor to myself any
other kind of *death*."

Commentaries

Samuel Johnson

Macbeth

Most of the notes which the present editor has sub-
joined to this play were published by him in a small
pamphlet in 1745.

I.i. *"Enter three* Witches." In order to make a true
estimate of the abilities and merit of a writer, it is always necessary to examine the genius of his age and the
opinions of his contemporaries. A poet who should now
make the whole action of his tragedy depend upon enchantment and produce the chief events by the assistance
of supernatural agents, would be censured as transgress-
ing the bounds of probability, be banished from the
theater to the nursery, and condemned to write fairy
tales instead of tragedies; but a survey of the notions
that prevailed at the time when this play was written will
prove that Shakespeare was in no danger of such censures, since he only turned the system that was then

From *The Plays of William Shakespeare* (1765).

universally admitted to his advantage and was far from overburdening the credulity of his audience.

The reality of witchcraft or enchantment, which, though not strictly the same, are confounded in this play, has in all ages and countries been credited by the common people, and in most, by the learned themselves. These phantoms have indeed appeared more frequently in proportion as the darkness of ignorance has been more gross; but it cannot be shown that the brightest gleams of knowledge have at any time been sufficient to drive them out of the world. The time in which this kind of credulity was at its height seems to have been that of the holy war, in which the Christians imputed all their defeats to enchantments or diabolical opposition, as they ascribed their success to the assistance of their military saints; and the learned Dr. Warburton appears to believe (*Supplement to the Introduction to "Don Quixote"*) that the first accounts of enchantments were brought into this part of the world by those who returned from their eastern expeditions. But there is always some distance between the birth and maturity of folly as of wickedness; this opinion had long existed, though perhaps application of it had in no foregoing age been so frequent, nor the reception so general. Olympiodorus, in Photius's extracts, tells us of one Libanius, who practiced this kind of military magic and having promised χωρὶς ὁπλιτῶν κατὰ βαρβάρων ἐνεργεῖν, *to perform great things against the barbarians without soldiers,* was, at the instances of the empress Placidia, put to death, when he was about to have given proof of his abilities. The empress showed some kindness in her anger by cutting him off at a time so convenient for his reputation.

But a more remarkable proof of the antiquity of this notion may be found in St. Chrysostom's book *de Sacerdotio,* which exhibits a scene of enchantments not exceeded by any romance of the Middle Age: he supposes a spectator overlooking a field of battle attended by one that points out all the various objects of horror, the engines of destruction, and the arts of slaughter. Δεικνύτο δὲ ἔτι παρὰ τοῖς ἐναντίοις καὶ πετομένους ἵππους διά τινος μαγγανείας, καὶ ὁπλίτας δὲ ἀέρος φερομένους, καὶ πάσην γοητείας δύναμιν καὶ ἰδέαν. "Let him then proceed to show him in the opposite armies horses flying by enchantment, armed men transported through the air, and every tower and form of magic." Whether St. Chrysostom believed that such performances were really to be seen in a day of battle, or only endeavored to enliven his description by adopting the notions of the vulgar, it is equally certain that such notions were in his time received, and that therefore they were not imported from the Saracens in a later age; the wars with the Saracens, however, gave occasion to their propagation, not only as bigotry naturally discovers prodigies, but as the scene of action was removed to a great distance.

The Reformation did not immediately arrive at its meridian, and though day was gradually increasing upon us, the goblins of witchcraft still continued to hover in the twilight. In the time of Queen Elizabeth was the remarkable trial of the witches of Warbois, whose conviction is still commemorated in an annual sermon at Huntingdon. But in the reign of King James, in which this tragedy was written, many circumstances concurred to propagate and confirm this opinion. The king, who was much celebrated for his knowledge, had, before his arrival in England, not only examined in person a woman accused of witchcraft but had given a very formal account of the practices and illusions of evil spirits, the compacts of witches, the ceremonies used by them, the manner of detecting them, and the justice of punishing them, in his dialogues of *Daemonologie*, written in the Scottish dialect, and published at Edinburgh. This book was, soon after his accession, reprinted at London, and as the ready way to gain King James's favor was to flatter his speculations, the system of *Daemonologie* was immediately adopted by all who desired either to gain preferment or not to lose it. Thus the doctrine of witchcraft was very powerfully inculcated; and as the greatest part of mankind have no other reason for their opinions than that they are in fashion, it cannot be doubted but this persuasion made a rapid progress, since vanity and credulity cooperated in its favor. The infection soon reached the Parliament, who, in the first year of King James, made a law, by which it was enacted, Chapter XII: That "if any person shall use any invocation or conjuration of any evil or wicked spirit; 2. or shall consult, covenant with, entertain, employ, feed or reward any evil or cursed spirit to or for any intent or purpose; 3. or take up any dead man, woman or child out of the grave,—or the skin, bone, or any part of the dead person, to be employed or used in any manner of witchcraft, sorcery, charm, or enchantment; 4. or shall use, practice, or exercise any sort of witchcraft, sorcery, charm, or enchantment; 5. whereby any person shall be destroyed, killed, wasted, consumed, pined, or lamed in any part of the body; 6. that every such person being convicted shall suffer death." This law was repealed in our own time.

Thus, in the time of Shakespeare, was the doctrine of witchcraft at once established by law and by the fashion, and it became not only unpolite, but criminal, to doubt it; and as prodigies are always seen in proportion as they are expected, witches were every day discovered and multiplied so fast in some places that Bishop Hall mentions a village in Lancashire where their number was greater than that of the houses. The Jesuits and sectaries took advantage of this universal error and endeavored to promote the interest of their parties by pretended cures of persons afflicted by evil spirits; but they were detected and exposed by the clergy of the Established Church.

Upon this general infatuation Shakespeare might be easily allowed to found a play, especially since he has followed with great exactness such histories as were then thought true; nor can it be doubted that the scenes of enchantment, however they may now be ridiculed, were both by himself and his audience thought awful and affecting.

I.vii.28. *"Enter* Lady Macbeth." The arguments by which Lady Macbeth persuades her husband to commit the murder afford a proof of Shakespeare's knowledge of human nature. She urges the excellence and dignity of courage, a glittering idea which has dazzled mankind from age to age and animated sometimes the housebreaker and sometimes the conqueror; but this sophism Macbeth has forever destroyed, by distinguishing true from false fortitude, in a line and a half; of which it may almost be said that they ought to bestow immortality on the author, though all his other productions had been lost;

> I dare do all that may become a man,
> Who dares do more, is none.

This topic, which has been always employed with too much success, is used in this scene with peculiar propriety, to a soldier by a woman. Courage is the distinguishing virtue of a soldier, and the reproach of cowardice cannot be borne by any man from a woman, without great impatience.

She then urges the oaths by which he had bound himself to murder Duncan, another art of sophistry by which men have sometimes deluded their consciences and persuaded themselves that what would be criminal in others is virtuous in them; this argument Shakespeare, whose plan obliged him to make Macbeth yield, has not confuted, though he might easily have shown that a former obligation could not be vacated by a latter; that obligations laid on us by a higher power could not be overruled by obligations which we lay upon ourselves.

II.i.49. *"Macbeth.* Now o'er the one half-world / Nature seems dead." That is, *over our hemisphere all action and motion seem to have ceased.* This image, which is perhaps the most striking that poetry can produce, has been adopted by Dryden in his *Conquest of Mexico:*

> All things are hush'd as Nature's self lay dead,
> The mountains seem to nod their drowsy head;
> The little birds in dreams their songs repeat,
> And sleeping flow'rs beneath the night dews sweat.
> Even lust and envy sleep!

These lines, though so well known, I have transcribed, that the contrast between them and this passage of Shakespeare may be more accurately observed.

Night is described by two great poets, but one describes a night of quiet, the other of perturbation. In the night of Dryden, all the disturbers of the world are laid asleep; in that of Shakespeare, nothing but sorcery, lust, and murder is awake. He that reads Dryden finds himself lulled with serenity and disposed to solitude and contemplation. He that peruses Shakespeare looks round alarmed and starts to find himself alone. One is the night of a lover, the other, of a murderer.

II.ii.55. "*Lady Macbeth.* gild the faces of the grooms withal; / For it must seem their guilt." Could Shakespeare possibly mean to play upon the similitude of *gild* and *guilt?*

II.iii.113–14. "*Macbeth.* Here lay Duncan, / His silver skin lac'd with his golden blood." Mr. Pope has endeavored to improve one of these lines by substituting *gory blood* for *golden blood;* but it may easily be admitted that he who could on such occasion talk of *lacing the silver skin* would *lace it* with *golden blood.* No amendment can be made to this line, of which every word is equally faulty, but by a general blot.

It is not improbable that Shakespeare put these forced and unnatural metaphors into the mouth of Macbeth as a mark of artifice and dissimulation, to show the difference between the studied language of hypocrisy and the natural outcries of sudden passion. This whole speech so considered is a remarkable instance of judgment, as it consists entirely of antithesis and metaphor.

III.i.68–69. "Mine eternal jewel / Giv'n to the common enemy of man." It is always an entertainment to an inquisitive reader, to trace a sentiment to its original source, and therefore though the term "enemy of man," applied to the devil, is in itself natural and obvious, yet some may be pleased with being informed, that Shakespeare probably borrowed it from the first lines of the destruction of Troy, a book which he is known to have read.

That this remark may not appear too trivial, I shall take occasion from it to point out a beautiful passage of Milton evidently copied from a book of no greater authority, in describing the gates of hell. Book 2. v. 879. he says,

> . . . On a sudden open fly,
> With impetuous recoil and jarring sound,
> Th' infernal doors, and on their hinges grate
> Harsh thunder.

In the history of Don Bellianis, when one of the knights approaches, as I remember, the castle of Brandezar, the gates are said to open "grating harsh thunder upon their brazen hinges."

IV.i. As this is the chief scene of enchantment in the play, it is proper in this place to observe, with how much judgment Shakespeare has selected all the circumstances of his infernal ceremonies, and how exactly he has conformed to common opinions and traditions.

> Thrice the brinded cat hath mew'd.

The usual form in which familiar spirits are reported to converse with witches, is that of a cat. A witch, who was tried about half a century before the time of Shakespeare, had a cat named Rutterkin, as the spirit of one of those witches was Grimalkin; and when any mischief was to be done she used to bid Rutterkin "go and fly," but once when she would have sent Rutterkin to torment a daughter of the countess of Rutland, instead of "going" or "flying," he only cried "mew," from whence she discovered that the lady was out of his power, the power of witches not being universal, but limited, as Shakespeare has taken care to inculcate.

> Though his bark cannot be lost,
> Yet it shall be tempest tost.

The common afflictions which the malice of witches produced were melancholy, fits, and loss of flesh, which are threatened by one of Shakespeare's witches.

> Weary sev'n-nights, nine times nine,
> Shall he dwindle, peak and pine.

It was likewise their practice to destroy the cattle of their neighbors, and the farmers have to this day many ceremonies to secure their cows and other cattle from witchcraft; but they seem to have been most suspected of malice against swine. Shakespeare has accordingly made one of his witches declare that she has been "killing swine," and Dr. Harsenet observes, that about that time, "a sow could not be ill of the measles, nor a girl of the sullens, but some old woman was charged with witchcraft."

> Toad, that under the cold stone,
> Days and nights has, thirty-one,
> Swelter'd venom sleeping got;
> Boil thou first i' th' charmed pot.

Toads have likewise long lain under the reproach of being by some means accessory to witchcraft, for which reason Shakespeare, in the first scene of this play, calls one of the spirits Padock or toad, and now takes care to put a toad first into the pot. When Vaninus was seized at Tholouse, there was found at his lodgings *ingens Bufo Vitro inclusus, a great Toad shut in a Vial,* upon which those that prosecuted him *Veneficium exprobrabant, charged him,* I suppose, with witchcraft.

> Fillet of a fenny snake,
> In the cauldron boil and bake;
> Eye of newt, and toe of frog . . .
> For a charm, &c.

The propriety of these ingredients may be known by consulting the books *de Viribus Animalium* and *de Mirabilibus Mundi,* ascribed to Albertus Magnus, in which the reader, who has time and credulity, may discover wonderful secrets.

> Finger of birth-strangled babes,
> Ditch-deliver'd by a drab. . . .

It has been already mentioned in the law against witches, that they are supposed to take up dead bodies to use in enchantments, which was confessed by the woman whom King James examined, and who had of a dead body that was divided in one of their assemblies, two fingers for her share. It is observable that Shakespeare, on this great occasion, which involves the fate of a king, multiplies all the circumstances of horror. The babe, whose finger is used, must be strangled in its birth; the grease must not only be human, but must have dropped from a gibbet, the gibbet of a murderer; and even the sow, whose blood is used, must have offended nature by devouring her own farrow. These are touches of judgment and genius.

> And now about the cauldron sing . . .
> Black spirits and white,
>   Blue spirits and grey,
> Mingle, mingle, mingle,
>   You that mingle may.

And in a former part,

> . . . weyward sisters, hand in hand, . . .
> Thus do go about, about,
> Thrice to thine, and thrice to mine,
> And thrice again to make up nine!

These two passages I have brought together, because they both seem subject to the objection of too much levity for the solemnity of enchantment, and may both be shown, by one quotation from Camden's account of Ireland, to be founded upon a practice really observed by the uncivilized natives of that country. "When any one gets a fall," says the informer of Camden, "he starts up, and *turning three times to the right* digs a hole in the earth; for they imagine that there is a spirit in the ground, and if he falls sick in two or three days, they send one of their women that is skilled in that way to the place, where she says, I call thee from the east, west, north and south, from the groves, the woods, the rivers, and the fens, from the *fairies red, black, white.*" There was likewise a book written before the time of Shakespeare, describing, amongst other properties, the colors of spirits.

Many other circumstances might be particularized, in which Shakespeare has shown his judgment and his knowledge.

General Observation. This play is deservedly celebrated for the propriety of its fictions, and solemnity, grandeur, and variety of its action; but it has no nice discriminations of character, the events are too great to admit the influence of particular dispositions, and the course of the action necessarily determines the conduct of the agents.

The danger of ambition is well described; and I know not whether it may not be said in defense of some parts which now seem improbable, that, in Shakespeare's time, it was necessary to warn credulity against vain and illusive predictions.

The passions are directed to their true end. Lady Macbeth is merely detested; and though the courage of Macbeth preserves some esteem, yet every reader rejoices at his fall.

A. C. Bradley

From *Shakespearean Tragedy*

From this murky background stand out the two great terrible figures who dwarf all the remaining characters of the drama. Both are sublime, and both inspire, far more than the other tragic heroes, the feeling of awe. They are never detached in imagination from the atmosphere which surrounds them and adds to their grandeur and terror. It is, as it were, continued into their souls. For within them is all that we felt without—the darkness of night, lit with the flame of tempest and the hues of blood, and haunted by wild and direful shapes, "murdering ministers," spirits of remorse, and maddening visions of peace lost and judgment to come. The way to be untrue to Shakespeare here, as always, is to relax the tension of imagination, to conventionalize, to conceive Macbeth, for example, as a halfhearted cowardly criminal, and Lady Macbeth as a wholehearted fiend.

These two characters are fired by one and the same passion of ambition; and to a considerable extent they are alike. The disposition of each is high, proud, and commanding. They are born to rule, if not to reign. They are peremptory or contemptuous to their inferiors. They are not children of light, like Brutus and Hamlet; they are of the world. We observe in them no love of country, and no interest in the welfare of anyone outside their fam-

From *Shakespearean Tragedy* by A. C. Bradley. London: Macmillan & Company, Ltd., 1904. Reprinted by permission of Macmillan & Company, Ltd. (London), St Martin's Press, Inc. (New York), and The Macmillan Company of Canada, Ltd. (Toronto).

ily. Their habitual thoughts and aims are, and, we imagine, long have been, all of station and power. And though in both there is something, and in one much, of what is higher—honor, conscience, humanity—they do not live consciously in the light of these things or speak their language. Not that they are egoists, like Iago; or, if they are egoists, theirs is an *egoïsme à deux*. They have no separate ambitions.[1] They support and love one another. They suffer together. And if, as time goes on, they drift a little apart, they are not vulgar souls, to be alienated and recriminate when they experience the fruitlessness of their ambition. They remain to the end tragic, even grand.

So far there is much likeness between them. Otherwise they are contrasted, and the action is built upon this contrast. Their attitudes towards the projected murder of Duncan are quite different; and it produces in them equally different effects. In consequence, they appear in the earlier part of the play as of equal importance, if indeed Lady Macbeth does not overshadow her husband; but afterwards she retires more and more into the background, and he becomes unmistakably the leading figure. His is indeed far the more complex character: and I will speak of it first.

Macbeth, the cousin of a King mild, just, and beloved, but now too old to lead his army, is introduced to us as a general of extraordinary prowess, who has covered himself with glory in putting down a rebellion and repelling the invasion of a foreign army. In these conflicts he showed great personal courage, a quality which he continues to display throughout the drama in regard to all plain dangers. It is difficult to be sure of his customary demeanor, for in the play we see him either in what appears to be an exceptional relation to his wife, or else in the throes of remorse and desperation; but from his behavior during his journey home after the war, from his

---

[1] The assertion that Lady Macbeth sought a crown for herself, or sought anything for herself, apart from her husband, is absolutely unjustified by anything in the play. It is based on a sentence of Holinshed's which Shakespeare did *not* use.

later conversations with Lady Macbeth, and from his language to the murderers of Banquo and to others, we
imagine him as a great warrior, somewhat masterful,
rough, and abrupt, a man to inspire some fear and much
admiration. He was thought "honest," or honorable; he
was trusted, apparently, by everyone; Macduff, a man of
the highest integrity, "loved him well." And there was, in
fact, much good in him. We have no warrant, I think,
for describing him, with many writers, as of a "noble"
nature, like Hamlet or Othello;[2] but he had a keen sense
both of honor and of the worth of a good name. The
phrase, again, "too full of the milk of human kindness,"
is applied to him in impatience by his wife, who did
not fully understand him; but certainly he was far from
devoid of humanity and pity.

At the same time he was exceedingly ambitious. He
must have been so by temper. The tendency must have
been greatly strengthened by his marriage. When we
see him, it has been further stimulated by his remarkable
success and by the consciousness of exceptional powers
and merit. It becomes a passion. The course of action
suggested by it is extremely perilous: it sets his good
name, his position, and even his life on the hazard. It is
also abhorrent to his better feelings. Their defeat in the
struggle with ambition leaves him utterly wretched, and
would have kept him so, however complete had been his
outward success and security. On the other hand, his
passion for power and his instinct of self-assertion are
so vehement that no inward misery could persuade him
to relinquish the fruits of crime, or to advance from remorse to repentance.

In the character as so far sketched there is nothing
very peculiar, though the strength of the forces contending in it is unusual. But there is in Macbeth one marked
peculiarity, the true apprehension of which is the key to
Shakespeare's conception.[3] This bold ambitious man of

---

[2] The word is used of him (I.ii.67), but not in a way that decides this question or even bears on it.

[3] This view, thus generally stated, is not original, but I cannot
say who first stated it.

action has, within certain limits, the imagination of a poet —an imagination on the one hand extremely sensitive to impressions of a certain kind, and, on the other, productive of violent disturbance both of mind and body. Through it he is kept in contact with supernatural impressions and is liable to supernatural fears. And through it, especially, come to him the intimations of conscience and honor. Macbeth's better nature—to put the matter for clearness' sake too broadly—instead of speaking to him in the overt language of moral ideas, commands, and prohibitions, incorporates itself in images which alarm and horrify. His imagination is thus the best of him, something usually deeper and higher than his conscious thoughts; and if he had obeyed it he would have been safe. But his wife quite misunderstands it, and he himself understands it only in part. The terrifying images which deter him from crime and follow its commission, and which are really the protest of his deepest self, seem to his wife the creations of mere nervous fear, and are sometimes referred by himself to the dread of vengeance or the restlessness of insecurity.[4] His conscious or reflective mind, that is, moves chiefly among considerations of outward success and failure, while his inner being is convulsed by conscience. And his inability to understand himself is repeated and exaggerated in the interpretations of actors and critics, who represent him as a coward, cold-blooded, calculating, and pitiless, who shrinks from crime simply because it is dangerous, and suffers afterwards simply because he is not safe. In reality his courage is frightful. He strides from crime to crime, though his soul never ceases to bar his advance with shapes of terror, or to clamor in his ears that he is murdering his peace and casting away his "eternal jewel."

It is of the first importance to realize the strength, and also (what has not been so clearly recognized) the limits, of Macbeth's imagination. It is not the universal meditative imagination of Hamlet. He came to see in man, as

---

[4] The latter, and more important, point was put quite clearly by Coleridge.

Hamlet sometimes did, the "quintessence of dust"; but he must always have been incapable of Hamlet's reflections on man's noble reason and infinite faculty, or of seeing with Hamlet's eyes "this brave o'erhanging firmament, this majestical roof fretted with golden fire." Nor could he feel, like Othello, the romance of war or the infinity of love. He shows no sign of any unusual sensitiveness to the glory or beauty in the world or the soul; and it is partly for this reason that we have no inclination to love him, and that we regard him with more of awe than of pity. His imagination is excitable and intense, but narrow. That which stimulates it is, almost solely, that which thrills with sudden, startling, and often supernatural fear.[5] There is a famous passage late in the play (V.v.10) which is here very significant, because it refers to a time before his conscience was burdened, and so shows his native disposition:

> The time has been, my senses would have cool'd
> To hear a night-shriek; and my fell of hair
> Would at a dismal treatise rise and stir
> As life were in't.

This "time" must have been in his youth, or at least before we see him. And, in the drama, everything which terrifies him is of this character, only it has now a deeper and a moral significance. Palpable dangers leave him unmoved or fill him with fire. He does himself mere justice when he asserts he "dare do all that may become a man," or when he exclaims to Banquo's ghost,

> What man dare, I dare:
> Approach thou like the rugged Russian bear,
> The arm'd rhinoceros, or the Hyrcan tiger;
> Take any shape but that, and my firm nerves
> Shall never tremble.

[5] It is the consequent insistence on the idea of fear, and the frequent repetition of the word, that have principally led to misinterpretation.

What appalls him is always the image of his own guilty heart or bloody deed, or some image which derives from them its terror or gloom. These, when they arise, hold him spellbound and possess him wholly, like a hypnotic trance which is at the same time the ecstasy of a poet. As the first "horrid image" of Duncan's murder—of himself murdering Duncan—rises from unconsciousness and confronts him, his hair stands on end and the outward scene vanishes from his eyes. Why? For fear of "consequences"? The idea is ridiculous. Or because the deed is bloody? The man who with his "smoking" steel "carved out his passage" to the rebel leader, and "unseam'd him from the nave to the chaps," would hardly be frightened by blood. How could fear of conscquences make the dagger he is to use hang suddenly glittering before him in the air, and then as suddenly dash it with gouts of blood? Even when he *talks* of consequences, and declares that if he were safe against them he would "jump the life to come," his imagination bears witness against him, and shows us that what really holds him back is the hideous vileness of the deed:

> He's here in double trust;
> First, as I am his kinsman and his subject,
> Strong both against the deed; then, as his host,
> Who should against his murderer shut the door,
> Not bear the knife myself. Besides, this Duncan
> Hath borne his faculties so meek, hath been
> So clear in his great office, that his virtues
> Will plead like angels, trumpet-tongued, against
> The deep damnation of his taking-off;
> And pity, like a naked new-born babe,
> Striding the blast, or heaven's cherubim, horsed
> Upon the sightless couriers of the air,
> Shall blow the horrid deed in every eye,
> That tears shall drown the wind.

It may be said that he is here thinking of the horror that others will feel at the deed—thinking therefore of consequences. Yes, but could he realize thus how horrible the deed would look to others if it were not equally horrible to himself?

It is the same when the murder is done. He is well-nigh mad with horror, but it is not the horror of detection. It is not he who thinks of washing his hands or getting his nightgown on. He has brought away the daggers he should have left on the pillows of the grooms, but what does he care for that? What *he* thinks of is that, when he heard one of the men awaked from sleep say "God bless us," he could not say "Amen"; for his imagination presents to him the parching of his throat as an immediate judgment from heaven. His wife heard the owl scream and the crickets cry; but what *he* heard was the voice that first cried "Macbeth doth murder sleep," and then, a minute later, with a change of tense, denounced on him, as if his three names gave him three personalities to suffer in, the doom of sleeplessness:

Glamis hath murdered sleep, and therefore Cawdor
Shall sleep no more, Macbeth shall sleep no more.

There comes a sound of knocking. It should be perfectly familiar to him; but he knows not whence, or from what world, it comes. He looks down at his hands, and starts violently: "What hands are here?" For they seem alive, they move, they mean to pluck out his eyes. He looks at one of them again; it does not move; but the blood upon it is enough to dye the whole ocean red. What has all this to do with fear of "consequences"? It is his soul speaking in the only shape in which it can speak freely, that of imagination.

So long as Macbeth's imagination is active, we watch him fascinated; we feel suspense, horror, awe; in which are latent, also, admiration and sympathy. But so soon as it is quiescent these feelings vanish. He is no longer "infirm of purpose": he becomes domineering, even brutal, or he becomes a cool pitiless hypocrite. He is generally said to be a very bad actor, but this is not wholly true. Whenever his imagination stirs, he acts badly. It so possesses him, and is so much stronger than his reason, that his face betrays him, and his voice utters the most improbable untruths[6] or the most artificial rhetoric.[7] But when it is asleep he is firm, self-controlled and practical, as in the conversation where he skillfully elicits from Banquo that information about his movements which is required for the successful arrangement of his murder.[8] Here he is hateful; and so he is in the conversation with the murderers, who are not professional cutthroats but old soldiers, and whom, without a vestige of remorse, he beguiles with calumnies against Banquo and with such appeals as his wife had used to him.[9] On the other hand, we feel much pity as well as anxiety in the scene (I.vii) where she overcomes his op-

---

[6] E.g., I.iii.149, where he excuses his abstraction by saying that his "dull brain was wrought with things forgotten," when nothing could be more natural than that he should be thinking of his new honor.

[7] E.g., in I.iv. This is so also in II.iii. 110 ff., though here there is some real imaginative excitement mingled with the rhetorical antitheses and balanced clauses and forced bombast.

[8] III.i. Lady Macbeth herself could not more naturally have introduced at intervals the questions "Ride you this afternoon?" (1. 19), "Is't far you ride?" (1. 23), "Goes Fleance with you?" (1. 35).

[9] We feel here, however, an underlying subdued frenzy which awakes some sympathy. There is an almost unendurable impatience expressed even in the rhythm of many of the lines; e.g.:

> Well then, now
> Have you consider'd of my speeches? Know
> That it was he in the times past which held you
> So under fortune, which you thought had been
> Our innocent self: this I made good to you
> In our last conference, pass'd in probation with you,
> How you were borne in hand, how cross'd, the instruments,
> Who wrought with them, and all things else that might
> To half a soul and to a notion crazed
> Say, "Thus did Banquo."

This effect is heard to the end of the play in Macbeth's less poetic speeches, and leaves the same impression of burning energy, though not of imaginative exaltation, as his great speeches. In these we find either violent, huge, sublime imagery, or a torrent of figurative expressions (as in the famous lines about "the innocent sleep"). Our impressions as to the diction of the play are largely derived from these speeches of the hero, but not wholly so. The writing almost throughout leaves an impression of intense, almost feverish, activity.

position to the murder; and we feel it (though his imagination is not specially active) because this scene shows
us how little he understands himself. This is his great mis-
fortune here. Not that he fails to realize in reflection the
baseness of the deed (the soliloquy with which the scene
opens shows that he does not). But he has never, to put it
pedantically, accepted as the principle of his conduct the
morality which takes shape in his imaginative fears. Had
he done so, and said plainly to his wife, "The thing is
vile, and, however much I have sworn to do it, I will
not," she would have been helpless; for all her arguments
proceed on the assumption that there is for them no
such point of view. Macbeth does approach this position
once, when, resenting the accusation of cowardice, he answers,

> I dare do all that may become a man;
> Who dares do more is none.

She feels in an instant that everything is at stake, and,
ignoring the point, overwhelms him with indignant and
contemptuous personal reproach. But he yields to it because he is himself half-ashamed of that answer of his,
and because, for want of habit, the simple idea which it
expresses has no hold on him comparable to the force
it acquires when it becomes incarnate in visionary fears
and warnings.

Yet these were so insistent, and they offered to his ambition a resistance so strong, that it is impossible to regard him as falling through the blindness or delusion of
passion. On the contrary, he himself feels with such intensity the enormity of his purpose that, it seems clear,
neither his ambition nor yet the prophecy of the Witches
would ever without the aid of Lady Macbeth have overcome this feeling. As it is, the deed is done in horror
and without the faintest desire or sense of glory—done,
one may almost say, as if it were an appalling duty;
and, the instant it is finished, its futility is revealed to
Macbeth as clearly as its vileness had been revealed be-

forehand. As he staggers from the scene he mutters in despair,

> Wake Duncan with thy knocking! I would thou could'st.

When, half an hour later, he returns with Lennox from the room of the murder, he breaks out:

> Had I but died an hour before this chance,
> I had lived a blessed time; for from this instant
> There's nothing serious in mortality:
> All is but toys: renown and grace is dead;
> The wine of life is drawn, and the mere lees
> Is left this vault to brag of.

This is no mere acting. The language here has none of the false rhetoric of his merely hypocritical speeches. It is meant to deceive, but it utters at the same time his profoundest feeling. And this he can henceforth never hide from himself for long. However he may try to drown it in further enormities, he hears it murmuring,

> Duncan is in his grave:
> After life's fitful fever he sleeps well:

or,

> better be with the dead:

or,

> I have lived long enough:

and it speaks its last words on the last day of his life:

> Out, out, brief candle!
> Life's but a walking shadow, a poor player
> That struts and frets his hour upon the stage
> And then is heard no more: it is a tale

> Told by an idiot, full of sound and fury,
> Signifying nothing.

How strange that this judgment on life, the despair of a man who had knowingly made mortal war on his own soul, should be frequently quoted as Shakespeare's own judgment, and should even be adduced, in serious criticism, as a proof of his pessimism!

It remains to look a little more fully at the history of Macbeth after the murder of Duncan. Unlike his first struggle this history excites little suspense or anxiety on his account: we have now no hope for him. But it is an engrossing spectacle, and psychologically it is perhaps the most remarkable exhibition of the *development* of a character to be found in Shakespeare's tragedies.

That heartsickness which comes from Macbeth's perception of the futility of his crime, and which never leaves him for long, is not, however, his habitual state. It could not be so, for two reasons. In the first place the consciousness of guilt is stronger in him than the consciousness of failure; and it keeps him in a perpetual agony of restlessness, and forbids him simply to droop and pine. His mind is "full of scorpions." He cannot sleep. He "keeps alone," moody and savage. "All that is within him does condemn itself for being there." There is a fever in his blood which urges him to ceaseless action in the search for oblivion. And, in the second place, ambition, the love of power, the instinct of self-assertion, are much too potent in Macbeth to permit him to resign, even in spirit, the prize for which he has put rancors in the vessel of his peace. The "will to live" is mighty in him. The forces which impelled him to aim at the crown reassert themselves. He faces the world, and his own conscience, desperate, but never dreaming of acknowledging defeat. He will see "the frame of things disjoint" first. He challenges fate into the lists.

The result is frightful. He speaks no more, as before Duncan's murder, of honor or pity. That sleepless torture, he tells himself, is nothing but the sense of insecurity and the fear of retaliation. If only he were safe, it would vanish. And he looks about for the cause of his fear; and his eye falls on Banquo. Banquo, who cannot fail to suspect him, has not fled or turned against him: Banquo has become his chief counselor. Why? Because, he answers, the kingdom was promised to Banquo's children. Banquo, then, is waiting to attack him, to make a way for them. The "bloody instructions" he himself taught when he murdered Duncan, are about to return, as he said they would, to plague the inventor. *This* then, he tells himself, is the fear that will not let him sleep; and it will die with Banquo. There is no hesitation now, and no remorse: he has nearly learned his lesson. He hastens feverishly, not to murder Banquo, but to procure his murder: some strange idea is in his mind that the thought of the dead man will not haunt him, like the memory of Duncan, if the deed is done by other hands.[10] The deed is done: but, instead of peace descending on him, from the depths of his nature his half-murdered conscience rises; his deed confronts him in the apparition of Banquo's Ghost, and the horror of the night of his first murder returns. But, alas, *it* has less power, and *he* has more will. Agonized and trembling, he still faces this rebel image, and it yields:

> Why, so: being gone,
> I am a man again.

Yes, but his secret is in the hands of the assembled lords. And, worse, this deed is as futile as the first. For, though Banquo is dead and even his Ghost is conquered, that inner torture is unassuaged. But he will not bear it. His guests have hardly left him when he turns roughly to his wife:

> How say'st thou, that Macduff denies his person
> At our great bidding?

---

10 See his first words to the Ghost: "Thou canst not say I did it."

Macduff it is that spoils his sleep. He shall perish,—he
and aught else that bars the road to peace.

> For mine own good
> All causes shall give way: I am in blood
> Stepp'd in so far that, should I wade no more,
> Returning were as tedious as go o'er:
> Strange things I have in head that will to hand,
> Which must be acted ere they may be scann'd.

She answers, sick at heart,

> You lack the season of all natures, sleep.

No doubt: but he has found the way to it now:

> Come, we'll to sleep. My strange and self abuse
> Is the initiate fear that wants hard use:
> We are yet but young in deed.

What a change from the man who thought of Duncan's
virtues, and of pity like a naked newborn babe! What a
frightful clearness of self-consciousness in this descent to
hell, and yet what a furious force in the instinct of life
and self-assertion that drives him on!

He goes to seek the Witches. He will know, by the
worst means, the worst. He has no longer any awe of
them.

> How now, you secret, black and midnight hags!

—so he greets them, and at once he demands and threatens. They tell him he is right to fear Macduff. They tell
him to fear nothing, for none of woman born can harm
him. He feels that the two statements are at variance; in-
fatuated, suspects no double meaning; but, that he may
"sleep in spite of thunder," determines not to spare Macduff. But his heart throbs to know one thing, and he
forces from the Witches the vision of Banquo's children

crowned. The old intolerable thought returns, "for Banquo's issue have I filed my mind"; and with it, for all the absolute security apparently promised him, there returns that inward fever. Will nothing quiet it? Nothing but destruction. Macduff, one comes to tell him, has escaped him; but that does not matter: he can still destroy: [11]

> And even now,
> To crown my thoughts with acts, be it thought and
>   done:
> The castle of Macduff I will surprise;
> Seize upon Fife; give to the edge o' the sword
> His wife, his babes, and all unfortunate souls
> That trace him in's line. No boasting like a fool;
> This deed I'll do before this purpose cool.
> But no more sights!

No, he need fear no more "sights." The Witches have done their work, and after this purposeless butchery his own imagination will trouble him no more.[12] He has dealt his last blow at the conscience and pity which spoke through it.

The whole flood of evil in his nature is now let loose.

---

[11]   For only in destroying I find ease
         To my relentless thoughts.—*Paradise Lost*, IX. 129.

Milton's portrait of Satan's misery here, and at the beginning of Book IV., might well have been suggested by *Macbeth*. Coleridge, after quoting Duncan's speech, I. iv. 35 ff., says: "It is a fancy; but I can never read this, and the following speeches of Macbeth, without involuntarily thinking of the Miltonic Messiah and Satan." I doubt if it was a mere fancy. (It will be remembered that Milton thought at one time of writing a tragedy on Macbeth.)

[12] The immediate reference in "But no more sights" is doubtless to the visions called up by the Witches; but one of these, the "blood-bolter'd Banquo," recalls to him the vision of the preceding night, of which he had said,

> You make me strange
> Even to the disposition that I owe,
> When now I think you can behold such *sights*,
> And keep the natural ruby of your cheeks,
> When mine is blanch'd with fear.

He becomes an open tyrant, dreaded by everyone about him, and a terror to his country. She "sinks beneath the yoke."

> Each new morn
> New widows howl, new orphans cry, new sorrows
> Strike heaven on the face.

She weeps, she bleeds, "and each new day a gash is added to her wounds." She is not the mother of her children, but their grave;

> where nothing,
> But who knows nothing, is once seen to smile:
> Where sighs and groans and shrieks that rend the air
> Are made, not mark'd.

For this wild rage and furious cruelty we are prepared; but vices of another kind start up as he plunges on his downward way.

> I grant him bloody,
> Luxurious, avaricious, false, deceitful,
> Sudden, malicious,

says Malcolm; and two of these epithets surprise us. Who would have expected avarice or lechery [13] in Macbeth? His ruin seems complete.

Yet it is never complete. To the end he never totally loses our sympathy; we never feel towards him as we do to those who appear the born children of darkness. There remains something sublime in the defiance with which, even when cheated of his last hope, he faces earth and hell and heaven. Nor would any soul to whom evil was congenial be capable of that heartsickness which over-

---

[13] "Luxurious" and "luxury" are used by Shakespeare only in this older sense. It must be remembered that these lines are spoken by Malcolm, but it seems likely that they are meant to be taken as true throughout.

comes him when he thinks of the "honor, love, obedience, troops of friends" which "he must not look to
have" (and which Iago would never have cared to have),
and contrasts with them

> Curses, not loud but deep, mouth-honor, breath,
> Which the poor heart would fain deny, and dare not,

(and which Iago would have accepted with indifference).
Neither can I agree with those who find in his reception
of the news of his wife's death proof of alienation or
utter carelessness. There is no proof of these in the words,

> She should have died hereafter;
> There would have been a time for such a word,

spoken as they are by a man already in some measure prepared for such news, and now transported by the
frenzy of his last fight for life. He has no time now to
feel.[14] Only, as he thinks of the morrow when time to
feel will come—if anything comes, the vanity of all hopes
and forward-lookings sinks deep into his soul with an
infinite weariness, and he murmurs,

> Tomorrow, and tomorrow, and tomorrow,
> Creeps in this petty pace from day to day
> To the last syllable of recorded time,
> And all our yesterdays have lighted fools
> The way to dusty death.

---

[14] I do not at all suggest that his love for his wife remains what
it was when he greeted her with the words "My dearest love,
Duncan comes here tonight." He has greatly changed; she has
ceased to help him, sunk in her own despair; and there is no
intensity of anxiety in the questions he puts to the doctor about
her. But his love for her was probably never unselfish, never the
love of Brutus, who, in somewhat similar circumstances, uses, on
the death of Cassius, words which remind us of Macbeth's:

> I shall find time, Cassius, I shall find time.

For the opposite strain of feeling cf. Sonnet 90:

> Then hate me if thou wilt; if ever, now,
> Now while the world is bent my deeds to cross.

In the very depths a gleam of his native love of goodness, and with it a touch of tragic grandeur, rests upon
him. The evil he has desperately embraced continues to
madden or to wither his inmost heart. No experience in
the world could bring him to glory in it or make his peace
with it, or to forget what he once was and Iago and
Goneril never were.

Elmer Edgar Stoll

Source and Motive in *Macbeth* and *Othello*

*The best tragedy—highest tragedy in short—is that
of the worthy encompassed by the inevitable.*

THOMAS HARDY

Shakespeare, of course, has, like the Greeks—unlike
the Bourbon French—no *règles,* neither rule nor
formula. But for all that, why in *Othello* and *Macbeth,*
two of the great tragedies that are not histories and that
apparently are not in any measure *rifacimenti* of previous
plays, does he, in the matter of motivation, deviate so
widely and so similarly from his source?

I

What in *Macbeth* he has omitted and what substituted
Sir Arthur Quiller-Couch has made admirably clear, but
has not considered the reasons for this or the similarity
of procedure in *Othello.* In Holinshed's Chronicle there
is the suggestion that, cut off by the nomination of Malcolm as successor to the throne from his own expectations, Macbeth had for his usurpation "a juste quarell so
to do (as he tooke the matter)." The crown was then not
strictly hereditary, and "by the old lawes of the realme,
if he that should succeed were not of able age to take
the charge upon himselfe, he that was next of blood

From *From Shakespeare to Joyce* by Elmer Edgar Stoll. New York:
Doubleday and Company, Inc., 1944. Copyright 1944 by Elmer Edgar
Stoll. Reprinted by permission of Doubleday and Company, Inc.

should be admitted." [1] "Did Shakespeare use that one
hint, enlarge that loophole?" asks Sir Arthur. "He did
not."

> Instead of using a paltry chance to condone Mac-
> beth's guilt, he seized on it and plunged it threefold
> deeper ...
> He made this man, a sworn soldier, murder Duncan,
> his liege-lord.
> He made this man, a host, murder Duncan, a guest
> within his gates.
> He made this man, strong and hale, murder Duncan,
> old, weak, asleep and defenceless.
> He made this man commit murder for nothing but
> his own advancement.
> He made this man murder Duncan, who had steadily
> advanced him hitherto, who had never been aught but
> trustful, and who (that no detail of reproach might
> be wanting) had that very night, as he retired, sent,
> in most kindly thought, the gift of a diamond to his
> hostess.
> To sum up: instead of extenuating Macbeth's crimi-
> nality, Shakespeare doubles and redoubles it. (*Shake-
> speare's Workmanship* [Holt, N. Y., 1930], pp.
> 19–20.)

And yet Macbeth is the protagonist, the hero, with
whom as such, for the right tragic effect, there must,
naturally, be some large measure of sympathy. So, having thus put him much farther beyond the reach of our
sympathy than in the original, what does the dramatist
then do but (indirectly) bring him back within it—in
general, by the power of poetry, in particular, by the
exhibition of the hero's bravery and virtue at the beginning, by emphasizing the influence of the supernatural

---

[1] *Boswell-Stone's Holinshed* (1896), p. 25. Sir Arthur's quotation,
preceding, is curtailed: "for that Duncane did what in him lay to
defraud him of all maner of title and claime, which he might, in
time to come, pretend unto the crowne."

presented, and of his wife's inordinate ambition distinctly mentioned, in the source.

There are additional devices which Sir Arthur dwells upon, such as the flattening of the other characters—that the hero and heroine may stand out in high relief, to absorb our interest and (presumably on the principle considered in the preceding chapter) our sympathy also; and such as the keeping of the murders, as the ancients do, in the background, off the stage. "There is some deep law in imaginative illusion," says Watts-Dunton,[2] "whereby the identification of the spectator's personality is with the active character in most dramatic actions rather than the passive." We share the emotions, the perturbations, of Macbeth and his Lady, as even of Clytemnestra and Phaedra, because they are the impassioned doers and speakers, constantly in the foreground; and it is with their ears that we hear the owl and the cricket, the voices in the castle and the knocking at the gate. And still more clearly than in the veiling of the horrors the method is that of the ancients. The central complication—the contrast—is that recommended by Aristotle,[3] the *good* man doing the dreadful deed, though not unwittingly, nor quite unwillingly either. As with the ancients, again, he is under the sway of fate; for the Weird Sisters and his Lady—"burning in unquenchable desire to beare the name of a queene"[4]—together amount to that.

This, of course, is not what we ordinarily call motivation, not psychology. For both—the narrative or external motivation and the internal—there was, positively and negatively, better provision in Holinshed—not only the "juste quarell (as he tooke the matter)" but also "the feeble and slouthfull administration of Duncane,"[5] no treachery or violation of the laws of hospitality in the killing, and the just and efficient rule (for ten years) in

[2] *Harper's* (November, 1906), p. 818.
[3] *Poetics, cap.* 13, 14.
[4] *Boswell-Stone's Holinshed* (1896), p. 25.
[5] *Ibid.*, p. 32. Cf. p. 20: "At length, Macbeth speaking much against the kings softnes and overmuch slacknesse in punishing offenders." . . .

the sequel.⁶ *La carrière ouverte aux talents,* and Macbeth had the justification of Napoleon, of Cromwell. But not Shakespeare's Macbeth.

Nor is this what we call drama, either, as it is ordinarily practiced today. It is as in Aristotle,—situation first and motivation or psychology afterwards, if at all. The effect is emotional, with which psychology or even simple narrative coherence often considerably interferes. To Schiller's neglect of careful motivation, and in a day of psychology and philosophy both, Goethe even attributes his superiority on the stage.⁷ Shakespeare sometimes neglects it because it can be counted upon as familiar; sometimes, as with Hamlet's feigning of lunacy and Lear's dividing of the kingdom, because, the motive in the old play not being a good one, it is better that it should be omitted or only hinted at; but in Macbeth the omission is for a positive purpose, and the contravention of psychological probability is so as well. Here, as generally in Shakespeare, *Coriolanus* being only a partial exception, character is not its own destiny, the action is not exclusively derived from it. For Shakespeare "a human being" is *not,* as in Galsworthy's words or as in his own and his fellows' practice, "the best plot there is." To his minor characters the words better apply. The hero's conduct, at the heart of the action, is often not in keeping with his essential nature but in contrast with it.

Manifestly, and, if not forthwith, certainly upon a moment's consideration, by all the motives prompting or circumstances attending the murder of Duncan that have been omitted, the big, sharply outlined, highly emotional contrast in the situation of a good man doing the deed of horror would be broken or obscured. If Macbeth had been thwarted or (to use Holinshed's word) "defrauded," as having, at this juncture, a better title to the throne than Malcolm, or had thought himself better fitted to rule; or, again, if Duncan had not borne his faculties so

⁶ *Ibid.,* p. 32: "he set his whole intention to maintaine justice and to punish all enormities and abuses which had chanced," etc.; "made manie holesome laws and statutes for the publike weale."

⁷ Eckermann (Castle), I, 400.

meek and been so clear in his great office, as in the tragedy but not the chronicle he is; why, then, Macbeth's conduct in killing him would have been more reasonable and more psychologically in keeping, to be sure, but less terrible, less truly tragic. Even if Duncan had been less affectionate and generous, less admiring and confiding, still the hero's conduct would have been less truly tragic! There is positive need of "the deep damnation of his taking off." For the tragedy is of the brave and honorable man suddenly and squarely—fatally, too—turned against the moral order. Sir Arthur compares him to Satan about to engage in the temptation: "Evil, be thou my good." Or "Fair is foul and foul is fair," as the Weird Sisters have it, which Macbeth on his first appearance echoes—

So foul and fair a day I have not seen.

And that situation, no question, is a contrast big and sharp enough.

Sir Arthur does not, indeed, pause to take notice how unpsychological the change here is. Others besides fallen archangels have so turned about, but evil they do not continue to call evil. Macbeth so does. He has scarcely a word of ambition beforehand, not a word of delight in the power when attained. As Mr. Firkins and even Mr. Bradley have noticed, it is the deterrents that he dwells upon, not the incentives; it is the spectral bloody dagger that he sees, not a glittering crown; it is "withered murder" that he follows to the chamber, not the call to sovereign sway and masterdom. In horror he commits the crime, even as he is to remember it. There is no satisfaction but only torment in the thought of it. The conscience in him, before and after, is that of a good man, not that of the man who can do such wickedness; first the voice of God, then either that or else—"accuser of mankind"!—the devil's. It is Macbeth himself that considers the "deep damnation," and neither before nor after does he deceive himself, as the good turning to wickedness necessarily do. But the contrast is kept clear and distinct; and the emotional effect—that the whole world has acknowledged.

If, on the other hand, Shakespeare had kept to history, to reality and psychology! If he had followed Holinshed—made more of Macbeth's grievances, dilated on Duncan's unfitness and his own fitness to rule, without bringing on his head the blood of an old man, asleep, his benefactor and guest! If he had dwelt on reasons for committing instead of not committing the crime! And if afterwards he had expressed the psychologically natural or appropriate opinions upon his own conduct, excusing or palliating it, perhaps even justifying it! If in short Macbeth (and his Lady, too, who invokes the powers of evil at the outset and is tormented by conscience at the end) had acted more like the human beings we know of; why, then we should have had decidedly less of contrast and excitement, of imaginative and emotional power generated and discharged, of poetry and drama.

II

The treatment of the material in *Othello*, probably an earlier play, is somewhat the same. In Cinthio there is no warrant for introducing the supernatural; but in Shakespeare's hands the villain takes the place of Fate—of the Weird Sisters and the Lady—and more completely than is usual in the tragedy of the Renaissance. He is a devil in the flesh, as Booth played him, as Coleridge and Lamb implied, and George Woodberry, J. J. Chapman, Lytton Strachey, John Palmer, not to mention others, have put it explicitly.[8] Iago himself practically acknowledges it in the soliloquies—"Hell and night," "Divinity of hell! when devils will the blackest sins put on"—and on that point apparently he and Othello at the end are agreed:

If that thou beest a devil, I cannot kill thee . . .

[*wounds Iago*]

I bleed, sir, but not kill'd.

[8] For their opinions see my *Shakespeare and Other Masters*, pp. 233, 238, 243–44.

Before that, to be sure, the Ancient is misapprehended by everybody; yet as Fate, as master of the show, he is holding nearly all the strings of the action in hand, and leading both heroine and hero to destruction. In the victim now, not the victimizer, is the great change; but from good to evil only under a complete delusion—"be thou my good" he neither says nor thinks, and the prince of villains himself has no need to say it. For again, as in *Macbeth,* the motives are dispensed with. The Ensign of the *novella* is deprived of the internal incentives to his wickedness, and the Moor relieved of the traits which might have provoked or somewhat warranted it.

As Professor Wolfgang Keller notices, the villainy is "better motived" in the source. That is, more plausibly, more realistically. Not a devil in the flesh, a "black angel," as Mr. Chapman calls him, Cinthio's Ensign is still of "the most depraved nature in the world" (*della più scelerata natura che mai fosse huomo del mondo*). But as such he has provocation enough. He is a rejected suitor, and really suspects the Captain (Shakespeare's Cassio) of being the favored one. Against both him and the lady he has a grudge; his love for her is turned to the "bitterest hate"; whereas in the tragedy his love for Desdemona and her intrigue with Cassio are, like Cassio's and Othello's with Emilia, pretexts and afterthoughts. There he has need of these. His genuine reason for resentment is against Othello, but only for promoting Cassio above him, and against Cassio (incidentally) for being promoted. In soliloquy, as always in drama, the truth will out. "I hate the Moor," he mutters,

> *And it is thought* abroad that 'twixt my sheets
> He has done my office.

And the next moment the pretext is made still plainer: "I know not if 't be true, but I for mere suspicion in that kind will do as if for surety." [9]

---

[9] Cf. *Shakespeare and Other Masters,* pp. 236–38, for the way that his suspicions become convictions.

So the Ensign is deprived of his motive as much as the Thane of Glamis—as much as Richard III of his, which was ambition, or as Goneril and Regan of theirs, which was envy,[10]—but without an external Fate to relieve him of the burden of his iniquity. He carries it indeed, like the Weird Sisters, lightly enough; and the Aristotelian contrast of the good man doing the deed of horror is presented in his victim, who, however, unlike Macbeth, is guilty only of a mistake in judgment—the *hamartia*—and is far from uttering Satan's cry. Othello never loses our sympathy, as Macbeth, despite the poignant presentation of his sufferings, cannot but in some measure do.

What is almost quite as important to the emotional effect—to the steep tragic contrast—as the apparently unmitigated wickedness of Iago, is, as in the Caledonian tragedy, the nature of the victim and the circumstances of the crime. As we have seen, Shakespeare's Moor has changed places with his wife in the villain's enmity. Love turned to hatred is too ambiguous and appealing a passion—it is that, moreover, into which the Moor himself is precipitated, and, as Strachey observes, the villain's must not be anything of a parallel. For the contrast, again, it must not be. Moreover, though Cinthio's Moor is given some noble and attractive traits, especially at the outset, Shakespeare's is both there and throughout on a far higher level of intelligence and feeling. He is not a stupid dupe or a vulgarly vindictive cuckold. He is not the man to call the informer in to do the killing, or the concealing of it afterwards. For his own safety, Shakespeare's, unlike Cinthio's Moor, shows no concern. Nor is there, for that matter, the slightest evidence in his conduct or his utterance, nor in the woman's either, of the love Iago suspects between him and Emilia—no more than there is in Iago's own conduct or utterance, indeed, of his own love for Desdemona—though of late there has been a

[10] In the old *King Leir*, envy of Cordelia's beauty, cf. E. E. Kellett, *Suggestions* (1923), p. 38. For Richard, cf. Brandl, *Shakespeare* (1937), p. 120.

fairly prominent critic to say there is.[11] That would be like thinking, with some Germans, that Hamlet had betrayed Ophelia, for which, to be sure, there is a little evidence, though far from enough; or with some Frenchmen, that Lady Macbeth as, re-enacting in memory the deed of blood, she whispers, "to bed, to bed! there's knocking at the gate ... to bed, to bed, to bed," she, having enticed her husband, is now for rewarding him. On the contrary, the black man is made the grandest and noblest of Shakespeare's lovers; and it is only through Iago's overwhelming reputation for honesty and sagacity, the impenetrableness of his mask together with the potency of his seductive arts, that he is led astray and succumbs. For the highest tragic effect it is the great and good man that succumbs. Like other supreme artists, Shakespeare has here created his own world, which holds together. Like Corneille (*les grands sujets de la tragédie doivent toujours aller au delà du vraisemblable*) Goethe holds that *in den höheren Regionen des künstlerischen Verfahrens, hat der Künstler ein freieres Spiel, und er darf sogar zu Fiktionen schreiten.*[12] This Shakespeare boldly does. No one else sees through Iago, including his own wife; so Othello, for not seeing, is no gull or dupe. In the matter of the Ancient's cleverness in maneuver and also of his success in hypocrisy the English is a little indebted to the Italian writer; but the Ensign's wife does see through him and only for fear of him holds her tongue.

[11] It is of course not enough to urge the probabilities upon us—that a healthy and vigorous soldier of the time would lead "a *man's* life," and that Emilia was none too good for taking up with him. As I have repeatedly reminded my readers, no character in fiction has a private life, beyond the reach of the writer, which a character in a biography or history, on the other hand, has, not being the writer's own creation. And in Shakespearean drama, as in the ancient or the classical French, none has the "past" or the "love life" that is more readily expected, and so more easily suggested, today.

[12] Eckermann, April 18, 1827.—I hope Corneille here does not go beyond the endurable.

III

In both *Macbeth* and *Othello,* then, it is the whole situation that is mainly important, not the character; it is the reciprocal matter of motivation (whether present or missing), of defects or qualities in both victim and victimizer together. Here lies the chief point of the present discussion. What if Shakespeare's Macbeth and Duncan had been like Holinshed's, or like Henry IV and Richard II, or like Cromwell and Charles I? And as I have elsewhere said, "How the scope and stature of Iago's wickedness (and of Othello's virtue) would be limited by any adequate grudge!" [18] How they would be also by a credulous or suspicious nature—a predisposition or a psychology—in the hero! Against that Shakespeare has guarded not only by Iago's impregnable reputation and by his all-prevailing arts but also by Othello's own reputation for capability and for virtue. (A world of reputation and circumstance here, not of motive!) Before the temptation begins, as in *Macbeth,* but much more fully and felicitously, the Moor has not only in his own right but through the admiration of everybody (and here even of the villain) been firmly established in our good opinion and our sympathies. So with Desdemona, too, and she is not deceitful or supersubtle as Mr. Shaw would have her, not enough so "to strengthen the case for Othello's jealousy"; the dramatic preparations are emotional, not analytical and psychological, primarily for the situation, not the character. And both women, Emilia at the last and Desdemona once the action is well started, are shocked at the discoveries they make in their husbands. But she is justified, when hers gives signs of jealousy, in being unable to believe it; "not easily jealous" he himself says (where a Shakespearean hero, or his best friend, is expected to know and everything comes to light) at the end. Even Iago, hearing that Othello is angry, exclaims,

> and is he angry?
> Something of moment, then. I will go meet him.
> There's matter in't indeed, if he be angry.

And in the fourth act, when the jealous rage is fully upon him, Lodovico, newly come from Venice, is moved to wonder and to grief.

> Is this the nature
> Whom passion could not shake? whose solid virtue
> The shot of accident nor dart of chance
> Could neither graze nor pierce?

"He is much chang'd," Iago coolly, and still not superfluously, replies. So he is, until, in the last scene, by Emilia's disclosures and Iago's self-betraying resentment, he recovers something of his old stately and generous self.

Macbeth too is changed, but for once and all. Othello had suffered from an overpowering delusion, and has just now, he thinks, performed an act of justice. Macbeth, not deluded, has come under the dominion of evil, his "eternal jewel given to the common enemy of man." Neither change is probable. In neither is there much of what can be called psychology. In life neither person would really have done what he did. In both tragedy and comedy, however, that is not exactly what is to be expected: for a Henry IV, a Cromwell, we should turn to history, not the stage. What is expected is what from life we do not get—enlargement, excitement, another world, not a copy of this. And that airy edifice, an imaginative structure, is the emotionally consistent story or situation as a whole—the conduct of characters both active and passive, perhaps also a motiving both external and internal, but in any case an interplay of relations or circumstances as important as the motives themselves; not to mention the apportionment of emphasis or relief whether in the framework or the expression, the poetry that informs both, and the individuality of the speech, which, real, though poetical, leads one to accept and delight in the improbable things said or done. "It is when their minds (those of the audience) are preoccupied with his personality," says Dr. Bridges of Macbeth, "that the actions follow as unquestionable realities." [14] Not merely, that is, when the actions proceed from the character; and the convincing quality of the speech is only a participating element in the consistent overpowering imaginative and emotional effect of the whole.

IV

"In tragedy and comedy both," I have said elsewhere, "life must be, as it has ever been, piled on life, or we have visited the theater in vain." It is not primarily to present characters in their convincing reality that Shakespeare and the Greeks have written, nor in an action strictly and wholly of their doing, but to set them in a state of high commotion, and thus to move and elevate the audience in turn. And here I fall back upon the authority of Mr. Santayana, a philosopher (but also a poet and critic) who, without my knowledge until of late, [15] expressed, though from a different point of view, similar opinions before me:

> Aristotle was justified in making the plot the chief element in fiction; for it is by virtue of the plot that the characters live, or, rather, that we live in them, and by virtue of the plot accordingly that our soul rises to the imaginative activity by which we tend at once to escape from the personal life and to realise its ideal. . . .

And as the eminent critic proceeds, he maintains that poetry is not

[14] *The Influence of the Audience on Shakespeare's Drama.*
[15] *Poetry and Religion* (1900). Cf. my *Shakespeare and Other Masters*, p. 369. The passage here quoted is as in the *Works* (Scribner, N. Y., 1936) ii. Cf. my "Plot and Character," to appear.

at its best when it depicts a further possible experience, but when it initiates us, by feigning something which as an experience is impossible, into the meaning of the experience which we have actually had.

And that is partly because "in the theater," as the producer Mr. Robert Edmond Jones has assured us, "the actual thing is never the exciting thing. Unless life is turned into art on the stage it stops being alive and goes dead." [16] It is by the excitement that the meaning is brought home to us. And that is true . . . even without a stage or without poetry, as in Dickens, who, according to Chesterton, "could only make his characters probable if he was allowed to make them impossible."

Cleanth Brooks

The Naked Babe and the Cloak of Manliness

The debate about the proper limits of metaphor has perhaps never been carried on in so spirited a fashion as it has been within the last twenty-five years. The tendency has been to argue for a much wider extension of those limits than critics like Dr. Johnson, say, were willing to allow—one wider even than the Romantic poets were willing to allow. Indeed, some alarm has been expressed of late, in one quarter or another, lest John Donne's characteristic treatment of metaphor be taken as the type and norm, measured against which other poets must, of necessity, come off badly. Yet, on the whole, I think that it must be conceded that the debate on metaphor has been stimulating and illuminating—and not least so with reference to those poets who lie quite outside the tradition of metaphysical wit.

Since the "new criticism," so called, has tended to center around the rehabilitation of Donne, and the Donne tradition, the latter point, I believe, needs to be emphasized. Actually, it would be a poor rehabilitation which, if exalting Donne above all his fellow poets, in fact succeeded in leaving him quite as much isolated from the rest of them as he was before. What the new awareness of the importance of metaphor—if it is actually new, and if its character is really that of a freshened awareness— what this new awareness of metaphor results in when ap-

From *The Well Wrought Urn* by Cleanth Brooks. New York: Harcourt, Brace & Co., Inc., 1947; London: Dennis Dobson, Ltd., 1949. Copyright 1947, by Cleanth Brooks. Reprinted by permission of Harcourt, Brace & World, Inc.

plied to poets other than Donne and his followers is
therefore a matter of first importance. Shakespeare provides, of course, the supremely interesting case.

But there are some misapprehensions to be avoided
at the outset. We tend to associate Donne with the self-
conscious and witty figure—his comparison of the souls
of the lovers to the two legs of the compass is the obvious example. Shakespeare's extended figures are elaborated in another fashion. They are, we are inclined to
feel, spontaneous comparisons struck out in the heat of
composition, and not carefully articulated, self-conscious
conceits at all. Indeed, for the average reader the con-
nection between spontaneity and seriously imaginative
poetry is so strong that he will probably reject as pre-
posterous any account of Shakespeare's poetry which
sees an elaborate pattern in the imagery. He will reject
it because to accept it means for him the assumption that
the writer was not a fervent poet but a preternaturally
cold and self-conscious monster.

Poems are certainly not made by formula and blue-
print. One rightly holds suspect a critical interpretation
that implies that they are. Shakespeare, we may be sure,
was no such monster of calculation. But neither, for that
matter, was Donne. Even in Donne's poetry, the elaborated
and logically developed comparisons are outnumbered by
the abrupt and succinct comparisons—by what T. S. Eliot
has called the "telescoped conceits." Moreover, the extended comparisons themselves are frequently knit together in the sudden and apparently uncalculated fashion of the telescoped images; and if one examines the
way in which the famous compass comparison is related
to the rest of the poem in which it occurs, he may feel
that even this elaborately "logical" figure was probably
the result of a happy accident.

The truth of the matter is that we know very little
of the various poets' methods of composition, and that
what may seem to us the product of deliberate choice
may well have been as "spontaneous" as anything else
in the poem. Certainly, the general vigor of metaphor
in the Elizabethan period—as testified to by pamphlets,

sermons, and plays—should warn us against putting the
literature of that period at the mercy of our own personal theories of poetic composition. In any case, we
shall probably speculate to better advantage—if speculate we must—on the possible significant interrelations of
image with image rather than on the possible amount of
pen-biting which the interrelations may have cost the
author.

I do not intend, however, to beg the case by over-
simplifying the relation between Shakespeare's intricate
figures and Donne's. There are most important differences;
and, indeed, Shakespeare's very similarities to the witty
poets will, for many readers, tell against the thesis proposed here. For those instances in which Shakespeare
most obviously resembles the witty poets occur in the
earlier plays or in *Venus and Adonis* and *The Rape of
Lucrece;* and these we are inclined to dismiss as early
experiments—trial pieces from the Shakespearean work-
shop. We demand, quite properly, instances from the
great style of the later plays.

Still, we will do well not to forget the witty examples
in the poems and earlier plays. They indicate that Shakespeare is in the beginning not too far removed from
Donne, and that, for certain effects at least, he was willing to play with the witty comparison. Dr. Johnson, in
teasing the metaphysical poets for their fanciful conceits
on the subject of tears, might well have added instances
from Shakespeare. One remembers, for example, from
Venus and Adonis:

> O, how her eyes and tears did lend and borrow!
> Her eyes seen in her tears, tears in her eye;
> Both crystals, where they view'd each other's
>   sorrow. . . .

Or, that more exquisite instance which Shakespeare, perhaps half-smiling, provided for the King in *Love's
Labor's Lost:*

> So sweet a kiss the golden sun gives not

To those fresh morning drops upon the rose,
As thy eye-beams, when their fresh rays have smote
The night of dew that on my cheeks down flows:
Nor shines the silver moon one half so bright
Through the transparent bosom of the deep,
As does thy face through tears of mine give light:
Thou shin'st in every tear that I do weep,
No drop but as a coach doth carry thee:
So ridest thou triumphing in my woe.
Do but behold the tears that swell in me,
And they thy glory through my grief will show:
But do not love thyself—then thou wilt keep
My tears for glasses, and still make me weep.

But Berowne, we know, at the end of the play, foreswears all such

> Taffeta phrases, silken terms precise,
> Three-piled hyperboles, spruce affectation,
> Figures pedantical. . . .

in favor of "russet yeas and honest kersey noes." It is sometimes assumed that Shakespeare did the same thing in his later dramas, and certainly the epithet "taffeta phrases" does not describe the great style of *Macbeth* and *Lear*. Theirs is assuredly of a tougher fabric. But "russet" and "honest kersey" do not describe it either. The weaving was not so simple as that.

The weaving was very intricate indeed—if anything, *more* rather than *less* intricate than that of *Venus and Adonis*, though obviously the pattern was fashioned in accordance with other designs, and yielded other kinds of poetry. But in suggesting that there is a real continuity between the imagery of *Venus and Adonis*, say, and that of a play like *Macbeth*, I am glad to be able to avail myself of Coleridge's support. I refer to the remarkable fifteenth chapter of the *Biographia*.

There Coleridge stresses not the beautiful tapestry work—the purely visual effect—of the images, but quite another quality. He suggests that Shakespeare was prompted by a secret dramatic instinct to realize, in the imagery itself, that "constant intervention and running comment by tone, look and gesture" ordinarily provided by the actor, and that Shakespeare's imagery becomes under this prompting "a series and never broken chain . . . always vivid and, because unbroken, often minute. . . ." Coleridge goes on, a few sentences later, to emphasize further "the perpetual activity of attention required on the part of the reader, . . . the rapid flow, the quick change, and the playful nature of the thoughts and images."

These characteristics, Coleridge hastens to say, are not in themselves enough to make superlative poetry. "They become proofs of original genius only as far as they are modified by a predominant passion; or by associated thoughts or images awakened by that passion; or when they have the effect of reducing multitude to unity, or succession to an instant; or lastly, when a human and intellectual life is transferred to them from the poet's own spirit."

Of the intellectual vigor which Shakespeare possessed, Coleridge then proceeds to speak—perhaps extravagantly. But he goes on to say: "In Shakespeare's *poems*, the creative power and the intellectual energy wrestle as in a war embrace. Each in its excess of strength seems to threaten the extinction of the other."

I am tempted to gloss Coleridge's comment here, perhaps too heavily, with remarks taken from Chapter XIII where he discusses the distinction between the Imagination and the Fancy—the modifying and creative power, on the one hand, and on the other, that "mode of Memory" . . . "blended with, and modified by . . . Choice." But if in *Venus and Adonis* and *The Rape of Lucrece* the powers grapple "in a war embrace," Coleridge goes on to pronounce: "At length, in the *Drama* they were reconciled, and fought each with its shield before the breast of the other."

It is a noble metaphor. I believe that it is also an accurate one, and that it comprises one of the most bril-

liant insights ever made into the nature of the dramatic
poetry of Shakespeare's mature style. If it is accurate,
we shall expect to find, even in the mature poetry, the
"never broken chain" of images, "always vivid and, because unbroken, often minute," but we shall expect to
find the individual images, not mechanically linked together in the mode of Fancy, but organically related, modified by "a predominant passion," and mutually modifying
each other.

T. S. Eliot has remarked that "The difference between
imagination and fancy, in view of [the] poetry of wit, is
a very narrow one." If I have interpreted Coleridge cor-
rectly, he is saying that in Shakespeare's greatest work,
the distinction lapses altogether—or rather, that one is
caught up and merged in the other. As his latest champion, I. A. Richards, observes: "Coleridge often insisted
—and would have insisted still more often had he been a
better judge of his reader's capacity for misunderstanding—that Fancy and Imagination are not exclusive of, or
inimical to, one another."

I began by suggesting that our reading of Donne
might contribute something to our reading of Shakespeare, though I tried to make plain the fact that I had no
design of trying to turn Shakespeare into Donne, or—
what I regard as nonsense—of trying to exalt Donne
above Shakespeare. I have in mind specifically some such
matter as this: that since the *Songs and Sonets* of Donne,
no less than *Venus and Adonis,* requires a "perpetual
activity of attention . . . on the part of the reader from
the rapid flow, the quick change, and the playful nature of
the thoughts and images," the discipline gained from reading Donne may allow us to see more clearly the survival
of such qualities in the later style of Shakespeare. And,
again, I have in mind some such matter as this: that if a
reading of Donne has taught us that the "rapid flow, the
quick change, and the playful nature of the thoughts
and images"—qualities which we are all too prone to associate merely with the fancy—can, on occasion, take on
imaginative power, we may, thus taught, better appreciate
details in Shakespeare which we shall otherwise dismiss

as merely fanciful, or, what is more likely, which we shall simply ignore altogether.

With Donne, of course, the chains of imagery, "always vivid" and "often minute" are perfectly evident. For many readers they are all too evident. The difficulty is not to prove that they exist, but that, on occasion, they may subserve a more imaginative unity. With Shakespeare, the difficulty may well be to prove that the chains exist at all. In general, we may say, Shakespeare has made it relatively easy for his admirers to choose what they like and neglect what they like. What he gives on one or another level is usually so magnificent that the reader finds it easy to ignore other levels.

Yet there are passages not easy to ignore and on which even critics with the conventional interests have been forced to comment. One of these passages occurs in *Macbeth*, Act I, Scene vii, where Macbeth compares the pity for his victim-to-be, Duncan, to

> a naked new-born babe,
> Striding the blast, or heaven's cherubim, hors'd
> Upon the sightless couriers of the air . . .

The comparison is odd, to say the least. Is the babe natural or supernatural—an ordinary, helpless baby, who, as newborn, could not, of course, even toddle, much less stride the blast? Or is it some infant Hercules, quite capable of striding the blast, but, since it is powerful and not helpless, hardly the typical pitiable object?

Shakespeare seems bent upon having it both ways—and, if we read on through the passage—bent upon having the best of both worlds; for he proceeds to give us the option: pity is like the babe "or heaven's cherubim" who quite appropriately, of course, do ride the blast. Yet, even if we waive the question of the legitimacy of the alternative (of which Shakespeare so promptly avails himself), is the cherubim comparison really any more successful than is the babe comparison? Would not one of the great warrior archangels be more appropriate to the scene than the cherub? Does Shakespeare mean for pity or for fear of retribution to be dominant in Macbeth's mind?

Or is it possible that Shakespeare could not make up his own mind? Was he merely writing hastily and loosely, and letting the word "pity" suggest the typically pitiable object, the babe naked in the blast, and then, stirred by the vague notion that some threat to Macbeth should be hinted, using "heaven's cherubim"—already suggested by "babe"—to convey the hint? Is the passage vague or precise? Loosely or tightly organized? Comments upon the passage have ranged all the way from one critic's calling it "pure rant, and intended to be so" to another's laudation: "Either like a mortal babe, terrible in helplessness; or like heaven's angel-children, mighty in love and compassion. This magnificent passage . . ."

An even more interesting, and perhaps more disturbing passage in the play is that in which Macbeth describes his discovery of the murder:

> Here lay Duncan,
> His silver skin lac'd with his golden blood;
> And his gash'd stabs look'd like a breach in nature
> For ruin's wasteful entrance: there, the murderers,
> Steep'd in the colors of their trade, their daggers
> Unmannerly breech'd with gore. . . .

It is amusing to watch the textual critics, particularly those of the eighteenth century, fight a stubborn rearguard action against the acceptance of "breech'd." Warburton emended "breech'd" to "reech'd"; Johnson, to "drench'd"; Seward, to "hatch'd." Other critics argued that the *breeches* implied were really the handles of the daggers, and that, accordingly, "breech'd" actually here meant "sheathed." The Variorum page witnesses the desperate character of the defense, but the position has had to be yielded, after all. *The Shakespeare Glossary* defines "breech'd" as meaning "covered as with breeches," and thus leaves the poet committed to a reading which must still shock the average reader as much as it shocked that nineteenth-century critic who pronounced upon it as follows: "A metaphor must not be far-fetched nor dwell upon the details of a disgusting picture, as in these lines. There is little, and that far-fetched, similarity between *gold lace* and *blood,* or between *bloody daggers* and *breech'd legs.* The slightness of the similarity, recalling the greatness of the dissimilarity, disgusts us with the attempted comparison."

The two passages are not of the utmost importance, I dare say, though the speeches (of which each is a part) are put in Macbeth's mouth and come at moments of great dramatic tension in the play. Yet, in neither case is there any warrant for thinking that Shakespeare was not trying to write as well as he could. Moreover, whether we like it or not, the imagery is fairly typical of Shakespeare's mature style. Either passage ought to raise some qualms among those who retreat to Shakespeare's authority when they seek to urge the claims of "noble simplicity." They are hardly simple. Yet it is possible that such passages as these may illustrate another poetic resource, another type of imagery which, even in spite of its apparent violence and complication, Shakespeare could absorb into the total structure of his work.

Shakespeare, I repeat, is not Donne—is a much greater poet than Donne; yet the example of his typical handling of imagery will scarcely render support to the usual attacks on Donne's imagery—for, with regard to the two passages in question, the second one, at any rate, is about as strained as Donne is at his most extreme pitch.

Yet I think that Shakespeare's daggers attired in their bloody breeches can be defended as poetry, and as characteristically Shakespearean poetry. Furthermore, both this passage and that about the newborn babe, it seems to me, are far more than excrescences, mere extravagances of detail: each, it seems to me, contains a central symbol of the play, and symbols which we must understand if we are to understand either the detailed passage or the play as a whole.

If this be true, then more is at stake than the merit of the quoted lines taken as lines. (The lines as constituting mere details of a larger structure could, of course, be omitted in the acting of the play without seriously damaging the total effect of the tragedy— though this argument obviously cuts two ways. Whole scenes, and admittedly fine scenes, might also be omitted —have in fact *been* omitted—without quite destroying the massive structure of the tragedy.) What is at stake is the whole matter of the relation of Shakespeare's imagery to the total structures of the plays themselves.

I should like to use the passages as convenient points of entry into the larger symbols which dominate the play. They *are* convenient because, even if we judge them to be faulty, they demonstrate how obsessive for Shakespeare the symbols were—they demonstrate how far the conscious (or unconscious) symbolism could take him.

If we see how the passages are related to these symbols, and they to the tragedy as a whole, the main matter is achieved; and having seen this, if we still prefer "to wish the lines away," that, of course, is our privilege. In the meantime, we may have learned something about Shakespeare's methods—not merely of building metaphors—but of encompassing his larger meanings.

One of the most startling things which has come out of Miss Spurgeon's book on Shakespeare's imagery is her discovery of the "old clothes" imagery in *Macbeth*. As she points out: "The idea constantly recurs that Macbeth's new honours sit ill upon him, like a loose and badly fitting garment, belonging to someone else." And she goes on to quote passage after passage in which the idea is expressed. But, though we are all in Miss Spurgeon's debt for having pointed this out, one has to observe that Miss Spurgeon has hardly explored the full implications of her discovery. Perhaps her interest in classifying and cataloguing the imagery of the plays has obscured for her some of the larger and more important relationships. At any rate, for reasons to be given below, she has realized only a part of the potentialities of her discovery.

Her comment on the clothes imagery reaches its climax with the following paragraphs:

> And, at the end, when the tyrant is at bay at Dunsinane, and the English troops are advancing, the Scottish lords still have this image in their minds. Caithness sees him as a man vainly trying to fasten a large garment on him with too small a belt:

> > He cannot buckle his distemper'd cause
> > Within the belt of rule;

> while Angus, in a similar image, vividly sums up the essence of what they all have been thinking ever since Macbeth's accession to power:

> > now does he feel his title
> > Hang loose about him, like a giant's robe
> > Upon a dwarfish thief.

This imaginative picture of a small, ignoble man encumbered and degraded by garments unsuited to him, should be put against the view emphasized by some critics (notably Coleridge and Bradley) of the likeness between Macbeth and Milton's Satan in grandeur and sublimity.

Undoubtedly Macbeth . . . is great, magnificently great . . . But he could never be put beside, say, Hamlet or Othello, in nobility of nature; and there *is* an aspect in which he is but a poor, vain, cruel, treacherous creature, snatching ruthlessly over the dead bodies of kinsman and friend at place and power he is utterly unfitted to possess. It is worth remembering that it is thus that Shakespeare, with his unshrinking clarity of vision, repeatedly *sees* him.

But this is to make primary what is only one aspect of

the old-clothes imagery! And there is no warrant for interpreting the garment imagery as used by Macbeth's enemies, Caithness and Angus, to mean that *Shakespeare*
sees Macbeth as a poor and somewhat comic figure.

The crucial point of the comparison, it seems to me,
lies not in the smallness of the man and the largeness of
the robes, but rather in the fact that—whether the man
be large or small—these are not *his* garments; in Macbeth's case they are actually stolen garments. Macbeth is
uncomfortable in them because he is continually conscious of the fact that they do not belong to him. There
is a further point, and it is one of the utmost importance; the oldest symbol for the hypocrite is that of the
man who cloaks his true nature under a disguise. Macbeth loathes playing the part of the hypocrite—and actually does not play it too well. If we keep this in mind
as we look back at the instances of the garment images
which Miss Spurgeon has collected for us, we shall see
that the pattern of imagery becomes very rich indeed.
Macbeth says in Act I:

> The Thane of Cawdor lives: why do you dress me
> In borrow'd robes?

Macbeth at this point wants no honors that are not
honestly his. Banquo says in Act I:

> New honors come upon him,
> Like our strange garments, cleave not to their mold,
> But with the aid of use.

But Banquo's remark, one must observe, is not cen-
sorious. It is indeed a compliment to say of one that he
wears new honors with some awkwardness. The observation becomes ironical only in terms of what is to occur
later.

Macbeth says in Act I:

> He hath honor'd me of late; and I have bought
> Golden opinions from all sorts of people,

Which would be worn now in their newest gloss,
Not cast aside so soon.

Macbeth here is proud of his new clothes: he is
happy to wear what he has truly earned. It is the part of
simple good husbandry not to throw aside these new garments and replace them with robes stolen from Duncan.

But Macbeth has already been wearing Duncan's garments in anticipation, as his wife implies in the metaphor
with which she answers him:

Was the hope drunk,
Wherein you dress'd yourself?

(The metaphor may seem hopelessly mixed, and a full
and accurate analysis of such mixed metaphors in terms
of the premises of Shakespeare's style waits upon some
critic who will have to consider not only this passage but
many more like it in Shakespeare.) For our purposes
here, however, one may observe that the psychological
line, the line of the basic symbolism, runs on unbroken.
A man dressed in a drunken hope is garbed in strange
attire indeed—a ridiculous dress which accords thoroughly with the contemptuous picture that Lady Macbeth
wishes to evoke. Macbeth's earlier dream of glory has
been a drunken fantasy merely, if he flinches from action now.

But the series of garment metaphors which run through
the play is paralleled by a series of masking or cloaking
images which—if we free ourselves of Miss Spurgeon's
rather mechanical scheme of classification—show themselves to be merely variants of the garments which hide
none too well his disgraceful self. He is consciously hid-
ing that self throughout the play.

"False face must hide what the false heart doth know,"
he counsels Lady Macbeth before the murder of Duncan;
and later, just before the murder of Banquo, he invokes
night to "Scarf up the eye of pitiful day."

One of the most powerful of these cloaking images

is given to Lady Macbeth in the famous speech in Act I:

> Come, thick night,
> And pall thee in the dunnest smoke of hell,
> That my keen knife see not the wound it makes,
> Nor heaven peep through the blanket of the dark,
> To cry, "Hold, Hold!"

I suppose that it is natural to conceive the "keen knife" here as held in her own hand. Lady Macbeth is capable of wielding it. And in this interpretation, the imagery is thoroughly significant. Night is to be doubly black so that not even her knife may see the wound it makes. But I think that there is good warrant for regarding her "keen knife" as Macbeth himself. She has just, a few lines above, given her analysis of Macbeth's character as one who would "not play false,/ And yet [would] wrongly win." To bring him to the point of action, she will have to "chastise [him] with the valor of [her] tongue." There is good reason, then, for her to invoke night to become blacker still—to pall itself in the "dunnest smoke of hell." For night must not only screen the deed from the eye of heaven—conceal it at least until it is too late for heaven to call out to Macbeth "Hold, Hold!" Lady Macbeth would have night blanket the deed from the hesitant doer. The imagery thus repeats and reinforces the substance of Macbeth's anguished aside uttered in the preceding scene:

> Let not light see my black and deep desires;
> The eye wink at the hand; yet let that be
> Which the eye fears, when it is done, to see.

I do not know whether "blanket" and "pall" qualify as garment metaphors in Miss Spurgeon's classification: yet one is the clothing of sleep, and the other, the clothing of death—they are the appropriate garments of night; and they carry on an important aspect of the gen-

eral clothes imagery. It is not necessary to attempt to give
here an exhaustive list of instances of the garment metaphor; but one should say a word about the remarkable
passage in II, iii.

Here, after the discovery of Duncan's murder, Banquo
says

> And when we have our naked frailties hid,
> That suffer in exposure, let us meet,
> And question this most bloody piece of work—

that is, "When we have clothed ourselves against the chill
morning air, let us meet to discuss this bloody piece of
work." Macbeth answers, as if his subconscious mind
were already taking Banquo's innocent phrase, "naked
frailties," in a deeper, ironic sense:

> Let's briefly put on manly readiness. . . .

It is ironic; for the "manly readiness" which he urges
the other lords to put on, is, in his own case, a hypocrite's garment: he can only pretend to be the loyal,
grief-stricken liege who is almost unstrung by the horror
of Duncan's murder.

But the word "manly" carries still a further ironic
implication: earlier, Macbeth had told Lady Macbeth
that he dared

> do all that may become a man;
> Who dares do more is none.

Under the weight of her reproaches of cowardice, however, he *has* dared do more, and has become less than
a man, a beast. He has already laid aside, therefore, one
kind of "manly readiness" and has assumed another:
he has garbed himself in a sterner composure than that
which he counsels to his fellows—the hard and inhuman
"manly readiness" of the resolved murderer.

The clothes imagery, used sometimes with emphasis on one aspect of it, sometimes, on another, does pervade the play. And it should be evident that the daggers "breech'd with gore"—though Miss Spurgeon does not include the passage in her examples of clothes imagery—represent one more variant of this general symbol. Consider the passage once more:

> Here lay Duncan,
> His silver skin lac'd with his golden blood;
> And his gash'd stabs look'd like a breach in nature
> For ruin's wasteful entrance: there, the murderers,
> Steep'd in the colors of their trade, their daggers
> Unmannerly breech'd with gore. . . .

The clothes imagery runs throughout the passage; the body of the king is dressed in the most precious of garments, the blood royal itself; and the daggers too are dressed—in the same garment. The daggers, "naked" except for their lower parts which are reddened with blood, are like men in "unmannerly" dress—men, naked except for their red breeches, lying beside the red-handed grooms. The figure, though vivid, is fantastic; granted. But the basis for the comparison is *not* slight and adventitious. The metaphor fits the real situation on the deepest levels. As Macbeth and Lennox burst into the room, they find the daggers wearing, as Macbeth knows all too well, a horrible masquerade. They have been carefully "clothed" to play a part. They are not honest daggers, honorably naked in readiness to guard the king, or, "mannerly" clothed in their own sheaths. Yet the disguise which they wear will enable Macbeth to assume the robes of Duncan—robes to which he is no more entitled than are the daggers to the royal garments which they now wear, grotesquely.

The reader will, of course, make up his own mind as to the value of the passage. But the metaphor in question, in the light of the other garment imagery, cannot be dismissed as merely a strained ingenuity, irrelevant to the play. And the reader who *does* accept it as poetry will

probably be that reader who knows the play best, not
the reader who knows it slightly and regards Shakespeare's poetry as a rhetoric more or less loosely draped
over the "content" of the play.

And now what can be said of pity, the "naked newborn babe"? Though Miss Spurgeon does not note it
(since the governing scheme of her book would have
hardly allowed her to see it), there are, by the way, a
great many references to babes in this play—references
which occur on a number of levels. The babe appears
sometimes as a character, such as Macduff's child; sometimes as a symbol, like the crowned babe and the
bloody babe which are raised by the witches on the
occasion of Macbeth's visit to them; sometimes, in a
metaphor, as in the passage under discussion. The number of such references can hardly be accidental; and the
babe turns out to be, as a matter of fact, perhaps the most
powerful symbol in the tragedy.

But to see this fully, it will be necessary to review the
motivation of the play. The stimulus to Duncan's murder, as we know, was the prophecy of the Weird Sisters.
But Macbeth's subsequent career of bloodshed stems
from the same prophecy. Macbeth was to have the
crown, but the crown was to pass to Banquo's children.
The second part of the prophecy troubles Macbeth from
the start. It does not oppress him, however, until the
crown has been won. But from this point on, the effect
of the prophecy is to hurry Macbeth into action and more
action until he is finally precipitated into ruin.

We need not spend much time in speculating on whether
Macbeth, had he been content with Duncan's murder,
had he tempted fate no further, had he been willing to
court the favor of his nobles, might not have died peace-
ably in bed. We are dealing, not with history, but with a
play. Yet, even in history the usurper sometimes succeeds; and he sometimes succeeds on the stage. Shakespeare himself knew of, and wrote plays about, usurpers
who successfully maintained possession of the crown. But,
in any case, this much is plain: the train of murders into

which Macbeth launches aggravates suspicions of his guilt and alienates the nobles.

Yet, a Macbeth who could act once, and then settle down to enjoy the fruits of this one attempt to meddle with the future would, of course, not be Macbeth. For it is not merely his great imagination and his warrior courage in defeat which redeem him for tragedy and place him beside the other great tragic protagonists: rather, it is his attempt to conquer the future, an attempt involving him, like Oedipus, in a desperate struggle with fate itself. It is this which holds our imaginative sympathy, even after he has degenerated into a bloody tyrant and has become the slayer of Macduff's wife and children.

To sum up, there can be no question that Macbeth stands at the height of his power after his murder of Duncan, and that the plan—as outlined by Lady Macbeth—has been relatively successful. The road turns toward disaster only when Macbeth decides to murder Banquo. Why does he make this decision? Shakespeare has pointed up the basic motivation very carefully:

> Then prophet-like,
> They hail'd him father to a line of kings.
> Upon my head they plac'd a fruitless crown,
> And put a barren scepter in my gripe,
> Thence to be wrench'd with an unlineal hand,
> No son of mine succeeding. If't be so,
> For Banquo's issue have I fil'd my mind;
> For them the gracious Duncan have I murder'd;
> Put rancors in the vessel of my peace
> Only for them; and mine eternal jewel
> Given to the common enemy of man,
> To make them kings, the seed of Banquo kings!

Presumably, Macbeth had entered upon his course from sheer personal ambition. Ironically, it is the more human part of Macbeth—his desire to have more than a limited personal satisfaction, his desire to found a line, his wish

to pass something on to later generations—which
prompts him to dispose of Banquo. There is, of course, a
resentment against Banquo, but that resentment is itself
closely related to Macbeth's desire to found a dynasty.
Banquo, who has risked nothing, who has remained up-
right, who has not defiled himself, will have kings for
children; Macbeth, none. Again, ironically, the Weird Sisters who have given Macbeth, so he has thought, the price-
less gift of knowledge of the future, have given the real
future to Banquo.

So Banquo's murder is decided upon, and accomplished. But Banquo's son escapes, and once more, the
future has eluded Macbeth. The murder of Banquo thus
becomes almost meaningless. This general point may be
obvious enough, but we shall do well to note some of the
further ways in which Shakespeare has pointed up the
significance of Macbeth's war with the future.

When Macbeth, at the beginning of Scene vii, Act I,
contemplates Duncan's murder, it is the future over
which he agonizes:

> If it were done, when 'tis done, then 'twere well
> It were done quickly; if the assassination
> Could trammel up the consequence, and catch
> With his surcease success; that but this blow
> Might be the be-all and the end-all here. . . .

But the continuum of time cannot be partitioned off; the
future is implicit in the present. There is no net strong
enough to trammel up the consequence—not even in this
world.

Lady Macbeth, of course, has fewer qualms. When Macbeth hesitates to repudiate the duties which he owes Duncan—duties which, by some accident of imagery perhaps
—I hesitate to press the significance—he has earlier actually called "children"—Lady Macbeth cries out that
she is willing to crush her own child in order to gain the
crown:

> I have given suck, and know
> How tender 'tis to love the babe that milks me;
> I would, while it was smiling in my face,
> Have pluck'd my nipple from his boneless gums
> And dash'd the brains out, had I so sworn as you
> Have done to this.

Robert Penn Warren has made the penetrating observation that all of Shakespeare's villains are rationalists.
Lady Macbeth is certainly of their company. She knows
what she wants; and she is ruthless in her consideration
of means. She will always "catch the nearest way."
This is not to say that she ignores the problem of scruples,
or that she is ready to oversimplify psychological com-
plexities. But scruples are to be used to entangle one's
enemies. One is not to become tangled in the mesh of
scruples himself. Even though she loves her husband and
though her ambition for herself is a part of her ambition
for him, still she seems willing to consider even Macbeth at times as pure instrument, playing upon his hopes
and fears and pride.

Her rationalism is quite sincere. She is apparently
thoroughly honest in declaring that

> The sleeping and the dead
> Are but as pictures; 'tis the eye of childhood
> That fears a painted devil. If he do bleed,
> I'll gild the faces of the grooms withal,
> For it must seem their guilt.

For her, there is no moral order: *guilt* is something like
gilt—one can wash it off or paint it on. Her pun is not
frivolous and it is deeply expressive.

Lady Macbeth abjures all pity; she is willing to
unsex herself; and her continual taunt to Macbeth, when
he falters, is that he is acting like a baby—not like a
man. This "manhood" Macbeth tries to learn. He is a
dogged pupil. For that reason he is almost pathetic when
the shallow rationalism which his wife urges upon him

fails. His tone is almost one of puzzled bewilderment at
nature's unfairness in failing to play the game according to the rules—the rules which have applied to other
murders:

> the time has been,
> That, when the brains were out, the man would die,
> And there an end; but now they rise again. . . .

Yet, after the harrowing scene, Macbeth can say, with a
sort of dogged weariness:

> Come, we'll to sleep. My strange and self-abuse
> Is the initiate fear that wants hard use:
> We are yet but young in deed.

Ironically, Macbeth is still echoing the dominant metaphor of Lady Macbeth's reproach. He has not yet attained
to "manhood"; that *must* be the explanation. He has not
yet succeeded in hardening himself into something inhuman.

Tempted by the Weird Sisters and urged on by his
wife, Macbeth is thus caught between the irrational and
the rational. There is a sense, of course, in which every
man is caught between them. Man must try to predict
and plan and control his destiny. That is man's fate; and
the struggle, if he is to realize himself as a man, cannot
be avoided. The question, of course, which has always interested the tragic dramatist involves the terms on
which the struggle is accepted and the protagonist's atti-
tude toward fate and toward himself. Macbeth in his general concern for the future is typical—is Every Man. He
becomes the typical tragic protagonist when he yields to
pride and *hybris*. The occasion for temptation is offered
by the prophecy of the Weird Sisters. They offer him
knowledge which cannot be arrived at rationally. They offer a key—if only a partial key—to what is otherwise
unpredictable. Lady Macbeth, on the other hand, by em-
ploying a ruthless clarity of perception, by discounting
all emotional claims, offers him the promise of bringing

about the course of events which he desires.

Now, in the middle of the play, though he has not lost confidence and though, as he himself says, there can be no turning back, doubts have begun to arise; and he returns to the Weird Sisters to secure unambiguous answers to his fears. But, pathetically and ironically for Macbeth, in returning to the Weird Sisters, he is really trying to impose rationality on what sets itself forth plainly as irrational: that is, Macbeth would force a rigid control on a future which, by definition—by the very fact that the Weird Sisters already know it—stands beyond his manipulation.

It is because of his hopes for his own children and his fears of Banquo's that he has returned to the witches for counsel. It is altogether appropriate, therefore, that two of the apparitions by which their counsel is revealed should be babes, the crowned babe and the bloody babe.

For the babe signifies the future which Macbeth would control and cannot control. It is the unpredictable thing itself—as Yeats has put it magnificently, "The uncontrollable mystery on the bestial floor." It is the one thing that can justify, even in Macbeth's mind, the murders which he has committed. Earlier in the play, Macbeth had declared that if the deed could "trammel up the consequence," he would be willing to "jump the life to come." But he cannot jump the life to come. In his own terms he is betrayed. For it is idle to speak of jumping the life to come if one yearns to found a line of kings. It is the babe that betrays Macbeth—his own babes, most of all.

The logic of Macbeth's distraught mind, thus, forces him to make war on children, a war which in itself reflects his desperation and is a confession of weakness. Macbeth's ruffians, for example, break into Macduff's castle and kill his wife and children. The scene in which the innocent child prattles with his mother about his absent father, and then is murdered, is typical Shakespearean "fourth act" pathos. But the pathos is not adventitious; the scene ties into the inner symbolism of the

play. For the child, in its helplessness, defies the murderers. Its defiance testifies to the force which threatens Macbeth and which Macbeth cannot destroy.

But we are not, of course, to placard the child as The
Future in a rather stiff and mechanical allegory. *Macbeth* is no such allegory. Shakespeare's symbols are richer
and more flexible than that. The babe signifies not only
the future; it symbolizes all those enlarging purposes
which make life meaningful, and it symbolizes, furthermore, all those emotional and—to Lady Macbeth—irrational ties which make man more than a machine—which
render him human. It signifies pre-eminently the pity
which Macbeth, under Lady Macbeth's tutelage, would
wean himself of as something "unmanly." Lady Macbeth's
great speeches early in the play become brilliantly ironical
when we realize that Shakespeare is using the same symbol for the unpredictable future that he uses for human
compassion. Lady Macbeth is willing to go to any
length to grasp the future: she would willingly dash out
the brains of her own child if it stood in her way to that
future. But this is to repudiate the future, for the child is
its symbol.

Shakespeare does not, of course, limit himself to the
symbolism of the child: he makes use of other symbols of
growth and development, notably that of the plant. And
this plant symbolism patterns itself to reflect the development of the play. For example, Banquo says to the Weird
Sisters, early in the play:

> If you can look into the seeds of time,
> And say which grain will grow and which will not,
> Speak then to me. . . .

A little later, on welcoming Macbeth, Duncan says to
him:

> I have begun to plant thee, and will labor
> To make thee full of growing.

After the murder of Duncan, Macbeth falls into the same

metaphor when he comes to resolve on Banquo's death.
The Weird Sisters, he reflects, had hailed Banquo as

> . . . father to a line of kings.
> Upon my head they placed a fruitless crown,
> And put a barren scepter in my gripe. . . .

Late in the play, Macbeth sees himself as the winter-stricken tree:

> I have liv'd long enough: my way of life
> Is fall'n into the sear, the yellow leaf. . . .

The plant symbolism, then, supplements the child symbolism. At points it merges with it, as when Macbeth ponders bitterly that he has damned himself

> To make them kings, the seed of Banquo kings!

And, in at least one brilliant example, the plant symbolism unites with the clothes symbolism. It is a crowning irony that one of the Weird Sisters' prophecies on which Macbeth has staked his hopes is fulfilled when Birnam Wood comes to Dunsinane. For, in a sense, Macbeth is here hoist on his own petard. Macbeth, who has invoked night to "Scarf up the tender eye of pitiful day," and who has, again and again, used the "false face" to "hide what the false heart doth know," here has the trick turned against him. But the garment which cloaks the avengers is the living green of nature itself, and nature seems, to the startled eyes of his sentinels, to be rising up against him.

But it is the babe, the child, that dominates the symbolism. Most fittingly, the last of the prophecies in which Macbeth has placed his confidence, concerns the child: and Macbeth comes to know the final worst when Macduff declares to him that he was not "born of woman" but was from his "mother's womb/ Untimely ripp'd." The babe here has defied even the thing which one feels may reasonably be predicted of him—his time of birth.

With Macduff's pronouncement, the unpredictable has broken through the last shred of the net of calculation. The future cannot be trammeled up. The naked babe confronts Macbeth to pronounce his doom.

The passage with which we began this essay, then, is an integral part of a larger context, and of a very rich context:

> And pity, like a naked new-born babe,
> Striding the blast, or heaven's cherubim, hors'd
> Upon the sightless couriers of the air,
> Shall blow the horrid deed in every eye,
> That tears shall drown the wind.

Pity is like the naked babe, the most sensitive and helpless thing; yet, almost as soon as the comparison is announced, the symbol of weakness begins to turn into a symbol of strength; for the babe, though newborn, is pictured as "Striding the blast" like an elemental force—like "heaven's cherubim, hors'd/ Upon the sightless couriers of the air." We can give an answer to the question put earlier: is Pity like the human and helpless babe, or powerful as the angel that rides the winds? It is both; and it is strong because of its very weakness. The paradox is inherent in the situation itself; and it is the paradox that will destroy the overbrittle rationalism on which Macbeth founds his career.

For what will it avail Macbeth to cover the deed with the blanket of the dark if the elemental forces that ride the winds will blow the horrid deed in every eye? And what will it avail Macbeth to clothe himself in "manliness"—to become bloody, bold, and resolute,—if he is to find himself again and again, viewing his bloody work through the "eye of childhood/ That fears a painted devil"? Certainly, the final and climactic appearance of the babe symbol merges all the contradictory elements of the symbol. For, with Macduff's statement about his birth, the naked babe rises before Macbeth as not only the future that eludes calculation but as avenging angel as well.

The clothed daggers and the naked babe—mechanism and life—instrument and end—death and birth—that which should be left bare and clean and that which should be clothed and warmed—these are facets of two of the great symbols which run throughout the play. They are not the only symbols, to be sure; they are not the most obvious symbols: darkness and blood appear more often. But with a flexibility which must amaze the reader, the image of the garment and the image of the babe are so used as to encompass an astonishingly large area of the total situation. And between them—the naked babe, essential humanity, humanity stripped down to the naked thing itself, and yet as various as the future—and the various garbs which humanity assumes, the robes of honor, the hypocrite's disguise, the inhuman "manliness" with which Macbeth endeavors to cover up his essential humanity—between them, they furnish Shakespeare with his most subtle and ironically telling instruments.

Oscar James Campbell

From "Shakespeare and the 'New' Critics"

One of the sanest of recent applications of the new critical method to a Shakespearean play is an essay on *Macbeth,* entitled "The Naked Babe and the Cloak of Manliness." [1] The article illustrates the virtues of the method but also exemplifies its dangers, even though it be applied by a critic of unusual sensitivity and insight. Mr. Brooks, discovering two principal chains of imagery in *Macbeth,* one composed of garments or "old clothes," the other of babes, undertakes to prove that each chain subserves a deep imaginative unity. Since he realizes that what is at stake in his investigation is the whole matter of the relation of Shakespeare's imagery to the structure of the play, he proceeds with caution and (if his premises be granted) with adequate logic.

Miss Spurgeon, in her study of the images in *Macbeth,* pointed out that "the idea constantly recurs that Macbeth's new honors sit ill upon him, like a loose and badly fitting garment belonging to someone else." [2] And she illustrates the point by showing how many times Shakespeare repeats and varies the clothes image in order to

From *Joseph Quincy Adams: Memorial Studies,* ed. James G. McManaway, Giles E. Dawson, and Edwin E. Willoughby. Copyright 1948 for the Folger Shakespeare Library by the Trustees of Amherst College. Reprinted by permission of the author, and the Folger Shakespeare Library.

[1] This essay appears in Cleanth Brooks' *The Well Wrought Urn* (1947), pp. 21–46.

[2] *Shakespeare's Imagery,* p. 324.

keep before our minds "this imaginative picture of a small ignoble man encumbered and degraded by garments unsuited to him." The poet's manipulation of this image, as described by Miss Spurgeon, is the reverse of metaphysical; it is direct and simple. The imaginative significance of Banquo's remark as he observes Macbeth ruminating over the "supernatural soliciting" of the witches—

> New honors come upon him,
> Like our strange garments, cleave not to their mold
> But with the aid of use (I.iii.144–46)—

is easily grasped without the intervention of a new critic. So is Angus's comment upon Macbeth's conduct after his accession to power:

> Now does he feel his title
> Hang loose about him, like a giant's robe
> Upon a dwarfish thief.

These two passages are typical of Shakespeare's use of the clothes metaphor as a descriptive tag to pin upon Macbeth.

Mr. Brooks, however, finds such simple employment of the figure merely an adumbration of its more subtle manifestations. After glancing with approval at Miss Spurgeon's analysis, he asserts that these undisguised appearances of the metaphor are paralleled by a series of cloaking or masking images, variants of garment figures. The purpose of those figures is to suggest that throughout the play Macbeth is seeking to hide his "disgraceful self" from his own eyes as well as from the eyes of others. Mr. Brooks seeks to prove that the cloaking images form a chain, in the manner of the metaphysicals new and old, to keep alive the ironical contrast between the wretched creature that Macbeth really is and the pompous disguises he assumes to conceal the fact.

In attempting to build a structure out of the clothes images Mr. Brooks is forced to distort the meaning of more than one passage. This is evident in the variant interpretation he offers for Lady Macbeth's

> Come, thick night,
> And pall thee in the dunnest smoke of hell,
> That my keen knife sees not the wound it makes,
> Nor heaven peep through the blanket of the dark
> To cry, Hold, Hold!

Mr. Brooks admits that it is natural to think of the "keen knife" as in Lady Macbeth's hand and that she is begging the night to be so dark that even her knife, much less herself, may not see the wound it makes. The interpretation is more than natural, considering the fact that the image comes at the end of a speech in which she seeks to suppress her woman's nature so that she can be capable of the horrid deed.

But since the figure thus interpreted cannot serve as a link in the chain the critic is forging, Mr. Brooks offers the over-ingenious suggestion that the "keen knife" may be Macbeth himself. Thus interpreted, the figure can be forced to serve as one more indication of the efforts of the two murderers to hide from themselves what they are and what they do. Lady Macbeth would then be invoking the pall, the clothing of death, to blanket the horrid deed from the reluctant doer. But such an interpretation seems to this writer to be strained beyond the limits of credulity.

It is obvious that *Macbeth* contains much clothes imagery, but it is equally undeniable that Shakespeare used it in his own characteristic fashion. Once having employed the figure as a swift and startling method of characterizing his villain hero, the poet found the image and the word so securely lodged in his mind that it arose repeatedly while he was at work on his drama. And instead of discarding it every time it demanded expression, he subtly varied its form and employed it on many occasions to intensify crucial moments in the action. A striking example of putting the figure to an original use occurs when, at the end of a highly mannered passage,

Macbeth describes the murderers' daggers as "unmanner-ly breeched with gore." Mr. Brooks properly charac-terizes this image as vivid and fantastic. But his efforts to make it play a part in developing the disguise motif seems as fantastic as the metaphor. The daggers, naked except for their red breeches, are not only "unmanner-ly" but have also been clothed, or so he believes, in a horrible masquerade in order to play in this disguise a villainous role. For their natural guise was honorable nakedness, the form in which they could have guarded the King. This interpretation quite ignores the value of the metaphor for the speech in which it occurs. There it flashes a sudden light upon Macbeth's state of mind at the moment when he utters it. Shakespeare has designed the series of extravagant images—of which the daggers "un-mannerly breeched with gore" is the last—as a means of revealing Macbeth's neurotic embarrassment, which is here on the verge of betraying his guilt to Macduff, Mal-colm, and Donalbain. In other words, the figure epit-omizes the murderer's state of mind and nerves at one of the play's high emotional moments. Mr. Brooks' an-alysis of the various clothes images does not establish the facts he desires. But it has the unconscious merit of throwing into sharp relief the difference between Shake-speare's habitual use of figurative language and the meth-ods of the metaphysical poets, which the new critics false-ly assume Shakespeare to have adopted.

Mr. Brooks' analysis of Shakespeare's employment of the image of the babe is less free of bias than his treat-ment of the clothes figure and leads to a less valid con-clusion. He begins with a brilliant interpretation of some lines which many commentators have stigmatized as pure fustian:

> And pity, like a naked new-born babe,
> Striding the blast, or heaven's cherubim, hors'd
> Upon the sightless couriers of the air,
> Shall blow the horrid deed in every eye,
> That tears shall drown the wind. (I.vii.21)

The poet means, so says Mr. Brooks, that the nature of pity is paradoxical. When first aroused it seems to be as helpless as a newborn babe. Yet when it is blown into the hearts and minds of multitudes of men, it becomes stronger than the blasts of tempestuous wind. That is, its strength lies in its very weakness.

Mr. Brooks' close attention to this passage has led him to note many other references to babes in *Macbeth*. "Sometimes," he writes, "it is a character such as Macduff's child" (who is not a babe at all); "sometimes a symbol, like the crowned babe and the bloody babe which are raised by the witches; . . . sometimes in a metaphor." This babe, the critic arbitrarily decides, "signifies the future which Macbeth would control and cannot control." Mr. Brooks makes this identification in spite of the fact that in the passage he has just analyzed the babe is a symbol of something quite different. But not satisfied with this concrete use of the symbol Mr. Brooks explains that "the babe signifies not only the future; it symbolizes all those enlarging purposes which make life meaningful, and it symbolizes, furthermore, all those emotional and—to Lady Macbeth—irrational ties which make man more than a machine—which render him human." By this time the hard concrete core of the symbol has developed so amorphous an aura that its "burning center" has been almost completely obscured. By interpreting the babe as a recurrent symbol of the future Mr. Brooks is able to discover that Macbeth's tragedy is that of man making futile efforts to control the future. But this erratic, neo-Hegelian judgment reduces the rich complexity of Macbeth's human nature to a bare general proposition. His tragedy lies not in a failure of his efforts to impose his will upon the future but in the multitudinous fears and superstitions that form the psychological punishment for his crime. Whatever the value of imagery as an objective correlative of emotion, it obviously must not be interpreted in such a way as to contradict directly the clear meaning of the plot.

If Mr. Brooks' conclusions be false, it is important to discover at what points his method has been at fault.

In general his errors of judgment result from efforts to force all the references to babes into one connected system of imagery to form a structural principle for the drama. For example, Macbeth's famous soliloquy ending

> If th' assassination
> Could trammel up the consequence, and catch
> With his surcease, success; that but this blow
> Might be the be-all and the end-all here,
> But here, upon this bank and shoal of time,
> We'd jump the life to come (I.vii.2–7)

to Mr. Brooks means that Macbeth is agonizing over the future. But Macbeth's case is hopeless, he proceeds, because "the continuum of time cannot be partitioned off, the future is implicit in the present." Such recourse to a philosophical generality is perverse. Macbeth, like all murderers in Elizabethan plays, is afraid, not of his inability to control the future, but of the knife in the hands of a human avenger. This fear he expresses in the lines:

> We but teach
> Bloody instructions, which, being taught, return
> To plague the inventor.

This expectation of inevitable revenge is the reason why his fears in Banquo stick deep—why, in spite of the witches' assurance that he need fear no man of woman born, he fears Macduff so greatly that he orders his death.

One reason for Mr. Brooks' misunderstanding of the above passage is his misinterpretation of the phrase "the life to come." In its context it clearly refers to life after death and not, as Mr. Brooks thinks, to the future of Macbeth and his line in this world. Can it be that the critic has taken "jump" to mean "leap over"—that is, "skip" —instead of the correct "risk"? His following statement suggests this as a distinct possibility. "It is idle," he says, "to speak of jumping the life to come if one yearns to found a line of kings."

Mr. Brooks forces other passages into distorted shapes in his valiant effort to forge a chain of imagery out of materials extracted from the poetry. For example, he gives a sophistical interpretation to one of Lady Macbeth's most revealing exclamations—her scornful cry that she would rather have torn her baby from her breast and dashed out its brains than be so cowardly as to fail to kill Duncan, as her husband had sworn to do. This, says the critic, means that she is willing to go to any lengths to grasp the future. But her cry, Mr. Brooks continues, is extremely ironical because "she will grasp the future by repudiating the future of which the child is the symbol." This over-ingenious reading obscures and enfeebles the stark simplicity of Lady Macbeth's utterance. What she says to her husband is this: Rather than be such an ir-resolute coward as you now are, I had rather be guilty of the most fiendishly unnatural deed of which a mother is capable.

More than once Brooks forces upon an image an interpretation which, by the wildest stretch of the imag-ination, it cannot be made to bear. For example, he in-sists that when Macduff's little boy defies the murderers the child, whom he persists in calling a babe, testifies to the strength of the future, the force that threatens Macbeth and which he cannot destroy. The child, whose real dramatic function, besides the evocation of pity, is to show the wild killer that Macbeth has become in his ef-forts to kill fear itself, in Mr. Brooks' view "ties into the inner symbolism of the play." The truth is that Shake-speare has not used the image of the babe any more in the manner of a metaphysical poet than he did that of the clothes image. The word and the image reappeared in the poet's mind, but each time he used it for an immediate imaginative purpose relevant only to a specific situation.

Mary McCarthy

General Macbeth

He is a general and has just won a battle; he enters the scene making a remark about the weather. "So fair and foul a day I have not seen." On this flat note Macbeth's character tone is set. "Terrible weather we're having." "The sun can't seem to make up its mind." "Is it hot/cold/wet enough for you?" A commonplace man who talks in commonplaces, a golfer, one might guess, on the Scottish fairways, Macbeth is the only Shakespeare hero who corresponds to a bourgeois type: a murderous Babbitt, let us say.

You might argue just the opposite, that Macbeth is over-imaginative, the prey of visions. It is true that he is impressionable. Banquo, when they come upon the witches, amuses himself at their expense, like a man of parts idly chaffing a fortune-teller. Macbeth, though, is deeply impressed. "Thane of Cawdor and King." He thinks this over aloud "How can I be Thane of Cawdor when the Thane of Cawdor is alive?" When this mental stumbling block has been cleared away for him (the Thane of Cawdor has received a death sentence), he turns his thoughts *sotto voce* to the next question. "How can I be king when Duncan is alive?" The answer comes back, "Kill him." It does fleetingly occur to Macbeth, as it would to most people, to leave matters alone and let destiny work it out. "If chance will have me king, why,

From *Harper's Magazine* (June, 1962). Copyright © 1962 by Mary McCarthy. Reprinted by permission of Mary McCarthy.

chance may crown me, without my stir." But this goes
against his grain. A reflective man might wonder how fate
would spin her plot, as the Virgin Mary wondered after
the Angel Gabriel's visit. But Macbeth does not trust to
fate, that is, to the unknown, the mystery of things; he
trusts only to a known quantity—himself—to put the
prophecy into action. In short, he has no faith, which requires imagination. He is literal-minded; that, in a word,
is his "tragedy" and his tragedy.

It was not *his* idea, he could plead in self-defense, but
the witches', that he should have the throne. *They*
said it first. But the witches only voiced a thought that was
already in his mind; after all, he was Duncan's cousin
and close to the crown. And once the thought has
been put into *words,* he is in a scrambling hurry. He cannot wait to get home to tell his wife about the promise;
in his excitement, he puts it in a letter, which he sends
on ahead, like a businessman briefing an associate on a
piece of good news for the firm.

Lady Macbeth—has this been noted?—takes very little
stock in the witches. She never pesters her husband, as
most wives would, with questions about the Weird Sisters: "What did they say, exactly?" "How did they look?"
"Are you sure?" She is less interested in "fate and metaphysical aid" than in the business at hand—how to nerve
her husband to do what he wants to do. And later, when
Macbeth announces that he is going out to consult the
Weird Sisters again, she refrains from comment. As
though she were keeping her opinion—"O proper stuff!"
—to herself. Lady Macbeth is not superstitious. Macbeth is. This makes her repeatedly impatient with him, for
Macbeth, like many men of his sort, is an old story to
his wife. A tale full of sound and fury signifying nothing.
Her contempt for him perhaps extends even to his ambition. "Wouldst not play false, And yet wouldst wrongly
win." As though to say, "All right, if that's what you
want, have the courage to get it." Lady Macbeth does
not so much give the impression of coveting the crown
herself as of being weary of watching Macbeth covet it.
Macbeth, by the way, is surely her second husband (she

has "given suck" and Macbeth "has no children"), and either her first husband was a better man than he, which galls her, or he was just another general, another superstitious golfer, which would gall her too.

Superstition here is the opposite of reason on the one hand and of imagination on the other. Macbeth is credulous, in contrast to Lady Macbeth, to Banquo, and, later, to Malcolm, who sets the audience an example of the right way by mistrusting Macduff until he has submitted him to an empirical test. Believing and knowing are paired in Malcolm's mind; what he *knows* he believes. Macbeth's eagerness to believe is the companion of his lack of faith. If all works out right for him in this world, Macbeth says, he can skip the next ("We'd jump the life to come"). Superstition whispers when true religion has been silenced, and Macbeth becomes the butt of his own know-nothing materialism incarnate in the jeering witches on the heath.

As in his first interview with them he is too quick to act literally on a dark saying, in the second he is too easily reassured. He will not be conquered till "Great Birnam Wood to High Dunsinane shall come against him." "Why, that can never happen!" he cries out in immediate relief, his brow clearing.

It never enters his mind to examine the saying more closely, test it, so to speak, for a double bottom, as was common in those days (Banquo even points this out to him) with prophetic utterances, which were known to be ambiguous and tricky. Any child knew that a prophecy often meant the reverse of what it seemed to say, and any man of imagination would ask himself how Birnam Wood *might* come to Dunsinane and take measures to prevent it, as King Laius took measures to prevent his own death by arranging to have the baby Oedipus killed. If Macbeth had thought it out, he could have had Birnam Wood chopped down and burned on the spot and the ashes dumped into the sea. True, the prophecy might still have turned against him (since destiny cannot be avoided and the appointment will be kept at Samarra), but that would have been another story, another tragedy, the tragedy of a clever man not clever enough to circumvent fate. Macbeth is not clever; he is taken in by surfaces, by appearance. He cannot think beyond the usual course of things. As with "No man of woman born." All men, he says to himself, sagely, are born of women; Malcolm and Macduff are men; therefore I am safe. This logic leaves out of account the extraordinary: the man brought into the world by Caesarean section. In the same way, it leaves out of account the supernatural—the very forces he is trafficking with. He might be overcome by an angel or a demon, as well as by Macduff.

Yet this pedestrian general sees ghosts and imaginary daggers in the air. Lady Macbeth does not, and this tendency in her husband grates on her nerves; she is sick of his terrors and fancies. A practical woman, Lady Macbeth, more a partner than a wife, though Macbeth treats her with a trite domestic fondness—"Love," "Dearest love," "Dearest chuck," "Sweet remembrancer." These endearments, this middle-aged, middle-class cuddliness, as though he called her "Honeybunch" or "Sweetheart," as well as the obligatory "Dear," are a master stroke of Shakespeare's and perfectly in keeping with the prosing about the weather, the heavy credulousness.

Naturally Macbeth is dominated by his wife. He is old Iron Pants in the field (as she bitterly reminds him), but at home she has to wear the pants; she has to unsex herself. No "chucks" or "dearests" escape her tightened lips, and yet she is more feeling, more human at bottom than Macbeth. She thinks of her father when she sees the old King asleep, and this natural thought will not let her kill him. Macbeth has to do it, just as the quailing husband of any modern virago is sent down to the basement to kill a rat or drown a set of kittens. An image of her father, irrelevant to her purpose, softens this monster woman; sleepwalking, she thinks of Lady Macduff. "The Thane of Fife had a wife. Where is she now?" Stronger than Macbeth, less suggestible, she is nevertheless imaginative, where he is not. She does not see ghosts and daggers; when she sleepwalks, it is simple reality that haunts her—the crime relived. "Who would have thought the old man to have had so much blood in him?" Over and over, the details of the crime repeat themselves on the screen of her consciousness. This nightly reliving is not penitence but more terrible—remorse, the agenbite of the restless deed. Lady Macbeth's uncontrollable imagination drives her to put herself in the place of others—the wife of the Thane of Fife—and to recognize a kinship between all human kind: the pathos of old age in Duncan makes her think, "Why, he might be my father!" This sense of a natural bond among men opens her to contrition—sorrowing with. To ask whether, waking, she is "sorry" for what she has done is impertinent. She lives with it and it kills her.

Macbeth has absolutely no feeling for others, except envy, a common middle-class trait. He *envies* the murdered Duncan his rest, which is a strange way of looking at your victim. What he suffers on his own account after the crimes is simple panic. He is never contrite or remorseful; it is not the deed but a shadow of it, Banquo's spook, that appears to him. The "scruples" that agitate him before Duncan's murder are mere echoes of conventional opinion, of what might be *said* about his deed: that Duncan was his king, his cousin, and a guest under his roof. "I have bought golden opinions," he says to himself (note the verb), "from all sorts of people"; now these people may ask for their opinions back if they suspect him of the murder. It is like a business firm's being reluctant to part with its "good will"—an asset. The fact that Duncan was such a good king bothers him, and why? Because there will be universal grief at his death. But his chief "scruple" is even simpler. "If we should fail?" he says timidly to Lady Macbeth. Sweet chuck tells him that they will not. Yet once she has ceased to be effectual as a partner, Dearest love is an embarrassment. He has no time for her; she should have died hereafter. That is, when he was not so busy. Again the general is speaking.

The idea of Macbeth as a conscience-tormented man is a platitude as false as Macbeth himself. Macbeth has no conscience. His main concern throughout the play is that most selfish of all concerns: to get a good night's sleep.

His invocation to sleep, while heartfelt, is perfectly conventional; sleep builds you up, enables you to start the day fresh. Thus the virtue of having a good conscience is seen by him in terms of bodily hygiene, as if it were a Simmons mattress or an electric blanket. Lady Macbeth shares these preoccupations. When he tells her he is going to see the witches, she remarks that he needs sleep.

Her wifely concern is mechanical and far from real solicitude. She is aware of Macbeth; she *knows* him (he does not know her at all, apparently), but she regards him coldly as a thing, a tool that must be oiled and polished. His soul-states do not interest her; her attention is narrowed on his morale, his public conduct, the shifting expressions of his face. But in a sense she is right, for there is nothing to Macbeth but fear and ambition, both of which he tries to hide, except from her. This naturally gives her a poor opinion of the inner man.

Why is it, though, that Lady Macbeth seems to us a monster while Macbeth does not? Partly because she is a woman and has "unsexed" herself, which makes her a monster by definition. Also because the very prospect of murder quickens an hysterical excitement in her, like the discovery of some object in a shop—a set of emeralds or a sable stole—which Macbeth can give her and which will be an "outlet" for all the repressed desires he cannot satisfy. She behaves as though Macbeth, through his weakness, will deprive her of self-realization; the unimpeded exercise of her will is the voluptuous end she seeks. That is why she makes naught of scruples, as inner brakes on her throbbing engines. Unlike Macbeth, she does not pretend to harbor a conscience, though this, on her part, by a curious turn, *is* a pretense, as the sleepwalking scene reveals. After the first crime, her will subsides, spent; the devil has brought her to climax and left her.

Macbeth is not a monster, like Richard III or Iago or Iachimo, though in the catalogue he might go for one because of the blackness of his deeds. But his deeds are only the wishes and fears of the average, undistinguished man translated halfheartedly into action. Pure

evil is a kind of transcendence that he does not aspire to.
He only wants to be king and sleep the sleep of the just,
undisturbed. He could never have been a good man, even
if he had not met the witches; hence we cannot see him as
a devil incarnate, for the devil is a fallen angel. Macbeth does not fall; if anything, he somewhat improves as
the result of his career of crime. He throws off his dependency and thus achieves the "greatness" he mistak-
enly sought in worldly symbols.

The isolation of Macbeth, which is at once a punishment and a tragic dignity or honor, takes place by
stages and by deliberate choice; it begins when he does
not tell Lady Macbeth that he has decided to kill Banquo and reaches its height in the final action. Up to this
time, though he has cut himself off from all human con-
tacts, he is relying on the witches as a substitute. When
he first hears the news that Macduff is not "of woman
born," he is unmanned; everything he trusted (the lit-
eral word) has betrayed him, and he screams in terror,
"I'll not fight with thee!" But Macduff's taunts make a man
of him; he cannot die like this, shamed. His death is his
first act of courage, though even here he has had to be
pricked to it by mockery, Lady Macbeth's old spur. Nevertheless, weaned by his very crimes from dependency,
nursed in a tyrant's solitude, he meets death on his own,
without metaphysical aid. "Lay on, Macduff."

What is modern and bourgeois in Macbeth's character
is his wholly *social* outlook. He has no feeling for others,
and yet until the end he is a vicarious creature, existing
in his own eyes through others, through what they may
say of him, through what they tell him or promise him.
This paradox is typical of the social being—at once a
wolf out for himself and a sheep. Macbeth, moreover, is
an expert buck-passer; he sees how others can be used.
It is he, not Lady Macbeth, who thinks of smearing the
drunken chamberlains with blood, so that they shall be
caught "red-handed" the next morning when Duncan's
murder is discovered. At this idea he brightens; suddenly,
he sees his way clear. It is the moment when at last he decides. The eternal executive, ready to fix responsibility

on a subordinate, has seen the deed finally take a *recognizable* form. Now he can do it. And the crackerjack thought of killing the grooms afterwards (dead men tell no tales—old adage) is again purely his own on-the-spot inspiration; no credit to Lady Macbeth.

It is the sort of thought that would have come to Claudius in *Hamlet,* another trepidant executive. Indeed, Macbeth is more like Claudius than like any other character in Shakespeare. Both are doting husbands; both rose to power by betraying their superior's trust; both are easily frightened and have difficulty saying their prayers. Macbeth's "Amen" sticks in his throat, he complains, and Claudius, on his knees, sighs that he cannot make what priests call a "good act of contrition." The desire to say his prayers like any pew-holder, quite regardless of his horrible crime, is merely a longing for respectability. Macbeth "repents" killing the grooms, but this is strictly for public consumption. "O, yet I do repent me of my fury, That I did kill them." In fact, it is the one deed he does *not* repent (i.e., doubt the wisdom of) either before or after. This hypocritical self-accusation, which is his sidelong way of announcing the embarrassing fact that he has just done away with the grooms, and his simulated grief at Duncan's murder ("All is but toys; renown and grace is dead; The wine of life is drawn," etc.) are his basest moments in the play, as well as his boldest; here is nearly a magnificent monster.

The dramatic effect, too, is one of great boldness on Shakespeare's part. Macbeth is speaking pure Shakespearean poetry, but in his mouth, since we know he is lying, it turns into facile verse, Shakespearean poetry parodied. The same with "Here lay Duncan, his silver skin lac'd with his golden blood. . . ." If the image were given to Macduff, it would be uncontaminated poetry; from Macbeth it is "proper stuff"—fustian. This opens the perilous question of sincerity in the arts: is a line of verse altered for us by the sincerity of the poet (or speaker)? In short, is poetry relative to the circumstances or absolute? Or, more particularly, are Macbeth's soliloquies poetry, which they sound like, or something

else? Did Shakespeare intend to make Macbeth a poet,
like Hamlet, Lear, and Othello? In that case, how can
Macbeth be an unimaginative mediocrity? My opinion is
that Macbeth's soliloquies are not poetry but rhetoric.
They are tirades. That is, they do not trace any pensive
motion of the soul or heart but are a volley of words
discharged. Macbeth is neither thinking nor feeling aloud;
he is declaiming. Like so many unfeeling men, he has a
facile emotionalism, which he turns on and off. Not that
his fear is insincere, but his loss of control provides
him with an excuse for histrionics.

These gibberings exasperate Lady Macbeth. "What do
you mean?" she says coldly after she has listened to a
short harangue on "Methought I heard a voice cry 'Sleep
no more.' " It is an allowable question—what *does* he
mean? And his funeral oration on *her,* if she could have
heard it, would have brought her back to life to protest.
"She should have died hereafter"—fine, that was the real
Macbeth. But then, as if conscious of the proprieties, he
at once begins on a series of bromides ("Tomorrow and
tomorrow . . .") that he seems to have had ready to hand
for the occasion like a black mourning suit. All Macbeth's soliloquies have that ready-to-hand, if not hand-
me-down, air, which is perhaps why they are given to
schoolchildren to memorize, often with the result of making them hate Shakespeare. What children resent in these
soliloquies is precisely their sententiousness—the sound
they have of being already memorized from a copybook.

Macbeth's speeches often recall the Player's speech in
Hamlet—Shakespeare's example of how-not-to-do-it. He
tears a passion to tatters. He has a rather Senecan
rhetoric, the fustian of the time; in the dagger speech,
for example, he works in Hecate, Tarquin, and the wolf
—recherché embellishment for a man who is about to
commit a real murder. His taste for hyperbole goes with
a habit of euphuism, as when he calls the sea "the green
one." And what of the remarkable line just preceding,
"the multitudinous seas incarnadine," with its onomat-
opoeia of the crested waves rising in the *t*'s and *d*'s of
"multitudinous" and subsiding in the long swell of the

verb? This is sometimes cited as an example of pure poetry, which it would be in an anthology of isolated lines, but in the context, dramatically, it is bombast, a kind of stuffing or padding.

The play between poetry and rhetoric, the *conversion* of poetry to rhetoric, is subtle and horrible in *Macbeth*, being itself a subversive process or treasonous manipulation. The suggestion seems to be that poetry used for an ulterior purpose (as Macbeth uses it) turns into rhetoric. Macbeth is the perfect utilitarian. If an explanation is needed, you might say he learned to *use* words through long practice in haranguing his troops, whipping them and himself into battle frenzy. Up to recent times a fighting general, like a football coach, was an orator.

But it must be noted that it is not only Macbeth who rants. Nor is it only Macbeth who talks about the weather. The play is stormy with atmosphere—the screaming and shrieking of owls, the howling of winds. Nature herself is ranting, like the witches, and Night, black Hecate, is queen of the scene. Bats are flitting about; ravens and crows are hoarse; the house-martin's nests on the battlements of Macbeth's castle give a misleading promise of peace and gentle domesticity. "It will be rain tonight," says Banquo simply, looking at the sky (note the difference between this and Macbeth's pompous generality), and the First Murderer growls at him, striking, "Let it come down." The disorder of Nature, as so often in Shakespeare, presages and reflects the disorder of the body politic. Guilty Macbeth cannot sleep, but the night of Duncan's murder, the whole house, as if guilty too, is restless; Malcolm and Donalbain talk and laugh in their sleep; the drunken porter, roused, plays that he is gatekeeper of hell.

Indeed, the whole action takes place in a kind of hell and is pitched to the demons' shriek of hyperbole. This would appear to be a peculiar setting for a study of the commonplace. But only at first sight. The fact that an ordinary philistine like Macbeth goes on the rampage and commits a series of murders is a sign that human nature, like Nature, is capable of any mischief if left to its "natural" self. The witches, unnatural beings, are Nature spirits, stirring their snake-filet and owl's wing, newt's eye and frog toe in a camp stew: earthy ingredients boil down to an unearthly broth. It is the same with the man Macbeth. Ordinary ambition, fear, and a kind of stupidity make a deadly combination. Macbeth, a self-made king, is not kingly, but simply the original Adam, the social animal, and Lady Macbeth is Mother Eve.

There is no play of Shakespeare's (I think) that contains the words *Nature* and *natural* so many times, and the word *Nature* within the same speech can mean first something good and then something evil, as though it were a pun. Nature is two-sided, double-talking, like the witches. "Fair is foul and foul is fair," they cry, and Macbeth enters the play unconsciously echoing them, for he is never original but chock-full of the "milk of human kindness," which does not mean kindness in the modern sense but simply human "nature," human kind. The play is about Nature, and its blind echo, human nature.

Macbeth, in short, shows life in the cave. Without religion, animism rules the outer world, and without faith, the human soul is beset by hobgoblins. This at any rate was Shakespeare's opinion, to which modern history, with the return of the irrational in the Fascist nightmare and its new specters of Communism, Socialism, etc., lends support. It is a troubling thought that Macbeth, of all Shakespeare's characters, should seem the most "modern," the only one you could transpose into contemporary battle dress or a sport shirt and slacks.

The contemporary Macbeth, a churchgoer, is indifferent to religion, to the categorical imperative or any group of principles that may be held to stand above and govern human behavior. Like the old Macbeth, he'd gladly skip the future life, not only for himself but for the rest of humanity. He listens to soothsayers and prophets and has been out on the heath and in the desert, interfering with Nature on a grand scale, lest his rivals for power get ahead of him and Banquo's stock, instead of his, inherit the earth—why this should have seemed such a catastrophe to the real Macbeth, who had no children, is a mystery the scholars never mention. Unloosing the potential destructiveness that was always there in Nature, as Shakespeare understood, the contemporary Macbeth, like the old one, is not even a monster, though he may breed monsters, thanks to his activities on the heath; he is timorous, unimaginative, and the prayer he would like to say most fervently is simply "Amen."

Joan Larsen Klein

Lady Macbeth:

"Infirm of Purpose"

In the Elizabethan marriage service, in the Elizabethan homily on marriage, in books like Vives's *Instruction of a Christen Woman* and Tilney's discourse on marriage, women were said to be weaker than men in reason and physical strength, prone to fears and subject to the vagaries of their imaginations. The second account of the creation in Genesis even suggests that the perfect woman was an afterthought, created later than the perfect man, shaped from his rib in order to forestall his loneliness and to be a "helpe meet for him" (Chapter II, verse 20). The serpent was able to seduce Eve, many theologians said, because she was the weaker vessel. When she seduced Adam, they concluded, she reversed the order and denied the purpose of her own creation. On account of the original created estate of woman and the curse of the Fall, therefore, it was said that women were bound by nature and law to obey their husbands as well as their God. Only when husbands acted in opposition to divine law, said all the treatises, could their wives disobey them, however, the chief duty of good wives was to try lovingly to bring their errant husbands back into virtuous ways.

Joan Larsen Klein, "Lady Macbeth: 'Infirm of Purpose,'" in *The Woman's Part: Feminist Criticism of Shakespeare*, eds. Carol Ruth Swift Lenz, Gayle Greene, and Carol Thomas Neely (Urbana: University of Illinois Press, 1980), pp. 240–51.

Lady Macbeth violates her chief duty to her husband and her God when she urges Macbeth to murder his king. For these and other reasons, most critics believe that Lady Macbeth, the "fiend-like queen" (v.viii.69), lapses from womanliness. I want to suggest, however, that Shakespeare intended us to think that Lady Macbeth, despite her attempt to unsex herself, is never able to separate herself completely from womankind—unlike her husband, who ultimately becomes less and worse than a man. At the beginning Lady Macbeth embodies certain Renaissance notions about women. But when she wills actions that are opposed to the dictates of charity and fails in her chief duty, her wifely roles of hostess and helpmate are perverted. She is deprived of even these perverted roles in the banquet scene as Macbeth abandons his roles of host and husband. Her occupation gone, Lady Macbeth is left anguished, alone, and guilty in ways which are particularly "feminine."

Lady Macbeth embodies in extremity, I think, the Renaissance commonplace that women reflect God's image less clearly than men and that consequently women are less reasonable than men. Right reason enables mankind to choose between good and evil and thus to know right from wrong. Lady Macbeth, however, seems to have repudiated whatever glimmerings of right reason she might once have possessed. She does not consider the ethical or the religious aspects of murder. She seems to believe, for instance, that ambition is attended with "illness" (I.v.21). That which one craves "highly," she says, cannot be got "holily" (21–22). The dying grooms' prayers for blessing and Macbeth's inability to say "Amen," she insists, must not be considered "so deeply" (II.ii.26–29). She refuses, in fact, to think of "These deeds . . . After these ways" (32–33). Thus she seems to have forgotten or repudiated the dictates of reason and her own conscience. Shakespeare may even intend us to conclude that she has renounced her God.

Having put away the knowledge of good, Lady Macbeth is without charity. She is without, in other words, the virtue enjoined on mankind by Christ when He told man to love his neighbor as himself, the virtue which gave man the will to act upon his knowledge of good. Macbeth him-

self appears to be imperfectly rational and infected in will.
That the witches wait for no other purpose than to meet
him suggests that he has long since opened his mind to
demonic temptation, for "that olde and craftie enemie of
ours, assailes none . . . except he first finde an entresse
reddy for him." In fact, it is Macbeth who seems originally
to have thought of murdering Duncan (see I.vii.47–48).
Yet Macbeth, unlike Lady Macbeth, can at first perceive
goodness. He knows that "Duncan . . . hath been / So
clear in his great office" (I.vii.16–18) and that Banquo is
royal "of nature" (III.i.50). He also, for one short moment, seems to understand that charity, not cruelty, ought
to motivate human action and that pity, not cruelty, is
strong—that pity strides the blast and tears drown the
wind. His momentary vision of pity as a newborn babe,
furthermore, evokes not only the image of Christ trium-
phant but also the emblem of charity—a naked babe
sucking the breast. We should remember, however, that
charity was associated more often with women than it was
with men because woman, like children, were thought to
be physically weak: "hit is natural for women to be kynde
and gentyll / bicause they be feble / and nede the ayde of
other," said Vives (sig. Mᵛ). But the woman who denies
her nature and is consumed with "outragious ire and
cruelte," said Vives, "hit is jeoperdye / leest she be dis-
troyed / and have everlastynge payne / bothe in this lyfe /
and in an other" (sig. Mᵛ-Mii). Portia argues for mercy;
Cordelia practices it. It is Macbeth, however, not Lady
Macbeth, who has right reason enough to glimpse both the
strength of pity and its chief resting place. But he never
acts upon his vision and she never sees it.

Having apparently denied her God, Lady Macbeth puts
her trust in the murdering ministers of Hell. Thus she dis-
obeys the first rule of marriage as it was formulated in the
sixteenth century. A wife, said Tilney in the language of
natural fruition common to *Macbeth,* must trust wholly in
God: a wife "must being of hir selfe weake, and unable
besides hir owne diligence, put hir whole trust in the first
. . . author thereof, whome if she serve faythfullye, wyll no
doubt, make thys Flower [of Friendship in holye Matri-

monie] to spring up in hir abundantly" (sig. E[7]). Nothing in life can prosper, say all the authorities, when faith is dead, and the commandments of Christ denied. Thus, despite her wish to aid her husband, Lady Macbeth cannot give him that lasting companionship under God which the *Homilies* saw as true marriage. Furthermore, although Lady Macbeth may once have had a child, its absence from her life and her willingness to contemplate its destruction contradict the *Homilies'* view that children are an end of marriage, a blessing upon their parents, and a means of enlarging God's kingdom. Macbeth at first tries crookedly to keep to the ways of faith even as he dwells on the prospect of damnation and feels the loss of grace: "Wherefore could not I pronounce 'Amen'?" he asks (II.ii.30). But Lady Macbeth refuses from the outset to consider the first author of her being, the last judge of her actions, and the life to come.

Perhaps because of her separation from God, Lady Macbeth is as mistaken about her own nature as she is about her marriage. She says she could dash out the brains of her suckling child. She thinks of wounding with her keen knife. But she has no child and can not murder the sleeping Duncan. She begs to be unsexed, but is never able to assume in fact what she wrongly believes is the masculine attribute of "direst cruelty" (I.v.41). Lady Macbeth, therefore, cannot act out of cruelty. But she refuses to act out of what Latimer called "charitable" love. As she forfeits the power for good which derives from the practice of pity, she is left only with loss and weakness. She is further enfeebled to the point of madness by what Bright called the awareness of sin. Along this path to despair, she does not even seem to notice that she also loses her husband. But Macbeth loses too. He exchanges the fellowship of his badly founded marriage to Lady Macbeth for union with the weird sisters. He exchanges his hopes for men-children born to his wife for the grisly finger of a birth-strangled babe and tormenting visions of the crowned children of other men.

Despite Lady Macbeth's heavy ignorance of Christian marriage, she conceives of herself almost exclusively as a

wife, a helpmate. Thus she epitomizes at the same time that
she perverts Renaissance views of the woman's role. Macbeth, she says, shall be what he is "promised" (i.v.17).
"Great Glamis" must have the "golden round" (23, 29).
When Lady Macbeth reads Macbeth's letter, she speaks
not to herself but to her husband: "Thou wouldst be great
... wouldst not play false, / And yet wouldst wrongly win"
(16–20). (Macbeth, on the contrary, absents himself in
soliloquy even in company.) Lady Macbeth will "chastise"
Macbeth with the "valor" of her tongue so that he, not she,
might have what he wants (28). Nowhere does she mention Macbeth's implied bribe—that she, too, has been
promised "greatness" (14). When Lady Macbeth later
speaks to Macbeth in person, she measures what she takes
to be his love for her by his willingness to murder. But love
for Lady Macbeth never figures in Macbeth's stated desires
for the kingdom or for an heir. Nor does he give in to her
persuasions out of love. On the contrary, he responds to
her only when she impeaches his manliness and arouses
his fear. "If we should fail?" (i.vii.59), he asks. In a grim
perversion of married companionship, Lady Macbeth responds by assuming the feminine role of comforter and
helper: "we'll not fail" (61). But Macbeth never includes
Lady Macbeth in any of his visions of the deed successfully
done.

Although Lady Macbeth always thinks of herself as a
wife, Macbeth thinks of himself as a husband only when
she forces him to do so. Otherwise he is concerned solely
for himself: "I am Thane of Cawdor . . . My thought . . .
Shakes . . . my single state of man" (i.iii.133–40). (The
witches recognize Macbeth's self-interest better than Lady
Macbeth does; they never discuss her with him.) In his
soliloquy during the first banquet, Macbeth uses the royal
we proleptically when he describes his readiness to jump
the life to come and the first person singular when he
thinks about his own ambition and his present relationship
to a loving king. Nowhere in this soliloquy does he speak
of a wife or future queen. When Macbeth goes to murder
Duncan, it is the fatal vision of his own mind that mate-
rializes before him. The "I" sees the dagger of his own

fantasy and the "I" draws the dagger of steel. After the murder of Duncan, there is almost no husband to talk to a wife, for Lady Macbeth can scarcely reach Macbeth. "What do you mean?" (II.ii.39), she asks him. "Be not lost / So poorly in your thoughts" (70–71), she begs him, quite uselessly. After the murder of Banquo, Macbeth is wholly dominated by self: "For mine own good / All causes shall give way" (III.iv.136–37).

In spite of the view of some critics that Lady Macbeth is the evil force behind Macbeth's unwilling villainy, she seems to epitomize the sixteenth-century belief that women are passive, men active: "nature made man more strong and couragiouse, the woman more weake fearefull and scrupulouse, to the intente that she for her feblenesse shulde be more circumspecte, the man for his strengthe moche more adventurouse." It is Macbeth, the man, who must be the "same in [his] own act and valor / As [he is] in desire" (I.vii.40–41), Macbeth, who must "screw [his] courage to the sticking-place" (60). Lady Macbeth's threats of violence, for all their force and cruelty, are empty fantasies. It is Macbeth who converts them to hard reality. He does so in terms of his single self and his singular act: "I am settled, and bend up / Each corporal agent to this terrible feat" (79–80).

One can suggest, I think, that the virtues which Lady Macbeth sees as defects in Macbeth's character and obstacles to his success are in fact the better parts of her own being—which she determines to suppress. She says that she fears Macbeth's nature because "It is too full o' th' milk of human kindness" (I.v.18), but we have never seen Macbeth "kind." On the contrary, we were told about a man whose sword "smoked with bloody execution" and were shown a man whose thought was taken over by murderous "imaginings" (I.ii.18; I.iii.138). It is Lady Macbeth who knows "How tender 'tis to love the babe that milks" her (I.vii.55). It is Lady Macbeth who could not kill because she remembered her father as he slept. Thus it is Lady Macbeth, not Macbeth, who feels the bonds of kind, Lady Macbeth who has, as women were supposed to have, something of the milk of human kindness in her, and who, to rid herself of it, begs murdering ministers to come to her woman's breasts and take that milk "for gall" (I.v.49). She also begs those demonic ministers to stop up in her "th' access and passage to remorse" and thus forestall the "compunctious visitings of nature" which result when bonds of kind are violated (I.v.45–46; "compunction" = the stings of conscience, *OED*, 1). But Lady Macbeth's prayers are never granted by any of the murdering ministers we see waiting on nature's mischief. Unlike Macbeth and until her own suicide, Lady Macbeth does not succeed in breaking that great bond which keeps him pale and ties her to her kind.

Remorse and guilt finally overtake Lady Macbeth. But she manages for a short time to slow their advent by occupying herself with the practical details of murder. Indeed, Lady Macbeth's preparations for the clearing up after Duncan's murder become a frightening perversion of Renaissance woman's domestic activity. As Vives said, "the busynes and charge within the house lyeth upon the womans hande" (sig. Kii'). Unlike Goneril, Regan, Cordelia, and Desdemona—all of whom take to the field of battle—Lady Macbeth waits for Macbeth at home, where good-conduct books told her to stay: "whan her husbande is forth a dores, than kepe her house moche more diligently shutte" (Vives, sig. Kii'). At home, Lady Macbeth remembers to give "tending" to the messenger who comes with the news of Duncan's arrival (I.v.32). She remembers that the king "that's coming / Must be provided for" (I.v.67–69). She is called "hostess," "Fair and noble hostess" (I.vi.10, 24, 31). As she connives at murder, she thinks to assail the grooms with "wine and wassail" (I.vii.64). Even the images she uses to describe her domestic battleground evoke the limbeck and fumes of home-brewed liquor (I.vii.66–67). Before Duncan's murder, it is Lady Macbeth who unlocks the king's doors and lays the daggers ready—although Macbeth draws one of his own. After the murder, it is Lady Macbeth who smears the grooms with blood. In her last act as housekeeper, Lady Macbeth remembers to wash Duncan's blood off their hands and to put on nightgowns.

As soon as Duncan's murder is a public fact, Lady Macbeth begins to lose her place in society and her position at
home. She does so because there is no room for her in the
exclusively male world of treason and revenge. Therefore,
her true weakness and lack of consequence are first revealed in the discovery scene. Lady Macbeth's feeble and
domestic response, for instance, to the news she expected
to hear—"What, in our house?" (II.iii.89)—is very different from the cries and clamors she said she would raise.
When she asks Macduff the domestic question, "What's the
business" that wakes the "sleepers of the house?" (83–85),
he refuses to answer a "gentle lady": " 'Tis not for you to
hear what I can speak" (86). It is apparent, therefore, that
Lady Macbeth has as little place in the male world of
revenge as she had in the male world of war. Thus it may
be that her faint is genuine, a confirmation of her debility.
On the other hand, if her faint is only pretended in order
to shield Macbeth, it is still a particularly feminine ploy.
True or false, it dramatically symbolizes weakness. It has
the further effect of removing her from the center of events
to the periphery, from whence she never returns. It is characteristic that Macbeth, busy defending himself, ignores
his lady's fall. Only Banquo and Macduff in the midst of
genuine grief take time to "Look to the lady" (121, 128).

After Macbeth becomes king, he, the man, so fully commands Lady Macbeth that he allows her no share in his
new business. No longer his accomplice, she loses her role
as housekeeper. Macbeth plans the next feast, not Lady
Macbeth. It is Macbeth who invites Banquo to it, not Lady
Macbeth, who had welcomed Duncan to Inverness by herself. When Macbeth commands his nobles to leave him
alone, Lady Macbeth withdraws silently and unnoticed
along with them (III.i.39–43). Macbeth does not tell Lady
Macbeth that he plans to murder Banquo before his feast
or even that he wanted Macduff to attend it. Although
Macbeth needed Lady Macbeth to keep house during
Duncan's murder, he disposes of Banquo well outside the
castle walls. Thus Lady Macbeth is now neither companion
nor helpmate. Finally, in the great banquet scene, she loses
even her faltering role as hostess. Because Macbeth is

there beyond her reach and her comprehension, she is powerless. Ross, not Lady Macbeth, gives the first command to rise. When Lady Macbeth twice tries to tell the nobles that Macbeth has been thus since his youth, no one pretends to believe her. When she attempts to preserve the "good meeting" (III.iv.110), even Macbeth ignores her. As soon as she is forced by Macbeth's actions to give over her last role, she dissolves in confusion the very society upon whose continuance that role depends. With her husband out of her reach and society in shambles, Lady Macbeth no longer has any reason for being.

As soon as Macbeth abandons her company for that of the witches, Lady Macbeth is totally alone. In fact, Macbeth's union with the witches symbolizes the culmination of Lady Macbeth's loss of womanly social roles as well as her loss of home and family. But her growing isolation had been apparent from the moment her husband became king. Unlike Portia or Desdemona or even Macbeth himself, Lady Macbeth was never seen with friends or woman-servants in whose presence she could take comfort. Even when she appeared in company, she was the only woman there. Consequently, once she begins to lose her husband, she has neither person nor occupation to stave off the visitings of nature. All she has is time, time to succumb to that human kindness which, said Bright, no one could forget and remain human. Thus, in Lady Macbeth's short soliloquy before Macbeth's feast, even though she still talks in terms of "we," she seems to be speaking only of herself. Alone and unoccupied, she is visited by the remorse and sorrow she had hoped to banish:

> Naught's had, all's spent,
> Where our desire is got without content.
> 'Tis safer to be that which we destroy
> Than by destruction dwell in doubtful joy. (III.ii.4–7)

Lady Macbeth's existence now is circumscribed by the present memory of past loss. Absent from her mind is the sense of future promise she had anticipated before Duncan's murder when she thought herself transported beyond the "ignorant present" and felt "The future in the instant" (I.v.58–59). In her words we also hear, I think, what Bright calls the afflictions of a guilt-ridden conscience, that "internal anguish [which] bereve[s] us of all delight" in "outward benefits." Even after Macbeth joins Lady Macbeth, her words seem to continue her own thoughts, not to describe his: "Why do you keep alone, / Of sorriest fancies your companions making" (III.ii.8–9). For we know, as Lady Macbeth does not, that Macbeth is thinking of the coming murder of Banquo, not the past murder of Duncan. We know his recent companions have been murderers, not "fancies." Only Lady Macbeth suffers now the "repetition" of the "horror" of Duncan's death which Macduff had feared "in a woman's ear / Would murder as it fell" (II.iii.82, 87–88). When Lady Macbeth thinks to quiet her husband, she does so with advice she has already revealed she cannot herself take: "Things without all remedy / Should be without regard" (III.ii.11–12). But Macbeth no longer needs her advice: "Duncan is in his grave," he says, "nothing, / Can touch him further" (22–26). Thus Shakespeare shows us that the differences between husband and wife are extreme. Macbeth wades deeper and deeper in blood in order to stifle the tortures of a mind which fears only the future: Banquo's increasing kingliness, Fleance and his unborn children, all living things and their seed. Lady Macbeth, her husband's "Sweet remembrancer" (III.iv.38), does little else but think of horrors past: of the "air drawn" dagger which led Macbeth to Duncan (63), of the king slaughtered and her hands bloodied, of Banquo dead and Lady Macduff in realms unknown.

In the banquet scene, Lady Macbeth's words reveal an increase in weakness, emphasize the loss of her womanly roles, and lay bare her present isolation. Her scolding, for instance, is no more than a weak, futile imitation of the cruelty of her earlier goading. Her images, correspondingly, are more obviously feminine: "these flaws and starts," she tells Macbeth, "would well become / A woman's story at a winter's fire, / Authorized by her grandam" (III.iv.64–67). But her images also evoke a kind of homeliness and comfort she can never know: the security that other women

feel when they sit at their warm hearths and tell tales to
their children. In fact, Lady Macbeth's words describe the
comforts of a home she so little knows that she uses the
picture her words evoke to castigate a man who will soon
destroy the only real home we see in the play. Thus it is
not surprising that Lady Macbeth at the end of the banquet
scene does not seem to realize that Macbeth is leaving her
as well as the community of men in order to join the unsexed witches in an unholy union—one wherein they joy
to "grieve his heart" (IV.i.110). As soon as Macbeth joins
the witches, Lady Macbeth no longer has any place anywhere. Offstage, she is neither wife, queen, housekeeper,
nor hostess. When we see her next, she will have lost the
memories of motherhood and childhood she remembered
so imperfectly and used so cruelly at the beginning of the
play. She will also have lost that fragmented glimpse of
womanly life she repudiates during her last banquet.

In her sleepwalking scene, Lady Macbeth exists (for she
cannot be said to *live*) in the perpetual darkness of the
soul which no candle can enlighten, although she has a
taper by her continually. This is the darkness of the soul
which, said Bright, "is above measure unhappy and most
miserable." Cut off from grace, Lady Macbeth is without
hope. Like the damned in the *Inferno,* she exists solely
within the present memory of past horrors. In fact, her
existence seems to exemplify—but only in relation to herself—medieval definitions of eternal time as the everlasting
"now," the present during which all things that have happened or will happen are happening. For she relives outside of any temporal sequence all Macbeth's murders and
senses, as if damnation were an already accomplished fact,
that "Hell is murky" (v.i.39). Without grace, Lady Macbeth cannot envision a world outside her own where Lady
Macduff might possess another kind of being. Nor can she
conceive of a power greater than that which she still seems
to think she and Macbeth possess, a power which might
call theirs "to accompt" (42). In the prison of her own
anguish, she is ignorant of good and the God she long ago
renounced. This is the illness that Bright said no physic
could cure: "Here no medicine, no purgation, no cordiall,

no tryacle or balme are able to assure the afflicted soule and trembling heart." This is the infection of the mind which the physician hired by Macbeth says only a divine can cure—although Shakespeare shows us no priest in Scotland.

It is painfully ironic that Lady Macbeth, who had once thought that drink could make "memory, the warder of the brain," into a fume and sleep into something "swinish" (I.vii.65–67), can now neither forget her guilt nor sleep the sleep of oblivion. Unlike Macbeth, however, who revealed his guilt before the assembled nobility of Scotland, Lady Macbeth confesses hers when she is alone. She does so because she has always been, as women were supposed to be, a private figure, living behind closed doors. She also reveals her anguish in sleep partly because she has no purposeful waking existence and partly, as Banquo said, because in repose the fallen, unblessed nature "gives way" to "cursèd thoughts" (II.i.8–9; see also v.i.69–72). Macbeth's guilty soul is as public as his acts. Lady Macbeth's is as private as memory, tormented by a self whose function is only to remember in isolation and unwillingly the deeds done by another. So tormented is Lady Macbeth that the gentlewoman—the first we ever see tending her—says she would not have that heart in her "bosom for the dignity of the whole body" (v.i.59).

Our final glimpse into the afflicted and brainsick mind of Lady Macbeth reveals that her doctor is either mistaken or lying when he says she is troubled with "thick-coming fancies" (v.iii.38). Her madness is not that melancholy which springs from delusion, but rather than which stems from true and substantial causes. Her mind, like her being as mother, child, wife, and hostess, has also been twisted by her destructive longing for Macbeth to murder cruelly and deliberately. When we see Lady Macbeth at the end, therefore, she is "womanly" only in that she is sick and weak. All the valor of her tongue is gone, as is her illusion of its power. The hands which she cannot sweeten with the perfumes of Arabia are the little hands of a woman. As long as she lives, Lady Macbeth is never unsexed in the only way she wanted to be unsexed—able to act with the cruelty she ignorantly and perversely identified with male strength. But she has lost that true strength which Shakespeare says elsewhere is based on pity and fostered by love.

She is not now—perhaps she never was—of real concern to her lord, whom she remembers and speaks to even as she sleepwalks. Macbeth does not think of her as he prepares himself for war. When her doctor forces Macbeth to speak about her troubled mind, Macbeth renounces physic on his own account, not hers. "I'll none of it," he says (v.iii.47). It is ironic, therefore, that Lady Macbeth, offstage and neglected, is able at the last to unsex herself only through the act of self-murder—in contrast to her husband, whose single attribute now is the "direst cruelty" she begged for, who wills himself to murder others tomorrow after tomorrow so long as he sees "lives" (v.viii.2). The cry of women which rises at his wife's death is no more than another proof to him that he is fearless, that no "horrors" can move him. (v.v.13). Even her death to him is only a "word," a word for which he has no "time" (v.v.18).

Sylvan Barnet

Macbeth on Stage and Screen

Macbeth is not open to a range of interpretations equal to, say, *King Lear, Hamlet,* or *The Merchant of Venice.* There have, of course, been younger and older Macbeths and Lady Macbeths, expressionistic sets (toppling walls, tilted arches) and realistic sets (based on medieval Scottish architecture), and no sets (beyond the bare stage). There have been ugly witches and seductive witches, and highly physical ghosts of Banquo (the man himself), more ethereal ghosts (a shadow, a light, a rustling curtain), and no ghosts (in such productions Macbeth looks, as Lady Macbeth says, "but on a stool"). But on the whole there has been great uniformity as to what the play is about. And because the text is fairly short—it is the shortest of Shakespeare's tragedies, not much more than half the length of *Hamlet*—it can easily be staged uncut. Not much can be accomplished, in the way of interpretation, by cutting, and, in fact, the cuts are usually limited to the Hecate scenes and the passage on the King's Evil in IV.iii, although this passage significantly serves to contrast the power of virtuous kingship with the demise of a wicked king.

The earliest specific reference to *Macbeth* on the stage appears in Simon Forman's *Book of Plays,* which includes his description of a performance at the Globe in 1611. The document, although thought by some to be a forgery, is now widely accepted as genuine. Alas, it is not terribly informative. We would like to know, for instance, what the witches looked like, and how they disappeared—did they disappear through traps, or did they fly on wires?

—but Forman does not mention the first two scenes. He begins with Macbeth and Banquo "riding thorowe a wod" and meeting "3 women feiries or Nimphes." But does "riding" really mean that Macbeth and Banquo were mounted on horses? Almost surely not, for in III.iii.11–14 Shakespeare goes out of his way to explain why horses are *not* present on the stage in a scene where we might expect them. Perhaps, then, Macbeth and Banquo were mounted on some sort of hobby-horses? Or perhaps (and this is the most likely) Forman's statement that they were "riding" is merely his way of saying what Macbeth and Banquo were *imagined* to be doing. (By the way, one reason that Forman's account has been suspected of being a nineteenth-century forgery rather than a seventeenth-century document is this very passage. It shows no real knowledge of a performance at all, and it may well be derived from Holinshed, Shakespeare's source, which speaks of "three women . . . nymphs or feiries." But of course Forman may have known his Holinshed, and drawn on it to refresh his memory when he came to write about his visit to the Globe Theatre.) Forman, then, is of little or no help, but we nevertheless can get a glimpse, from stage directions in the earliest published text (1623) of the play, of what *Macbeth* at the Globe was like. Take, for instance, the first direction in the play: "Thunder and lightning. Enter three Witches." We know, from other sources, that lightning was produced by fireworks and by blowing resin through a candle, thunder by rolling a cannonball in a wooden trough. References to "Banquet prepared" and "Drum and colors" strengthen our impression that the Globe offered realism of a spectacular sort. But aside from what the text of 1623 tells us, or implies, we know nothing further about the staging of *Macbeth* for the next forty years.

Between 1664 and 1669 Samuel Pepys saw the play at least nine times. Here are two samples of entries from his diary. On November 5, 1664 he writes, "Macbeth, a pretty good play"; on April 19, 1667 he writes, "Here we saw Macbeth, which though I have seen it often yet it is one of the best plays for a stage, and variety of dancing and music, that ever I saw." Dancing and music in *Macbeth*? Yes, because Sir William Davenant adapted the play into operatic form in 1663, adding dancing and singing to the roles of the witches, who flew through the air on machines.

Davenant made other changes, as well, of two sorts: 1) he expanded the roles of Macduff and especially of Lady Macduff, making them more evident foils to Macbeth and Lady Macbeth, and 2) he simplified the language. For instance, his witches do not say, "Fair is foul, and foul is fair"; instead, they say, "To us, fair weather's foul, and foul is fair." Davenant thus simplifies a rich, paradoxical statement with thematic implications into a statement about the weather. Here is another example of a simplified speech: In II.ii, in place of Shakespeare's

> Will all great Neptune's ocean wash this blood
> Clean from my hand? No; this my hand will rather
> The multitudinous seas incarnadine,
> Making the green one red,

Davenant gives us this:

> Can the sea afford
> Water enough to wash away the stains?
> No, they would sooner add a tincture to
> The sea, and turn the green into a red.

Davenant's most infamous alteration, in V.iii.11–12, is of Macbeth's nearly hysterical words to the terrified servant who comes to report that Birnam Wood is on the move:

> The devil damn thee black, thou cream-faced loon!
> Where got'st thou that goose look?

becomes, in Davenant's more decorous text,

> Now friend, what means thy change of countenance?

Davenant's adaptation held the stage until 1744, when David Garrick brought back, to great acclaim, what can be thought of as Shakespeare's *Macbeth*. Garrick's claim that he would perform *Macbeth* as Shakespeare wrote it baffled the actor James Quin who had for two decades been performing in Davenant's adaptation: "What does he mean? Don't I play Macbeth as Shakespeare wrote it?" It is said that Quin, especially puzzled by Shakespeare's line about the "goose look," asked Garrick where he got such an odd expression. Although Garrick restored much of the play, he did not restore it all. (In fact, though he kept the goose look, he seems to have omitted the "The devil damn thee black.") The chief changes are these:

1) following Davenant, he heightened the parts of Macduff and Lady Macduff;

2) his witches, like Davenant's, still danced and sang some added songs, and they remained somewhat comic (though unlike Davenant's witches they disappeared through traps, rather than flew through the air);

3) he reduced the dagger scene;

4) he eliminated 269 lines of Shakespeare's play (for instance, he eliminated most of the scene showing the murder of Lady Macduff's son, preferring to have Ross report it later, and he altered the drunken porter into a respectable servant;

5) he killed Banquo offstage;

6) he did not bring on the severed head of Macbeth at the end;

7) he added some lines of his own, notably a dying speech for Macbeth:

'Tis done! The scene of life will quickly close.
Ambitions vain, delusive dreams are fled,
And now I wake to darkness, guilt and horror.
I cannot bear it! let me shake it off—
Two' [sic] not be; my soul is clogged with blood—

>   I cannot rise! I dare not ask for mercy—
>   It is too late, hell drags me down. I sink,
>   I sink—Oh!—my soul is lost forever.
>   Oh!

Today it is difficult to see the appeal of this speech, but
Garrick's contemporaries praised it. Francis Gentleman, a
drama critic of the time, gives us some idea of how it was
regarded:

> Shakespeare's idea of having [Macbeth's] head brought
> on by Macduff is either ludicrous or horrid, therefore
> commendably changed to visible punishment—a dying
> speech and a very good one has been furnished by Mr.
> Garrick, to give the actor more éclat.

Garrick's costumes for the play were, as was customary
in the period, the costumes of his own age; late in his
career he toyed with the idea of doing *Macbeth* in some
sort of "ancient dress," but he never put the motion into
practice. Apparently the earliest use of Scottish dress in
Macbeth was in a production in Scotland in 1757; the
first use of it on the English stage was in Charles Macklin's
production of 1773. But even Macklin's production was
only a first step toward historical realism, since he used
sixteenth-century dress for Macbeth rather than some pre-
Norman Conquest costume, and Lady Macbeth wore fash-
ionable modern attire. The argument in favor of historical
realism (as the eighteenth century saw it) was that it
made the play more probable; the argument against historical realism was that it endangered the dignity of
tragedy and therefore made the play less probable.
   In the late eighteenth century and early nineteenth the
chief Macbeth was John Philip Kemble, and the chief
Lady Macbeth was Kemble's sister, Sarah Siddons. Kemble, who is always characterized (doubtless with some
injustice) as a "formal" or "statuesque" or "classical"
actor, emphasized Macbeth's greatness as a soldier, and
tended to avoid any suggestion that Macbeth degenerates
and becomes cowardly. One critic complained that at the

sight of Banquo's ghost, Kemble "seemed not to fear while yet he said he 'trembled.'" His text was very close to Shakespeare's, and in costuming he made an effort at what was thought to be historical realism, wearing chain mail, a plaid, and a bonnet with a single feather, in the manner of some clan chieftains. Possibly in accord with his desire to make the play somewhat more rational, Kemble in 1794 dared to break with tradition by not showing the ghost of Banquo, though in 1809 (against his better judgment), he restored the ghost at the request of the public.

Sarah Siddons played Lady Macbeth for forty years, from 1777 to 1817. Like her brother, she is known as a great representative of the late eighteenth-century classical school of acting. In the early nineteenth century, toward the end of her career, when the public taste was changing, and grandeur was less valued, some spectators were unimpressed by her long pauses, her slow delivery, and her solemnity, but somehow all such reports are less impressive than the anecdote telling how she struck terror into the heart of a clerk in a drygoods shop when, before deciding to buy, she asked, "But will it wash?" Nor, according to the American actor Edwin Forrest, did she seem remote and stagy to James Sheridan Knowles, who had often seen Mrs. Siddons act. Forrest reports a conversation with Knowles:

> We have read all the high-flown descriptions of the critics, and they fall short. I want you to tell me in a plain blunt phrase just what impression she produced on you. Knowles replied, with a sort of shudder, . . . "Well, sir, I smelt blood! I swear that I smelt blood."

Other accounts insist that in the sleepwalking scene she marvelously retained her dignity while conveying her anguish, moving the audience with pity and awe. In her "Remarks on the Character of Lady Macbeth," a longish essay reprinted in Thomas Campbell's *Life of Mrs. Siddons* and elsewhere, Mrs. Siddons emphasizes, Stanislavsky-like, the importance of becoming the character and the importance of careful observation. To this end she observed a real sleepwalker. Curiously, however, reports of her acting often differ from the view of the character that she sets forth in her essay. For instance, she says that Lady Macbeth, like Macbeth, sees the ghost of Banquo, but none of the reports of her performances indicates that she conveyed this to the audience.

If the Kembles represent classical acting, Edmund Kean represents romantic acting. He first performed Macbeth in London in 1814, and immediately established himself as Kemble's rival, though many reviewers found Kean was too given to fits and starts. (One thinks of Coleridge's famous comment that watching Kean act was like reading Shakespeare by lightning.) Kean, perhaps reacting against Kemble's heroic Macbeth, emphasized Macbeth's disintegration, so much so that some reviewers believed he went too far and lost the dignity (and the pathos) of the tragic hero. Interestingly, the difference was not obtained by cutting anything in one version or the other, for Kean's text (like Kemble's) seems to have been very close to Garrick's; certainly he retained the speech Garrick had written for the dying Macbeth. And, like Kemble, he used Highland costumes.

In 1847 Samuel Phelps restored the drunken porter in II.iii, presenting a text whose only noticeable departure from Shakespeare's was the omission of the English doctor in IV.iii. Following the Folio, he even killed Macbeth offstage and then brought in the head on a pole. Furthermore, in an effort at historical realism, he abandoned the by then conventional tartans and introduced primitive mantles. But after Kean, the most famous nineteenth-century actor to play the role was not Phelps but Henry Irving, who staged *Macbeth* in 1875, when it ran for eighty performances. Irving revived it in 1888, with Ellen Terry as Lady Macbeth. It is customary to say that Ellen Terry was a softer, frailer, more sympathetic Lady Macbeth than was Sarah Siddons, and there must be something to this view, especially given the difference in their physiques. But when one reads accounts of how heart-rending Mrs. Siddons was in the sleepwalking scene, one begins to suspect that Terry's performance was not so much softer as more sentimental.

Irving's 1888 production was, in his usual style, lavishly mounted with three-dimensional illusionistic sets that were as archaeologically accurate as the age could produce. The lighting effects were elaborate, and the costumes were splendid, though Oscar Wilde commented that although Lady Macbeth patronized local manufacturers for the clothes of her husband and the servants, she bought her own clothing in Byzantium. Because the sets took considerable time to assemble and strike, not all of Shakespeare's scenes could be given, and not always in Shakespeare's order. For instance, in Shakespeare, II.iii and III.i are set in Macbeth's household, but between them comes II.iv, the brief scene between Ross and the Old Man, which takes place somewhere outside. One will hardly strike the set of a castle for such a minor scene—so one can either alter its position in the play or delete it. Irving chose to delete it. His cuts amounted to almost one-quarter of the play, but it should be mentioned that not all of them were made to enable him to use elaborate scenery. Some cuts, for instance the report of the bleeding soldier in I.ii, were based on current scholarly opinions, which held that the passage was not authentic.

One point about Irving's interpretation of his role must be mentioned. In 1875 he took the view that Macbeth is a good man who is destroyed by the fates, but in his second (1888) production he assumed (and tried to convey in his acting) that the witches initiate nothing. They meet Macbeth, Irving came to believe, because Macbeth's mind has already turned to evil thoughts. Irving's changing conception of Banquo's ghost is also worth mentioning: in 1877 some sort of optical illusion produced a transparent greenish silhouette; in 1888 the ghost was a real man, who rose from a trick chair, and who later emerged from the crowd; in 1895 the ghost was not an actor but simply a shaft of blue limelight.

In 1911 Herbert Beerbohm Tree presented a *Macbeth* that was in the elaborate tradition of Irving. Thus, Duncan was escorted by a train that included a harp player; the singing turned into a hymn as the king blessed the kneeling company, and when the stage was empty after Duncan had gone to bed, the witches entered and cackled with satisfaction. This sort of slow-moving pictorial amplification had been under attack by William Poel, who from the last decade of the nineteenth century argued that Shakespeare's plays should be done on the stage for which they were written—that is, on a stage unencumbered with scenery so that the action could flow continuously from scene to scene. If the plays were done on a Shakespeare-like stage, Poel argued, they would not have to be cut, their scenes would not have to be rearranged, and there would not have to be long pauses when new scenery was being set up. In 1895 he directed the Shakespeare Reading Society in a production of *Macbeth*. Bernard Shaw, an enemy of Irving's method, was then serving as drama critic for *The Saturday Review*. Shaw wrote of the production:

It is one of my eccentricities to be old-fashioned in my artistic tastes. For instance, I am fond—unaffectedly fond—of Shakespear's plays. I do not mean actor-managers' editions and revivals; I mean the plays as Shakespeare wrote them, played straight through line by line and scene by scene as nearly as possible under the conditions of representation for which they were designed. I have seen the suburban amateurs of the Shakespeare Reading Society, seated like Christy minstrels on the platform of the lecture hall at the London Institution produce, at a moderate computation, about sixty-six times as much effect by reading straight through *Much Ado about Nothing* as Mr. Irving with his expensively mounted and superlatively dull Lyceum version. When these same amateurs invited me to a regular stage performance of *Macbeth* in aid of the Siddons Memorial Fund, I went, not for the sake of Sarah the Respectable, whose great memory can take care of itself, . . . but simply because I wanted to see *Macbeth*.

Although Shaw goes on to say that the acting was, predictably, weak ("As to this performance of *Macbeth* at St George's Hall, of course it was, from the ordinary professional standpoint, a very bad one"), what is important here is the support he offers to a method of production that was antithetical to Irving's and Tree's method. (It is easy to laugh at Irving and Tree, and to approve of Poel, but one should recall that some sensitive students of Shakespeare—G. Wilson Knight, for instance—have believed that the elaborate Victorian style conferred on the plays the "richness and dignity," in Knight's words, which they require.) In 1909 Poel staged the play again, in what he claimed was "the Elizabethan manner." By this he meant not only that it was done on a stage without sets, but also that it was done not in Scottish garb but, Elizabethan garb. As we will see in a moment, it required only a small additional step to argue that since the Elizabethans staged their plays in the garb of the performers' day, we should stage the plays in the garb of our own. Against this view, however, it can be argued that modern-dress productions make the play too local, too bound to the present, and rob the play—any play—of its archetypal dimension.

Barry Jackson's modern dress *Macbeth* (1928), in which Macbeth was a general who wore khaki, riding breeches, and boots, and in which Lady Macduff was murdered while taking afternoon tea, can be seen as part of the anti-Victorian movement that Poel began. In 1925 Jackson had staged, with considerable success, a modern-dress *Hamlet*, but the *Macbeth* was widely considered (except for the drunken porter and for the scene in which Macduff received the news of the slaughter of his family) a failure. Why? Any Elizabethan play done in modern dress will present some problems (e.g. why do people engage in sword fights when they have pistols at hand?), but *Macbeth* seemed especially troublesome. First of all, since a murder had been committed in the house, why didn't they call the police? More seriously, what was gained by associating the play with World War I? Further, the witches were a problem, since witches are not a part of modern society. (As we'll see, various solutions have been proposed in other modern versions of *Macbeth*.) Jackson himself said he engaged in the experiment partly to see how it would come out. He had trouble getting an actor to play Macbeth, and finally settled on Eric Maturin, a realistic actor who could not speak verse effectively.

In 1933 Theodore Komisarjevsky, a Russian émigré who served as a visiting director at Stratford-upon-Avon, did another modern-dress version. Macbeth, dressed rather like a German officer of World War I, met the witches against the background of a ruined château. The witches (who were the only characters to speak with Scottish accents) were not supernatural creatures but were hags plundering corpses on the battlefield; they told the fortunes of Macbeth and Banquo by palmistry. In keeping with this diminution of the supernatural, Banquo's ghost in the banquet scene was Macbeth's own immense shadow, and Macbeth's second encounter with the witches was conceived as Macbeth's dream. In fact, the entire production, though evocative of World War I in certain details, was somewhat dreamlike and expressionistic, with aluminum screens forming labyrinthine sets.

Three years later, in 1936, Orson Welles, working with the WPA Negro Theatre, presented in New York a black *Macbeth*. Jack Carter (who had played Crown in *Porgy and Bess*) played Macbeth, Edna Thomas played Lady Macbeth, and Canada Lee played Banquo. (Carter and Thomas, being light-skinned blacks, had to darken themselves for the parts.) Virgil Thomson provided orchestrations of nineteenth-century waltzes for court scenes, and African drummers provided other music. This *Macbeth*, set in Haiti early in the nineteenth century (Napoleonic uniforms, with lots of gold braid), began by showing a jungle, through which sounded drums and the chants of voodoo celebrants. The play was a great hit, both in Harlem and later on tour, though some white journalists complained that the verse was not delivered in the usual declamatory style then expected in productions of Shakespeare. Welles's script, thought for decades to have been lost, turned up in 1974, and in 1977 Woodie King, Jr.

staged it at New York City's New Federal Theatre, with Lex Monson as Macbeth and Esther Rolle (of the television series *Good Times*) as Lady Macbeth, but the revival did not prove exciting.

There have, of course, been many productions of *Macbeth* since Welles did his black *Macbeth* in 1936. Among the most famous are a *Macbeth* directed by John Gielgud in 1952 (Gielgud pointedly rejected all suggestions of Scottish history); a *Macbeth* directed by Glen Byam Shaw in 1955, with Laurence Olivier in the title role, using sets that evoked medieval architecture but were at the same time expressionistic; a *Macbeth* directed by Joan Littlewood in 1957, using modern dress (Littlewood in her program note said she wanted "to wipe away the dust of three hundred years" and to strip away the interpretations of the "nineteenth-century sentimentalists," so she gave her Macbeth and Lady Macbeth no tragic dignity); a *Macbeth* directed by Trevor Nunn at Stratford-upon-Avon in 1976, with Ian McKellen as Macbeth and Judi Dench as Lady Macbeth, in which the Christian background was emphasized, for example by having the saintly Duncan dressed in white, and by having Malcolm and Macduff converse before a cross. But no *Macbeth* in the theater seems to have established itself as the great production of our age.

Three film versions, however, are of interest. Orson Welles's film, shot in 1947 and released in the following year, cast Welles as Macbeth, Jeanette Nolan as Lady Macbeth, and Roddy McDowall played Malcolm. Welles cut the text fairly heavily, introduced some novel business (in the sleepwalking scene, this Macbeth awakens Lady Macbeth with a kiss), and added a character, the Holy Father, some of whose lines were invented by Welles while others were salvaged from characters whom Welles cut. The underlying idea seems to be that Macbeth is a doomed figure, not so much a man who made a wrong decision but a man whose fate has been long decided. To this end, expressionistic shots (rough stone walls, figures looming in the foreground, minute figures in the distance) offer images of Macbeth's tormented mind. Welles was trying

to make a film version of *Macbeth*—a cinematic work,
rather than a mere film recording of the play—but inevitably a viewer who knows the play is disturbed by the
liberties taken with the text, and is also disturbed by the
extremely poor sound track, which makes many speeches
unintelligible.

The sense of Macbeth as a powerful warrior, missed by
Welles, is strongly present in Akira Kurosawa's *Throne of
Blood* (1957, in Japanese entitled *The Castle of the
Spider's Web*). Kurosawa, using conventions of the Noh
drama and the samurai movie, gives his characters Japanese names, and freely changes the story, so that his film
is not so much *Macbeth* as a spinoff of Shakespeare's play,
and perhaps that is why it is so much more satisfactory
than most movies (or productions?) of Shakespeare's
plays. That is, unlike an English-language film or production of the play, Kurosawa's work does not claim to be
Shakespeare in plot, in character, scene, or even in any of
its language. Without worrying about fidelity to the
original, we can easily enjoy it for itself.

The most recent film of *Macbeth*, Roman Polanski's
version (released in 1971), has been criticized as being
excessively bloody; but Polanski might well plead that
since Shakespeare's play includes the stage direction, "Enter Macduff, with Macbeth's head," blood might just as
well flow abundantly in a film. Still, it is evident that
Polanski (who shows us such sights as Macbeth repeatedly
plunging a dagger into Duncan, and an arrow striking
Seyton between the eyes) is influenced not only by Shakespeare but by Antonin Artaud's Theater of Cruelty. Many
viewers find such stuff hard to take; only a few viewers—
persons highly familiar with Shakespeare's play—find
Polanski's tinkering with the ending equally hard to take,
but for them Polanski is engaged in yet further violence.
At the end of this film, as Malcolm is being crowned, his
younger brother, Donalbain, rides off to listen to the
witches. The implication is that he will conspire against
the king, just as Macbeth had conspired against King
Duncan, and so the play ends not with Shakespeare's

suggestions of union ("loves," "friends"), fertility ("planted newly"), piety ("by the grace of Grace"), and order ("measure, time, and place"), but with a suggestion of unending treachery. Almost equally unusual, and more interesting, is the casting of a relatively young Macbeth (Jon Finch) and Lady Macbeth (Francesca Annis), emphasizing their sexuality and presumably also emphasizing the contrast between a fair exterior and an ugly interior. What is most lacking in the film, however, is a sense that Macbeth is a heroic figure, a man who has a moral sense— even if he wars against it.

BIBLIOGRAPHIC NOTE: A very large book, a medium-size book, and a very small book have been devoted to productions of *Macbeth*. They are, in that order, Marvin Rosenberg, *The Masks of Macbeth* (1978); Dennis Bartholomeusz, *Macbeth and the Players* (1969); and Gordon Williams, *Macbeth: Text and Performance* (1985). Rosenberg and Bartholomeusz cover numerous productions, old and new; Williams concentrates on a few recent productions including Polanski's film version. For further reviews of productions from the middle of this century to the present, consult *Shakespeare Survey* (an annual publication) and *Shakespeare Quarterly*. For a survey of twentieth-century developments in staging Shakespeare's plays, see J. L. Styan, *The Shakespeare Revolution* (1977).

More specialized studies include Kalman Burnim, *David Garrick, Director* (1961); Arthur Colby Sprague, *Shakespearian Players and Performances* (1954, on William Macready as Macbeth and Sarah Siddons as Lady Macbeth); Alan Hughes, *Henry Irving, Shakespearean* (1981); John Houseman, *Run-Through* (1972, on Welles's black *Macbeth*); Jack J. Jorgens, *Shakespeare on Film* (1977). An article by Carol J. Carlisle in *Shakespeare Survey 16* (1983) is devoted to Helen Faucit's mid-nineteenth-century Lady Macbeth but includes also information about Sarah Siddons's interpretation of the role.

Suggested References

The number of possible references is vast and grows alarmingly. (The *Shakespeare Quarterly* devotes one issue each year to a list of the previous year's work, and *Shakespeare Survey* —an annual publication—includes a substantial review of recent scholarship, as well as an occasional essay surveying a few decades of scholarship on a chosen topic.) Though no works are indispensable, those listed below have been found especially helpful.

1. Shakespeare's Times

Byrne, M. St. Clare. *Elizabethan Life in Town and Country.* Rev. ed. New York: Barnes & Noble, 1961. Chapters on manners, beliefs, education, etc., with illustrations.

Joseph, B. L. *Shakespeare's Eden: The Commonwealth of England, 1558–1629.* New York: Barnes & Noble, 1971. An account of the social, political, economic, and cultural life of England.

Schoenbaum, S. *Shakespeare: The Globe and the World.* New York: Oxford University Press, 1979. A readable, handsomely illustrated book on the world of the Elizabethans.

Shakespeare's England. 2 vols. London: Oxford University Press, 1916. A large collection of scholarly essays on a wide variety of topics (e.g. astrology, costume, gardening, horsemanship), with special attention to Shakespeare's references to these topics.

Stone, Lawrence. *The Crisis of the Aristocracy, 1558–1641,* abridged edition. London: Oxford University Press, 1967.

2. Shakespeare

Barnet, Sylvan. *A Short Guide to Shakespeare.* New York: Harcourt Brace Jovanovich, 1974. An introduction to all of the works and to the dramatic traditions behind them.

Bentley, Gerald E. *Shakespeare: A Biographical Handbook.* New Haven, Conn.: Yale University Press, 1961. The facts about Shakespeare, with virtually no conjecture intermingled.

Bush, Geoffrey. *Shakespeare and the Natural Condition.* Cambridge, Mass.: Harvard University Press, 1956. A short, sensitive account of Shakespeare's view of "Nature," touching most of the works.

Chambers, E. K. *William Shakespeare: A Study of Facts and Problems.* 2 vols. London: Oxford University Press, 1930.

An invaluable, detailed reference work; not for the casual reader.

Chute, Marchette. *Shakespeare of London*. New York: Dutton, 1949. A readable biography fused with portraits of Stratford and London life.

Clemen, Wolfgang H. *The Development of Shakespeare's Imagery*. Cambridge, Mass.: Harvard University Press, 1951. (Originally published in German, 1936.) A temperate account of a subject often abused.

Granville-Barker, Harley. *Prefaces to Shakespeare*. 2 vols. Princeton, N.J.: Princeton University Press, 1946–47. Essays on ten plays by a scholarly man of the theater.

Harbage, Alfred. *As They Liked It*. New York: Macmillan, 1947. A long, sensitive essay on Shakespeare, morality, and the audience's expectations.

Kernan, Alvin B., ed. *Modern Shakespearean Criticism: Essays on Style, Dramaturgy, and the Major Plays*. New York: Harcourt Brace Jovanovich, 1970. A collection of major formalist criticism.

————. "The Plays and the Playwrights." In *The Revels History of Drama in English*, general editors Clifford Leech and T. W. Craik. Vol. III. London: Methuen, 1975. A book-length essay surveying Elizabethan drama with substantial discussions of Shakespeare's plays.

Schoenbaum, S. *Shakespeare's Lives*. Oxford: Clarendon Press, 1970. A review of the evidence, and an examination of many biographies, including those by Baconians and other heretics.

————. *William Shakespeare: A Compact Documentary Life*. New York: Oxford University Press, 1977. A readable presentation of all that the documents tell us about Shakespeare.

Traversi, D. A. *An Approach to Shakespeare*. 3rd rev. ed. 2 vols. New York: Doubleday, 1968–69. An analysis of the plays beginning with words, images, and themes, rather than with characters.

Van Doren, Mark. *Shakespeare*. New York: Holt, 1939. Brief, perceptive readings of all of the plays.

3. Shakespeare's Theater

Beckerman, Bernard. *Shakespeare at the Globe, 1599–1609*. New York: Macmillan, 1962. On the playhouse and on Elizabethan dramaturgy, acting, and staging.

Chambers, E. K. *The Elizabethan Stage*. 4 vols. New York:

Oxford University Press, 1945. A major reference work on theaters, theatrical companies, and staging at court.

Cook, Ann Jennalie. *The Privileged Playgoers of Shakespeare's London, 1576–1642*. Princeton: N.J.: Princeton University Press, 1981. Sees Shakespeare's audience as more middle-class and more intellectual than Harbage (below) does.

Gurr, Andrew. *The Shakespearean Stage: 1574–1642*. 2d edition. Cambridge: Cambridge University Press, 1981. On the acting companies, the actors, the playhouses, the stages, and the audiences.

Harbage, Alfred. *Shakespeare's Audience*. New York: Columbia University Press, 1941. A study of the size and nature of the theatrical public, emphasizing its representativeness.

Hodges, C. Walter. *The Globe Restored*. London: Ernest Benn, 1953. A well-illustrated and readable attempt to reconstruct the Globe Theatre.

Hosley, Richard. "The Playhouses." In *The Revels History of Drama in English*, general editors Clifford Leech and T. W. Craik. Vol. III. London: Methuen, 1975. An essay of one hundred pages on the physical aspects of the playhouses.

Kernodle, George R. *From Art to Theatre: Form and Convention in the Renaissance*. Chicago: University of Chicago Press, 1944. Pioneering and stimulating work on the symbolic and cultural meanings of theater construction.

Nagler, A. M. *Shakespeare's Stage*. Trans. Ralph Manheim. New Haven, Conn.: Yale University Press, 1958. A very brief introduction to the physical aspects of the playhouse.

Slater, Ann Pasternak. *Shakespeare the Director*. Totowa, N.J.: Barnes & Noble, 1982. An analysis of theatrical effects (e.g., kissing, kneeling) in stage directions and dialogue.

Thomson, Peter. *Shakespeare's Theatre*. London: Routledge and Kegan Paul, 1983. A discussion of how plays were staged in Shakespeare's time.

4. Miscellaneous Reference Works

Abbott, E. A. *A Shakespearean Grammar*. New Edition. New York: Macmillan, 1877. An examination of differences between Elizabethan and modern grammar.

Bevington, David. *Shakespeare*. Arlington Heights, Ill.: A. H. M. Publishing, 1978. A short guide to hundreds of important writings on the works.

Bullough, Geoffrey. *Narrative and Dramatic Sources of Shake-*

speare. 8 vols. New York: Columbia University Press, 1957–75. A collection of many of the books Shakespeare drew upon, with judicious comments.

Campbell, Oscar James, and Edward G. Quinn. *The Reader's Encyclopedia of Shakespeare.* New York: Crowell, 1966. More than 2,600 entries, from a few sentences to a few pages, on everything related to Shakespeare.

Greg, W. W. *The Shakespeare First Folio.* New York: Oxford University Press, 1955. A detailed yet readable history of the first collection (1623) of Shakespeare's plays.

Kökeritz, Helge. *Shakespeare's Names.* New Haven, Conn.: Yale University Press, 1959. A guide to the pronunciation of some 1,800 names appearing in Shakespeare.

———. *Shakespeare's Pronunciation.* New Haven, Conn.: Yale University Press, 1953. Contains much information about puns and rhymes.

Muir, Kenneth. *The Sources of Shakespeare's Plays.* New Haven, Conn.: Yale University Press, 1978. An account of Shakespeare's use of his reading.

The Norton Facsimile: The First Folio of Shakespeare. Prepared by Charlton Hinman. New York: Norton, 1968. A handsome and accurate facsimile of the first collection (1623) of Shakespeare's plays.

Onions, C. T. *A Shakespeare Glossary.* 2d ed., rev., with enlarged addenda. London: Oxford University Press, 1953. Definitions of words (or senses of words) now obsolete.

Partridge, Eric. *Shakespeare's Bawdy.* Rev. ed. New York: Dutton, 1955. A glossary of bawdy words and phrases. ·

Shakespeare Quarterly. See headnote to Suggested References.

Shakespeare Survey. See headnote to Suggested References.

Shakespeare's Plays in Quarto. A Facsimile Edition. Ed. Michael J. B. Allen and Kenneth Muir. Berkeley, Calif.: University of California Press, 1981. A book of nine hundred pages, containing facsimiles of twenty-two of the quarto editions of Shakespeare's plays. An invaluable complement to *The Norton Facsimile: The First Folio of Shakespeare* (see above).

Smith, Gordon Ross. *A Classified Shakespeare Bibliography 1936–1958.* University Park, Pa.: Pennsylvania State University Press, 1963. A list of some twenty thousand items on Shakespeare.

Spevack, Marvin. *The Harvard Concordance to Shakespeare.* Cambridge, Mass.: Harvard University Press, 1973. An index to Shakespeare's words.

Wells, Stanley, ed. *Shakespeare: Select Bibliographies*. London: Oxford University Press, 1973. Seventeen essays surveying scholarship and criticism of Shakespeare's life, work, and theater.

5. Macbeth

Baxter, John. *Shakespeare's Poetic Style*. London: Routledge and Kegan Paul, 1980.

Berger, Harry. "The Text Against Performance in Shakespeare: The Example of *Macbeth*." In *The Power of Forms in the English Renaissance*. Ed. Stephen Greenblatt. Norman, Okla.: Pilgrim Books, 1982. 49–79.

Blissett, William. "The Secret'st Man of Blood. A Study of Dramatic Irony in Macbeth," *Shakespeare Quarterly*, 10 (1959), 397–408.

Bradley, A. C. *Shakespearean Tragedy*. London: Macmillan, 1904. Part of the material in *Macbeth* is reprinted above.

Brown, John Russell, ed. *Focus on "Macbeth."* London: Routledge and Kegan Paul, 1982.

Champion, Larry S. *Shakespeare's Tragic Perspective*. Athens, Ga.: University of Georgia Press, 1976.

Kahn, Coppélia. *Man's Estate: Masculine Identity in Shakespeare*. Berkeley, Cal.: University of California Press, 1981.

Knights, L. C. *Some Shakespearean Themes*. Stanford, Cal.: Stanford University Press, 1960.

Mack, Maynard. "The Jacobean Shakespeare: Some Observations on the Construction of the Tragedies," *Stratford-upon-Avon Studies I: Jacobean Theatre*. London: Edward Arnold, 1960. Reprinted in the Signet Classic edition of *Othello*.

Mack, Maynard Jr. *Killing the King*. New Haven, Conn.: Yale University Press, 1973.

Muir, Kenneth, ed. *Shakespeare Survey*, 19 (1966).

Paul, Henry N. *The Royal Play of Macbeth*. New York and London: Macmillan, 1950.

Rosen, William. *Shakespeare and the Craft of Tragedy*. Cambridge, Mass.: Harvard University Press, 1960.

Slights, Camille Wells. *The Casuistical Tradition*. Princeton, N.J.: Princeton University Press, 1981.

Walker, Roy. *The Time Is Free*. New York: Macmillan, 1949.